Street Scene in Jerusalem ......

Paul's Life
and
Letters

PAUL'S LIFE
AND
LETTERS

By

SIDNEY B. SPERRY

Director, Graduate Studies
in Religion

Brigham Young University
Provo, Utah

Bookcraft
Salt Lake City, Utah

25 26 27 28 29 30   89 88 87 86 85 84 83

Lithographed in the United States of America
PUBLISHERS PRSS
Salt Lake City, Utah

PREFACE

Because Paul was one of the greatest men that have ever graced the earth, books and articles on the great Apostle are legion. I shall not apologize for adding another little work to the already large list of books on the man of Tarsus. Long after this one is forgotten, men will continue to write about him. The writing of a book is a difficult task, but one who would catch the power of Paul in the fullest measure needs not only the Spirit but the discipline and love of adventure that the writing of a book on his life and Epistles entails. I have written this book to deepen my own understanding and appreciation of the great Apostle and to provide a text that will help Latter-day Saint students get at the essential facts about him in a minimum of time.

The topical headings in this book should make it easy for the average reader to follow what he is interested in and to pass over any technicalities that may be of interest only to students of the New Testament.

I have outlined Paul's Epistles so that one may get the gist of what the Apostle was writing. Most of the Epistles make difficult—very difficult—reading. Just how difficult, one may determine for himself by trying to outline what Paul was trying to say in a given Epistle. I cannot hope that my efforts in outlining the Epistles will always please or meet the approval of my readers. But I have tried earnestly to give them a fair idea of what the Apostle was writing about.

One who deals with Paul is everywhere dependent on those scholars who have preceded him. Over the years I have read numerous books and articles by them. I have attempted to give proper credit for unusual contributions but cannot hope in every case to have given credit where it is due. My thanks are due to all the authors of books on

Paul that I have read. The bibliography will give a partial list of books that I have used over the years. Some of these publications contain useful bibliographies on Paul.

I am particularly indebted to the classical works on Paul by Conybeare and Howson David Smith, Ramsey, and Farrar; and especially in matters pertaining to the Epistles and their organization have I been dependent on suggestions from the excellent works of J. E. Steinmueller, *A Companion to Scripture Studies*, Vol. III, and of C. J. Callan, *The Epistles of St. Paul*, (2 vols.), both of which are published by Joseph F. Wagner (Inc.) of New York.

My good friend and colleague, Bishop Ralph Britsch, has again obliged me by looking over the entire manuscript, and I am indebted to him for numerous suggestions that have bettered it.

I want to express warm thanks to my young colleague, Robert L. Layton, of the geography faculty of Brigham Young University and son of my old friends, Lynn and Leone Layton, for working out the maps in this volume. At my suggestion Professor Layton has made them as simple as possible, so that Paul's journeys can be easily followed by the eye.

We are living in a day and age when men doubt that Christ is the very Son of God, the Redeemer and Savior of the world, who was literally raised from the dead and who, by the shedding of His blood, wrought out an atonement for all mankind. In the face of these facts, we need today Paul's positive, unimpeachable testimony that he saw the risen, redeemed Lord. Without this testimony there is little reason to study Paul. It is to be hoped that this modest little volume will help Latter-day Saints better to appreciate the great Apostle's testimony and contribution to the world.

—Sidney B. Sperry

Brigham Young University
October 25, 1955

CONTENTS

ABBREVIATIONS

Mss., mss......... Manuscripts

Abbreviations of books in the
Standard Works of the Church
are those in common use.

Paul's Life

and

Letters

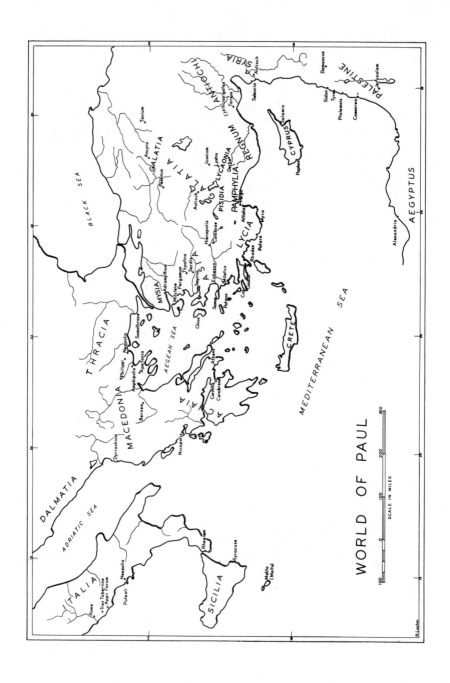

WORLD OF PAUL

SCALE IN MILES

100   0   100   200   300

R. Leaften

Chapter 1

SAUL'S EARLY BACKGROUND AND TRAINING

Saul's Name and Family.—The Hebrew name of the most illustrious of the sons of Tarsus was Saul ("asked for"), but it is by his Roman name of Paulus ("little") or Paul that we know him best. In the Acts, it is significant that Luke calls him "Saul" until the great Apostle-to-be meets the Roman Proconsul Sergius Paulus on the island of Cyprus during his first missionary journey. (Acts 13:6-9) Thereafter, because he seems to have sensed the appropriateness of a Roman name for a missionary to the Roman Empire, Luke generally calls him "Paul." (See Acts 13:13; 14:9, 12; 15:35, etc.)

Saul was born a free Roman citizen, and in this fact he seems to have taken great pride. (Acts 16:37-39; 22:28) Nevertheless, he was brought up as a Jew, being the son of a Pharisee from the tribe of Benjamin. (Acts 21:39; 23:6; Rom. 11:1) He strongly emphasizes his Hebrew background in these words:

> Circumcised the eighth day, of the stock of Israel, of the tribe of Benjamin, an Hebrew of the Hebrews; as touching the law, a Pharisee. (Phil. 3:5)

The Acts of the Apostles and Paul's own letters give us but scanty information about his parents and their family. It was common in ancient times for a son to inherit the trade of his father, and inasmuch as Paul in the days of his Apostleship often supported himself as a tentmaker, we may assume that his father plied the same trade. (See Acts 18:3; 20:34; 1 Cor. 4:12; 2 Cor. 11:7-9; 1 Thess. 2:9; 2 Thess. 3:8.) The very name of Paul's father is unknown; the same is true of his mother's.

We know that Paul had a sister who later married and lived in Jerusalem. It was her son who became the means of saving the Apostle's life. (Acts 23:16) Unfortunately, again, we do not know the name of the son, but a later account says that the name of Paul's sister was Rachel. If Paul had other sisters or even brothers we have not been told of it. History is silent on the matter.

St. Jerome (A.D. 400) records a rather doubtful tradition which states that Paul was born in the Galilean city of Gischala and brought to Tarsus when the legions of Varus wrought devastation in the province.

On the other hand, we now know that a body of Jews settled in Tarsus in 171 B.C., when assurances were given them of the rights of citizenship. It may be, therefore, that Paul inherited his citizenship from a family line that went back many generations in that city of Cilicia. Some authorities suppose that in return for some signal service to the Roman Republic by Paul's father or grandfather, the family may have received their citizenship from Mark Antony, who visited the city along with Cleopatra (41 B.C.).

There is little or no evidence to show that Paul's father was a wealthy man as some have supposed. Neither, on the other hand, is there any evidence that he was poor. That he was able to send Paul to school in Jerusalem may argue for his having been in fairly comfortable circumstances.

When Was Saul Born?—In our day and time we are prone to be exacting in matters of chronology. But ancient record keepers seem not to have been so concerned with them. Many of us are often quite frustrated when we can not date important historical events with some exactness. Thus, we would like to know the date of Paul's conversion, the date of his first missionary journey, the date of his epistle to the Galatians, and the dates of many other happenings, not to mention the date of his birth. As to this last, we should bear in mind that Luke made no pretense of giving a life of Paul. Had he done so, we could have expected from him some indications of the time of the Apostle's birth. In Luke's narrative in the Acts, we meet Saul for the first time as a young man, present at the stoning of Stephen. (Acts 7:58) Luke follows his career with more or less fulness until the Roman imprisonment, where he drops his story of the Apostle's career. Nor do Paul's epistles help us much more in our quest, though a few hints are given. Thus, when he writes to Philemon, he does so "as Paul the aged." (Vs. 9) And notice that in Acts 7:58 he is referred to as a "young man" at the time of Stephen's stoning. In Acts 26:10 Paul speaks of his career of persecuting in these words: ". . . when they [the saints] were put to death, I gave my voice [vote] against them." These words, taken naturally, would seem to indicate that Paul was a member of the Sanhedrin; indeed, there does not appear to be any very good reason why we shouldn't assume the fact.[1] If he was a member of that high tribunal, he must have been at least thirty years of age at the time his voice was given against the saints. From considerations growing out of the author's study of the Book of Mormon, he believes that the Savior was crucified in the year A.D. 33. Now, using this year as our point of departure, let us make a calculation that may come very close to the date of Paul's birth. It may be safely assumed that three years passed after the Savior's death before the young Church had grown to such proportions that it received the very active attention of Paul and its other persecutors. If this be true, the time of the Apostle's conversion was about A.D. 36. If, now, we subtract from this date the highly probable thirty or thirty-one years of his age at the time of his conversion, we come up with A.D. 5 or A.D. 6 as the approximate time of his birth. The validity of these dates,

[1]See A. T. Robertson, *Epochs in the Life of Paul*, p. 33; David Smith, *The Life and Letters of Paul*, p. 45; W. J. Conybeare and J. S. Howson, *The Life And Epistles of St. Paul*, p. 64.

as has been seen, depends on three crucial factors: (1) the
date of our Lord's crucifixion being A.D. 33; (2) the fact
that approximately three years had passed after the Savior's
death before the Church's growth brought on Paul's persecuting activities; and (3) the statement in Acts 7:58 that
he was a "young man" coupled with that in Acts 26:10,
which, read naturally, indicates that he must have been
attached to the Sanhedrin, membership in which would
require, among other things, that a man should be at least
thirty years of age.[2]

But let it be remembered that we do not know with
absolute certainty the date of a single event in Paul's whole
life. The time of his birth arrived at above will, in the writer's
personal opinion, someday be found very close to the true
date. But possibly most authorities on Paul at the present
time believe that he was born about A.D. 1; some differ
from this considerably, Dr. E. J. Goodspeed, for example,
placing it A.D. 10-15.[3]

Saul's Early Training in Tarsus.—Tarsus, the city in
which Saul was brought up, was one of which the Apostle
in later years could rightly boast as being "no mean [undis-
tinguished] city." (Acts 21:39) In Saul's youth the city was
already centuries old, and combined very well within itself
old Oriental qualities and the characteristics of its Greek
citizens whose forbears had settled in it long before, particularly after the conquering Alexander the Great had
entered it in 334 B.C. The city's fame and prosperity were
at their pinnacle near the time of our Lord's birth. Tarsus
was the capital of Cilicia, a narrow province (varying from
thirty to sixty miles in width and having a length of possibly three hundred miles) situated between the Taurus
mountains and the Mediterranean. The country round
about the city was fertile, and the metropolis also enjoyed

[2]See Conybeare and Howson, p. 56.
[3]*Paul*, p. 2.

a very lucrative commerce which passed through her port of Rhegma at the mouth of the Cydnus River. This river, whose cold waters issued from the mountains to the north, passed through Tarsus, about twelve miles from the Mediterranean.

But of even more significance is the fact that Tarsus was one of the three greatest centers of learning in the world of Saul's day, if not the greatest one. It was one of the great university cities, and students flocked to it from many places, but the natives of Tarsus are said to have surpassed all students of the time in their academic zeal. The learned sons of Tarsus were famous for their number and quality, and their influence was widely felt. We may notice among these the Stoic philosophers Athenodorus (teacher of the Roman Emperor Augustus), Archedamus, Athenodorus Cordulio (Cato's teacher), Antipater, and Nestor; notice also the grammarians Artemidorus and Diodorus, not to mention other philosophers like Nestor the Academic, the teacher of Marcellus, who was the son of Augustus' sister Octavia. We ought not to forget the poets, of whom Dionysius the tragedian is a good example.[4]

We might recite at much greater length the intellectual fame of Saul's native city, as many writers have done, but insofar as the Apostle is concerned, to do so would be of academic interest only. The reason for this is not far to see, inasmuch as Saul was the son of a strict Pharisee for whom pagan schools and customs were anathema. Saul's parents would not fail to teach him and indoctrinate him at an early age in their Sacred Law. His upbringing would be almost exclusively Jewish and narrow viewed in the light of some of our present standards. Although we do not know the Judaism of his age too well, it is probable that at about six

[4]See the brilliant exposition of Tarsus' intellectual fame in David Smith, *Life and Letters of St. Paul*, pp. 18f. But see Ramsay, *The Cities of St. Paul*, pp. 231-235, for a more conservative view.

years of age Saul was sent to an elementary school, in a room
connected with the Jewish synagogue. Here, with other
Jewish boys of his age, he would be instructed in the reading
of Scripture. This may have been in the Greek version known
to us as the Septuagint, because in later years he seems to
have quoted extensively from it. It is difficult not to believe
that he knew the Scriptures in their original Hebrew and
Aramaic languages, because Aramaic would be the vernacular of his home, and for a would-be Rabbi not to know
Hebrew would be unthinkable. It should be kept in mind
that although Aramaic may have been the vernacular in his
Jewish home, Saul would always be exposed to Greek on the
street. His writings display a good knowledge of it. In after
years, Paul found no difficulty in speaking Hebrew (possibly
Aramaic is meant) to a Jewish mob that sought his life. (Acts
21:40; see also verse 37.) So well would the future Apostle
learn the Scriptures, the Old Testament, that they would be
practically memorized by him and become an important
part of his mental equipment. In the home and in the synagogue, the growing boy would hear his elders year after year
discuss, interpret and debate them. Not without reason were
the Jews called the "people of the Book."

When he became thirteen years of age, we may presume that Saul, like other Jewish boys, would become "a
son of the commandment," leave the "House of the Book"
where he had so long studied the Scriptures, and take his
place along with the men of his people.

In a university city like Tarsus, it may be expected
that Saul would pick up some elements of philosophic jargon,
the Cynic-Stoic diatribe, and the figures of rhetoric taught in
the schools, not to mention scraps of Greek poetry and
history. But his knowledge of Greek learning should not be
emphasized; he seems not to have been deeply versed. The
mastery of the Scriptures, of Hebrew history, and of Jewish
traditions was the more important goal of a strict Pharisee.

Saul At The Feet of Gamaliel in Jerusalem.—Saul's parents must have been ambitious to see his theological or rabbinical training advanced, because they sent him to Jerusalem to sit at the feet of Gamaliel, one of the most celebrated Jewish teachers of the age. To study in the "Beth Hammidrash" or "House of Interpretation" in the Holy City was a coveted honor among young Jews. Possibly another reason Saul's parents sent him on to Jerusalem was the fact that his married sister may have been living there at the time. (Cf. Acts 23:16.) He could stay at her home during the time of his schooling. Saul was doubtless about fifteen years of age when he left home for Jerusalem to enter on his advanced Jewish studies. The phrase "to sit at the feet of Gamaliel" gives a true description of the method of his study. The great master would sit on a raised stand, and about him, sitting on the floor at his feet, would be his eager disciples.

Gamaliel the Elder appears before us once in the New Testament, and that in a noble role. When the Apostles were brought before the Sanhedrin, its members were disposed to kill them, but Gamaliel's words carried conviction and saved the Lord's servants. "Refrain from these men," he pleaded, "and let them alone: for if this counsel or this work be of men, it will come to nought; but if it be of God, ye cannot overthrow it; lest haply ye be found even to fight against God." (Acts 5:38-39) Christian peoples have always been kindly disposed towards Saul's great master for these words. Gamaliel was a grandson of Hillel the Great, whose kindliness and liberality were often contrasted with that of Rabbi Shammai, a famous but stern and uncompromising colleague of another school.

It was Gamaliel who instructed the promising scholar Saul in the strict acceptation of the Law, and helped him acquire his unusual knowledge of the Scriptures and skill in dialectics, which are everywhere noticeable in his Epistles.

We may suppose with some reason that Saul's study of the
Law, Prophets, and Writings comprehended what the Jews
knew as *halachah* and *haggadah*. In the words of David Smith,

> *Halachah* was the systematisation of the precepts of the Law, the
> definition, application, and reconciliation of the legal code; and
> it issued in a vast complexity of casuistical distinctions and vex-
> atious restrictions. *Haggadah*, on the other hand, dealt with the
> historical and didactic portions of the Scriptures, elaborating
> and elucidating them by the aid of parable and legend. It pur-
> sued the method of allegorical exegesis, recognizing in Scripture
> a fourfold meaning, denoted by the consonants of the word
> 'Paradise': *peshat*, the simple or literal meaning; *remaz*, the sug-
> gested meaning; *derush*, the meaning evolved by investigation;
> and *sod*, the mystic meaning.[5]

In the classroom, questions were welcomed and even
argumentation was encouraged. That student was best who
was most adept in defending his views regarding a disputed
point of law against those of his teacher and fellow students.
Josephus, the Jewish historian, in later years said:

> They give to that man the testimony of being a wise man, who
> is fully acquainted with our laws, and is able to interpret their
> meaning.[6]

That Saul learned his lessons well in the school of
Gamaliel, however imperfect may be our knowledge of
how it was conducted, can not be doubted in view of the
events that were to take place in the years to come.

A Period of Uncertainty.—We do not know how long
Saul remained under Gamaliel's tutelage or how long he
stayed in Jerusalem. It is quite probable that he returned
to his native Tarsus as a trained Rabbi, prepared when of
age to carry on his ministry in the local synagogue as well
as to engage in his craft of tent-making. All this would de-
light his parents no end, for their sacrifices in bringing up

[5]Found in *The Life and Letters of St. Paul*, by David Smith, p. 27. Used by permission of
Harper & Brothers, Publishers. Morton Scott Enslin, *The Ethics of Paul*, p. 11, though
admitting Paul's fanatic keeping of the Law and following the teaching of the Pharisees,
would deny there is much evidence of rabbinic training on his part. Indeed, Enslin cannot see that Paul's writings bear the slightest trace of any technical halakic training. This
difference of opinion on the part of reputable scholars only serves to emphasize our lack
of knowledge of the Judaistic training of Paul.

[6]*Ant.* XX. 11, 2.

their son as a strict Pharisee would be thought by them to have resulted in much fruit. That Saul remained in Tarsus or wherever he went until after the death of our Lord in A.D. 33 would seem reasonable to believe, in view of the fact that he never gives the slightest hint in his Epistles that he knew either the Savior or any of His Apostles during the days of His ministry.

Another problem remains to be considered concerning Saul's life during these years of uncertainty. Was he married? In our opinion, the answer to this must be an emphatic Yes. First of all, we know that it was the custom among the Jews for their young men to marry at an early age, generally between the years of sixteen and eighteen. And secondly, it is well known that the Jews considered marriage to be a religious obligation. The literature may be cited at length on this point.[7] There would seem to be no good reason that we know of why Saul, a trained and ardent Pharisee, should fail to honor an obligation esteemed so sacred in the eyes of his people. Finally, it should be noted that if Saul was a member of the Jewish Sanhedrin, as we believe he was (see above), it may be taken for granted that he was married, because it was required of one who belonged to that tribunal to be not only a married man but a father as well. The theory was that fathers would be more likely disposed to show mercy in their judgments than men with fewer domestic ties and presumably less affection.[8]

There will be those who will object to our views concerning Saul's marriage on the ground that 1 Corinthians 7 seems to argue otherwise. We shall consider that chapter in some detail later on in this volume and show that it does not necessarily prove that Saul had never married.

[7]See David Smith, *op. cit.*, p. 30f.
[8]*Ibid.*

Chapter 2

SAUL'S ROLE AS PERSECUTOR
OF THE CHURCH

What Brought Saul to Jerusalem as Persecutor?—
Saul is first called to our attention as a persecutor of the
early Christians in Acts 7:58, where we are told that the
witnesses to Stephen's martyrdom "laid down their clothes
at a young man's feet, whose name was Saul." Evidently
Saul had been in Jerusalem for some time engaged in re-
sisting with violence the peaceful but sure advances of the
early Church. But what had brought Saul to Jerusalem to
engage in his new role of persecutor to the Church? We
find him suddenly on the scene, with no direct explanation
given as to what caused him to forsake Tarsus, where he
had probably gone after leaving the school of Gamaliel in
Jerusalem years before. We can only conjecture that Saul's
zeal and talents were remembered by some of his former
friends in Jerusalem when the numbers and influence of
the followers of Jesus began to be thought of as a genuine
menace to Judaism. Shortly after the death of the Christ,
on the day of Pentecost, there came into the Church "about
three thousand souls." (Acts 2:41) And after Pentecost, just
how long we do not know, the number in the Church was
reckoned at "about five thousand" (Acts 4:4)—or is this
number another major addition to the Church that should
be added to those who were baptized on the day of Pentecost? At any rate, the young Church was growing by leaps
and bounds and numbered at least five thousand, not count-
ing women and children. Saul may well have been called
to Jerusalem by Pharisaic rulers to help combat the grow-

ing menace to their power. If that does not explain his presence in Jerusalem, it is just possible that a suggestion based on a passage from the Acts may provide the answer.[1] When Stephen was preaching and performing great miracles and wonders, we are told by Luke that "there arose certain of the synagogue, which is called the synagogue of the Libertines, and Cyrenians, and Alexandrians, and of them of Cilicia [Saul's original home] and of Asia, disputing with Stephen." (Acts 6:9) Drawn by this Passover and the stirring events in Judea, Saul may have been present representing Cilicia when Stephen made his attacks on the citadel of Pharisaism. But the enemies of the Church were "not able to resist the wisdom and the spirit by which he [Stephen] spake." (Acts 6:10) The defeat of the learned Jews at the hands of an unknown upstart rankled and embittered their souls. Before the Spirit their cleverness and theological casuistry went for nought. For that very reason, Saul and his Pharisaic colleagues were more than ever determined to fight the followers of the Church to a finish. Saul's natural zeal and ability rose to the occasion, for he felt that he was doing God a service if he could help stem the threatening advance of the followers of Christ.

Among these considerations we have reason enough for Saul's being in Jerusalem and for remaining there, if necessary, long enough to smother the threat to Judaism.

Saul's Official Presence at the Martyrdom of Stephen. —Stephen's piercing accusations against the Jews maddened them, particularly when he said:

> Which of the prophets have not your fathers persecuted? and they have slain them which shewed before of the coming of the Just One; of whom ye have been now the betrayers and murderers. (Acts 7:52)

If this were not enough to bring about his death, Stephen's declaration that he could see the heavens opened

---

[1]See A. T. Robertson, *Epochs in the Life of Paul*, pp. 23f.

and the Son of Man standing on the right hand of God
(Acts 7:56) triggered the dastardly act. Luke's account says
that they "cried out with a loud voice, and stopped their
ears, and ran upon him with one accord, and cast him out
of the city, and stoned him." (Acts 7:57-58)

The forthright account of Luke indicates that the Sanhedrin gave but scant justice to Stephen. The Council
doubtless took the view that he had blasphemed, and they
voted for his death, with Saul's vote probably among them.
(Acts 26:10) The stoning of Stephen was a flagrant viola-
tion of law. The Sanhedrin had the right to pass a sentence
of death, but only the Roman procurator, in this case
Pontius Pilate, could legally permit the judgment to be
carried out. The fact that Pilate seems not to have been
consulted shows how weak and uninfluential he had by this
time become. The Jews did as they pleased. The account in
Acts, as was pointed out above, tells us that Saul was present
at Stephen's execution. (Acts 7:58) The witnesses threw off
their outer garments and gave them into Saul's care. The
term "witnesses" is amply explained by this quotation from
the Hebrew Scriptures:

> At the mouth of two witnesses, or three witnesses, shall he that
> is worthy of death be put to death; but at the mouth of one
> witness he shall not be put to death. The hands of the witnesses
> shall be first upon him to put him to death; and afterward the
> hands of all the people. So thou shalt put the evil away from
> among you. (Deut. 17:6-7)

It would hardly seem probable that Saul was at the
scene of Stephen's death as a mere spectator. More probable is the belief that he was present in an official capacity
from the Sanhedrin to see that the Deuteronomic injunction was properly carried out. The two or three "witnesses"
who had testified against Stephen (see Acts 6:13-14) would
suitably identify themselves to Saul and leave their outer
garments with him before stepping forth to be the first in
the stoning of the victim. Saul was a willing and clever

agent of the Jewish rulers in bringing about their purpose, the complete destruction of the Church.

Saul Continues to Harass the Church.—"And Saul was consenting unto his death." (Acts 8:1) So the Acts describes the future Apostle's attitude toward Stephen's execution. Nor did his zeal abate with the bloody death of the Martyr. We are told that there was a great persecution against the Church in Jerusalem; so bad was it that all members, the Apostles excepted, were scattered throughout Judea and Samaria. (*Ibid.*) Saul's part in this affair is told in these graphic words:

> As for Saul, he made havoc of the Church, entering into every house, and haling men and women committed them to prison. (Acts 8:3)

The one happy circumstance about the scattering of the members of the Church in Jerusalem was the fact that they "went every where preaching the word." (Acts 8:4)

In later years Saul describes with great sorrow his own part in the heartless persecution of the Church. Let us look at his words:

> I verily thought with myself, that I ought to do many things contrary to the name of Jesus of Nazareth. Which thing I also did in Jerusalem: and many of the saints did I shut up in prison, having received authority from the chief priests; and when they were put to death, I gave my voice [vote] against them. And I punished them oft in every synagogue, and compelled them to blaspheme; and being exceedingly mad against them, I persecuted them even unto strange cities. (Acts 26:9-11)
>
> * * *
>
> For I am the least of the Apostles, that am not meet to be called an apostle, because I persecuted the Church of God. (1 Cor. 15:9)
>
> * * *
>
> For ye have heard in my conversation in time past in the Jews' religion, how that beyond measure I persecuted the Church of God, and wasted it. (Gal. 1:13)
>
> * * *
>
> Who was before a blasphemer, and a persecutor, and injurious. (I Tim. 1:13)

These "confessions" of Saul in the days of his Apostleship indicate the very serious nature of his offenses against
God and his fellowmen during the formative years of the
Church. One does not shut up men in prison without fair
trial, vote to put some of them to death, punish others in
their synagogues and compel them to blaspheme, be "injurious" and become in turn a blasphemer, without being
regarded by righteous men as a criminal offender. There
is no need to minimize the gravity of Saul's sins; the great
Apostle certainly did not. In his First Epistle to Timothy,
Paul records in his old age that he obtained mercy from
our Lord because he had sinned "ignorantly in unbelief."
(1:13)

Chapter 3

SAUL'S CONVERSION

Saul Obtains Authority to Persecute the Church in Damascus.—Saul and his colleagues had done so well in scattering the followers of Jesus in Jerusalem that he now felt it incumbent upon himself to break up their concentrations elsewhere. The future Apostle did nothing by halves. Like a physician who knows that centers of infection in a patient must be cleared up if a cure is to be effected, Saul felt it necessary to clear out the local branches of hated Christ-followers in distant centers if the threat to his beloved Judaism was to be allayed.

Damascus was deemed to be a "hot" metropolis that demanded immediate attention. His zeal unabated, indeed, "yet breathing out threatenings and slaughter against the disciples of the Lord, [Saul] went unto the high priest, and desired of him letters to Damascus to the synagogues, that if he found any of this Way, whether they were men or women, he might bring them bound unto Jerusalem." (Acts 9:1-2) If it be a puzzle to the modern reader how Saul could legally bring back prisoners from a city beyond the borders of Palestine, we may explain that by Roman sufferance every Jewish colony in her Empire was considered subject in religious matters to the local synagogue, which in turn was under the control of the Sanhedrin in Jerusalem. That a Jew belonged to the Church of Christ, or to some other strange group, would make no difference to the Jerusalem authorities; he would be looked upon merely as a member of a Jewish sect like any Pharisee or Sadducee. A. T. Robertson makes a comment of interest to us in this respect:

The Jew, like the modern Roman Catholic, owed a double allegiance, one to his state, the other to the ecclesiastical or temple authorities at Jerusalem.[1]

The reader may also have been interested in the reference to "this Way" in the passage we quoted from Acts. By it is simply meant the "Gospel" or the "Way of the Lord." The most frequently used word in Scripture for road is "way," and this word or its cognates are often used in describing religions.

Having received the necessary papers giving him the authorization he desired, Saul went on his cruel—yes, murderous—mission to Damascus. He was doubtless attended by the needed servants and officers of the Sanhedrin. We need not pause to speculate on the route he took; the fact is that he was only too willing to walk the one hundred and forty miles separating him from the ancient Syrian capital. The Greek words used in the narration suggest that he walked, not to mention the fact that on coming into the city his companions "led him by the hand." (Acts 9:8) When the author once traversed the distance between Jerusalem and Damascus in a modern car (which was bad enough), he couldn't help but think of Saul's zeal and determination in doing a job he thought was right. The fact that the future Apostle walked is perhaps of little importance in itself, but it does tend to reveal certain aspects of his character and state of mind.

The Turning Point in Saul's Life, A Heavenly Vision.—The epigram, so well known to us all, that "man proposes, but God disposes"[2] takes on particular significance when applied to Saul's life. The fiery Cilician and his Pharisaic colleagues had thus far played havoc with the Church and were determined to bring about its complete destruction. Saul had no reason to doubt that his Damascus mission would prove as successful as the one in Jerusalem. But as

[1]*Epochs in the Life of Paul*, p. 36. Charles Scribner's Sons, Publishers.
[2]From Thomas a Kempis' *Imitation of Christ*.

he drew near to Damascus, having, most likely, a grim satisfaction within himself for what he was about to do to those misguided followers of Jesus, the Almighty determined to have a reckoning with him. And that reckoning was to have tremendous repercussions, not only upon Saul, but upon the world. The story is told in the simple, straightforward and sober manner that we have learned to expect from Luke:

> And as he journeyed, he came near Damascus: and suddenly there shined [flashed, or gleamed around like lightning] round about him a light from heaven: and he fell to the earth, and heard a voice saying unto him, Saul, Saul, why persecutest thou Me? And he said, Who art thou, Lord? And the Lord said, I am Jesus whom thou persecutest: it is hard for thee to kick against the pricks [goads]. And he trembling and astonished said, Lord, what wilt thou have me to do? And the Lord said unto him, Arise, and go into the city, and it shall be told thee what thou must do. (Acts 9:3-6)

That this vision was real and no mere "subjective phantasm," to quote David Smith,[3] was the repeated testimony of Saul in later years. When his very Apostleship was challenged by the Judaizers on the grounds that he had never seen Jesus or had never been commissioned by Him, his answer was clear: "Am I not an Apostle? am I not free? have I not seen Jesus Christ our Lord?" (I Cor. 9:1) In two places in Acts, Saul personally tells of his experience on the way to Damascus. The first is in 22:6-8 and the second in 26:12-18. All three accounts (including the one in Acts 9:3-6) differ in certain minor respects, as might be expected, and the one in Acts 26 contains certain words to which we call attention. The Lord said to Saul:

> But rise, and stand upon thy feet: for I have *appeared* unto thee for this purpose, to make thee a minister and a witness both of these things which thou hast seen, and of those things in the which I will appear unto thee. (Acts 26:16; italics ours.)

The Greek word translated "appeared" in this passage seems clearly to indicate that Saul actually saw the risen

[3]*The Life and Letters of St. Paul*, p. 51.

Christ. The same word is used in Luke 24:34 in connection with our Lord's appearance to Simon, and also in I Cor. 15:5-7, where it is translated by the Authorized Version as "He was seen" when referring to His appearance to the Apostles and others.

That some very unusual but objective experience happened to Saul is to be seen in the conduct of his companions at the time. In Acts 9:7-8 (Authorized Version), we are told that they "stood speechless, hearing a voice, but seeing no man," and found it necessary, because Saul had been blinded, to lead him "by the hand" into Damascus. In the account in Acts 22:9 we are told that Saul's companions "saw indeed the light, . . . but they heard not the voice of him that spake. . ." The discrepancy in these two accounts was cleared up by the prophet Joseph Smith, who made known by the spirit of revelation that the one in Acts 22 is to be regarded as correct. (See "Inspired" revision of the Bible.)

— Unfortunately for the religious welfare of mankind, modern rationalists, in their open opposition to the supernatural, have given wide publicity to their "natural" explanations of Saul's vision and conversion. To Latter-day Saints a brief summary of their views may be of profit and interest if only because of the fact that the prophet Joseph Smith's accounts of his first and subsequent visions have been attacked in much the same manner. The rationalist hypotheses may be reduced to two:[4] (1) Saul was by nature nervous and excitable, subject to attacks of hysteria and epilepsy, and predisposed to visions and ecstasies. The appearance of Christ to him, therefore, on his mission to Damascus, was but the first of those ecstatic experiences which were repeated at intervals thereafter. (2) Saul's conversion, with the extraordinary phenomena that accompa-

[4]The author is here heavily indebted to the fine analysis of Charles J. Callan, O.P., *The Epistles of St. Paul*, I, xiii. By permission of Joseph F. Wagner (Inc.), Publishers. New York.

nied it, was but the final crisis of a great mental and soul-searching struggle that had shaken him profoundly since the death of Stephen. All during his trip to Damascus Saul was questioning his own motives in persecuting the Church. By day and by night he was harried and haunted with thoughts and feelings of fear, remorse and uncertainty. Finally, when he was near the great Oriental metropolis, Saul's great interior struggle reached its climax. A psychological transformation took place in him which Luke has erroneously materialized.

So much for the critics. But the evidence does not bear out their conclusions. As many believers in Saul's remarkable vision have not been slow to point out, his own words ascribe his conversion absolutely and without question to God's grace and the personal intervention of the Christ.

> It pleased God, who separated me from my mother's womb, and called me by His grace, to reveal His Son in me, that I might preach him among the heathen [Gentiles]. (Gal. 1:15-16)

Nowhere in the New Testament records is it possible to find any hint of Saul's having a soul-searching struggle while on the way to Damascus. He seems to have been caught unawares when our Lord vouchsafed him his first great vision.

The charge that Saul was subject to attacks of hysteria and epilepsy is difficult to maintain in view of the fact that the men with him at the time of his vision also saw the light and were speechless and afraid. (Acts 9:7; 22:9)

The evidence points to the fact that Saul was miraculously turned from carrying out a plan which he zealously believed to be right. To make him about-face, the Lord delivered a spiritual "jolt" that the proud Pharisee never forgot. The arisen Christ made him out as a persecutor, instead of a good man in God's service. But, quickly and effectually convinced that he was in the service of the wrong master, Saul asked the Lord what he should do. The Master

did not berate him, but gave to him a divine commission
which the Apostle was to recall in later years before King
Agrippa. Part of it we have already quoted above, but a
repetition of that part may be pardoned.

> But rise, and stand upon thy feet: for I have appeared unto
> thee for this purpose, to make thee a minister and a witness
> both of these things which thou hast seen, and of those things
> in the which I will appear unto thee; delivering thee from the
> people, and from the Gentiles, unto whom now I send thee, to
> open their eyes, and to turn them from darkness to light, and
> from the power of Satan unto God, that they may receive for-
> giveness of sins, and inheritance among them which are sancti-
> fied by faith that is in me. (Acts 26:16-18)

Saul now knew his real life's work, and he entered
into the Lord's service with the same vigor and zeal that
had characterized his career as a Pharisee. Like Alma the
Younger and the four sons of King Mosiah of Book of
Mormon fame (Mosiah 27:8-37), who years before on the
American continent, had had a very similar conversion to
his, Saul anxiously embarked upon a course tending not
only to undo the damage he had wrought upon the Church,
but also to spread its fame and increase its membership
throughout the Roman Empire.

Chapter 4

SAUL'S PERIOD OF PREPARATION

Saul is Led to Damascus.—Saul's interview with the risen, glorified Master had left him in spiritual concussion, nor could he see with his natural eyes when he arose from the ground where he had fallen when the light from heaven flashed round him. (Acts 9:3) Our Lord gave him a physical reminder that must have puzzled Saul's colleagues for a time, because they had to lead him by the hand into Damascus. Possibly their chief gave them a partial explanation of what had befallen him while on the way. The Master had bidden Saul to go into the city and await instructions. (Acts 9:6) The text does not inform us whether or not the Lord had directed him to go to some specific house; it is probable that Saul and his men proceeded directly to the home of a man called Judas on the street called Straight as per prior arrangements in Jerusalem. For three days the stricken Saul remained without sight, neither did he eat or drink. In this state he had ample time to think and ponder over the sudden change in his life.

The Lord Speaks to Ananias Concerning Saul.— Meanwhile, the Lord spoke in vision to one Ananias, a member of the Church (disciple), who was held in high repute by all the Jews of the city because of his piety and obedience to the Law, and directed him to go to Saul's side in the house of Judas. In the vision, Ananias was told that Saul was even then praying and had seen him (in vision) enter his room and lay hands upon him so that he might recover his sight. (Acts 9:10-12; 22:12) But Ananias seemed averse to visiting Saul, not only because he had

heard of his terrible activities in Jerusalem, but also because he knew of Saul's authorization by the High Priests
to arrest the Saints in Damascus. (Acts 9:13-14) Nevertheless, the Lord told Ananias to go to Saul, because he was
a chosen instrument to carry His name to the Gentiles and
to kings and to the sons of Israel. "For," said the Lord,
"I will show him how great things he must suffer for my
name's sake." (Acts 9:15-16)

Ananias Heals Saul.—Obedient to the Lord's call,
Ananias went to the house of Judas. Laying his hands upon
the sightless man of Tarsus, he addressed him as a brother:

> Brother Saul, the Lord, even Jesus, that appeared unto thee in
> the way as thou camest, hath sent me, that thou mightest receive
> thy sight, and be filled with the Holy Ghost. (Acts 9:17)

Something like scales fell from Saul's eyes, and he
could look upon Ananias, who addressed these further
words to Saul:

> The God of our fathers hath chosen thee, that thou shouldst
> know His will, and see that Just One, and shouldst hear the
> voice of His mouth. For thou shalt be His witness unto all men
> of what thou hast seen and heard. And now why tarriest thou?
> arise, and be baptized, and wash away thy sins, calling on the
> name of the Lord. (Acts 22:14-16; see also 9:18; 22:13)

Saul Joins the Church and Preaches.—Saul immediately acted upon the suggestion of Ananias and was baptized
even before receiving food, although he had been three
days without it. As Latter-day Saints, we feel it reasonable
to suppose that Ananias also laid hands upon the repentant
Saul, confirmed him a member of the Church, and blessed
him with the gift of the Holy Ghost. The reader should
notice that Paul was dealt with by a proper authority of
the Church in Damascus.

After baptism Saul remained with the disciples "certain
days," and, obedient to his heavenly vision, immediately
proclaimed Christ in the synagogues as the Son of God. He
also emphasized that men "should repent and turn to God,

and do works meet for repentance." (Acts 9:19-20; 26:19-20)
The doctrines of repentance, baptism, and belief in the
arisen Christ as the Son of God were about all that he could
preach with great conviction at the time, because he had
not been in the Church sufficiently long to digest all the
principles taught by it. Saul was a master of the Scriptures
as taught by Pharisee teachers, but it would take him some
time to reconcile and harmonize his great knowledge with
the Gospel as taught by our Lord. Much that he had been
taught in his earlier life would prove to be chaff, not in
accord with the true principles of religion he would now be
required to teach. Nevertheless, Saul had a ready mind,
and his great knowledge of the letter of Scripture put him
in an excellent position to receive quickly deep insights into
the Gospel, with the aid of the Holy Ghost. That this is so
is shown by the fact that after the initial period of amaze-
ment at his about-face was over, he "increased the more in
strength, and confounded the Jews which dwelt at Damascus, proving that this is very Christ." (Acts 9:21-22)

Little Known of Ananias or of Saul's Companions.
—In after years Saul spoke graciously of the part taken by
Ananias in this early period of his ministry. (Acts 22:12-13)
But he never mentions him in his Epistles, and aside from
what has been said in the Acts, we know nothing about him.

We may wonder about what happened to Saul's companions who came with him from Damascus. Did any of
them follow his example and join the Church? If not, did
they join in turning against him? But nothing is said of
them in the Acts or in any of the Epistles.

Saul Retires to Arabia.—Saul's conversion was such
an upsetting experience that he must have thought it necessary to seek retirement in a quiet place, think through his
changed situation, and seek the spiritual instruction and
uplift required for his coming mission to the Gentiles. It is
to Saul rather than to Luke that we owe the knowledge of

what he did after his "certain days" (Acts 9:19) with the disciples in Damascus were up. And this part of his story would fit in well after Acts 9:22. Without consulting anyone, including those who were Apostles, he went into Arabia and returned again to Damascus. (Gal. 1:16-17)

We are uncertain how long Saul remained in Arabia; neither are we told just where he sojourned in that land. Some suppose that he went to the peninsula of Sinai, where Moses gave the Law from the mountain of smoke and thunder; others say that he may not have been far from Damascus, because Arabia in that day encompassed also the region east of the Jordan, with Damascus itself included.[1] Indeed we cannot determine with any precision the exact place where he went, but wherever it was he probably stayed from one to three years, judging from what he says in Gal. 1:18. But we can be sure that through prayer and meditation Saul came to peace with himself and his God in the desert place. Like Moses and the Christ before him, in such solitary places was he prepared for his ministry; doubtless, during this desert sojourn, he became the recipient of divine revelations instructing him in the truths of his new faith (cf. 2 Cor. 12:1-7). Saul in later years emphasized the fact that the Gospel which he taught came not from man, neither did he receive it of ordinary mortals, but by revelation from the Lord:

> But I certify you, brethren, that the gospel which was preached of me is not after man. For I neither received it of man, neither was I taught it, but by the revelation of Jesus Christ. (Gal. 1:11-12)

Like Moses before him, Saul was instructed in the essentials of the faith through the revelations of Jesus Christ. It is undoubtedly true that before his conversion Saul knew many general principles of our Lord's teachings through the reports he received of the preaching of the Apostles.

---

[1]See Conybeare and Howson, *The Life and Epistles of St. Paul*, pp. 79f.; David Smith, *The Life and Letters of St. Paul*, pp. 56f., especially the notes.

But these would become spiritually meaningful to him only after he became heir to the ministrations of the Holy Ghost. That Saul received little or no direct instruction from men is strongly implied in Gal. 2:1-10, where he insists that his Gospel is not opposed to that of the leaders of the Church, but had had their direct approval; in fact, he did not even receive any new suggestions from them.

In due time, whether one year or two years, and part of another year, Saul finished the period of his preparation for the service of his new Master, and was prepared to leave the desert and its solitary places.

Chapter 5

FROM DAMASCUS TO ANTIOCH

Saul Returns to Damascus.—Leaving Arabia and
the scenes of his spiritual adjustment and preparation, Saul
returned to Damascus. Here he plunged directly into the
work of his ministry, and so vigorous and effective must
his testimony have been for "many days" that "the Jews
took counsel to kill him." (Acts 9:23) Now Saul got a taste
of persecution himself—sinister persecution that did not
scruple at the taking of life. In one sense this was poetic
justice, for Saul had only a short time before breathed out
"threatenings and slaughter" (Acts 9:1) against the Saints.
Furthermore, the persecution against him was in the very
city where he had hoped to clean out a nest of hated
Christ-followers.

Saul learned of the plot against him and of the fact
that his enemies watched the gates of Damascus day and
night to kill him. (Acts 9:24) The plotters enlisted the
active help of the ethnarch of Damascus, who was the
representative of King Aretas, the Roman-recognized ruler
of the city. The ethnarch, as guardian of the metropolis,
gave instructions to the guards at each of the gates to
apprehend Saul if he should attempt to escape. (2 Cor.
11:32) The situation became so tense that Saul finally
decided upon flight. It is a wise man who knows when to
hold his ground and when to flee. A dead man could not
very well carry the Gospel to the Gentiles, so flight it was.
Saul was aided by the disciples (same mss. read "his
disciples") in Damascus to make a clever escape. Certain
houses on the wall of the city had windows overhanging

the fosse, and one or more of those houses may have belonged to the loyal friends of Saul. It was decided to put the fleeing man through a window in a basket and lower him down the wall under cover of darkness. (Acts 9:25; 2 Cor. 11:33) Thus the beleaguered Saul made good his escape.

Saul Visits Jerusalem.—Three years had passed since Saul's conversion, and he felt it wise to go to Jerusalem (A.D. 39?), make himself known to the Church which he had so cruelly mistreated, and pay his respects to the Apostles, particularly to Peter. (Gal. 1:18) This first visit to the Palestinian metropolis after his conversion, was of great importance to him throughout his life. On arriving in Jerusalem he made attempts to associate with the Church membership, but they were all afraid of him, having doubts that he was a bonafide disciple. (Acts 9:26) These actions must have hurt Saul's feelings, but he could readily understand their suspicious attitude toward him. He could not very well blame them for their cool reception.

Barnabas Befriends Saul.—One of the Church members, quite happily, came to Saul's aid. This generous and discerning man was Barnabas ("the son of consolation" or "the son of exhortation"), whose proper name was Joseph, a Levite, hailing originally from the island of Cyprus. (Acts 4:36) He was a Hellenist,[1] therefore, and like his well-known kinswoman Mary, the mother of John Mark, he had been well endowed with this world's goods, which he had devoted to the welfare of the Church. (Acts 4:37; 12:12; Col. 4:10) Possessed of a winsome personality, he was also a man of distinguished appearance, and in later years the people of Lystra took him for Zeus, the King of the Gods. (Acts 14:11-12)

---

[1]The term is usually applied to Jews who had adopted the Greek language, and with it often Greek practices and opinions. The Authorized Version calls them "Grecians."

Convinced of Saul's sincerity and of the reality of his conversion, Barnabas took the unpopular man in hand, brought him to the Apostles, and told them of the miraculous conversion of their visitor. Barnabas emphasized the important parts of Saul's testimony, namely, the personal appearance of the risen Lord to him and his bold preaching to the Jews in Damascus. (Acts 9:27) Although the Acts bears testimony that Saul was taken to the Apostles, it should be remembered that only two of the Twelve were in Jerusalem at the time, according to Saul's own words, and these were Peter and James, the brother of the Lord. (Gal. 1:18-19) According to this last reference, Peter must have invited Saul to stay at his home, where he "abode with him fifteen days." It was more especially Peter that Saul had come to Jerusalem to see. Saul would learn much firsthand from Peter concerning the ministry and work of the Savior.

Saul Preaches in Jerusalem.—Under the sponsorship of Peter and James, Saul could mingle freely with the disciples in Jerusalem, who would now be anxious to hear him bear testimony concerning his conversion. His preaching and unusual testimony doubtless thrilled these disciples whom he had once persecuted.

But Saul's restless spirit yearned to cross swords with and reason with the Greek-speaking Jews who had once been confederate with him. With his usual courage he stepped into the Hellenistic synagogues and "disputed against the Grecians." (Acts 9:29) In these encounters Saul found himself up against the arguments which he had once employed against the disciples. But his keen knowledge of the Scriptures, aided and abetted by his absolute knowledge that Jesus was the Christ, would prove too strong a weapon for his adversaries. Saul now wielded the sword of the Spirit, and his opponents, who were not convinced by the truth, resorted to debate by violence and "went about to slay him." (Acts 9:29)

Saul's Vision in the Temple.—While yet in Jerusalem and apparently during the time of his encounters with the Hellenistic Jews, Saul came into the Temple to engage in prayer. Let him tell what followed:

> While I prayed in the temple, I was in a trance; and saw Him saying unto me, Make haste, and get thee quickly out of Jerusalem: for they will not receive thy testimony concerning Me. And I said, Lord, they know that I imprisoned and beat in every synagogue them that believed on thee: and when the blood of Thy martyr Stephen was shed, I also was standing by, and consenting unto his death, and kept the raiment of them that slew him. And He said unto me, Depart: for I will send thee far hence unto the Gentiles. (Acts 22:17-21)

Saul Leaves Jerusalem for Caesarea and Tarsus.— When Saul's brethren heard that the Jews were plotting to slay him, "they brought him down to Caesarea [some mss. add 'by night'], and sent him forth to Tarsus." (Acts 9:30)

After Luke had recounted Saul's flight from Jerusalem and the uproar he had caused, he added this interesting comment:

> Then had the churches rest throughout all Judea and Galilee and Samaria, and were edified; and walking in the fear of the Lord, and in the comfort of the Holy Ghost, were multiplied. (Acts 9:31)

Although we are not expressly told Saul's route from Caesarea to Tarsus, the natural presumption would be that he went by sea, for why would the disciples go as far with him to a seaport if not to get him upon the water completely out of the way of his adversaries? For aught we know, Saul may even have suffered shipwreck on his way to Tarsus. He tells us in 2 Cor. 11:25 that he had been shipwrecked three times, but in the narrative of Acts it is very difficult to find a place for any of these shipwrecks.

We can only imagine Saul's reception by his family and former associates upon his return to Tarsus. Yet it would very probably be a sad one, marked by the sorrow and evident displeasure of his father, a strict old Pharisee, at his son's conversion to the hated sect composed of the followers of Christ. Saul never once in later years refers to the encounter with his family and former friends. He doubtless chose to forget a scene that had caused another tragedy in his life. Surely he would have mentioned his father and mother if they had turned to Christ through his preaching; he mentions the names of so many other converts in his Epistles. And what, in the meantime, became of his wife and child (or children) whom we believe he had[2] before Stephen's martyrdom? Perhaps there is still another tragedy here. His wife may have completely forsaken him also, after his conversion. But of this we can only speculate; the record is silent.

Saul Preaches in Syria and Cilicia.—Whatever reception awaited him at his old home in Tarsus, we can be assured that Saul would soon be busy preaching. And years later, when he wrote his Epistle to the Galatians, he tells us that he preached in the regions of Syria and Cilicia with such success that the churches in Judea, to whom he was "unknown by face" (except in Jerusalem), heard of his work and glorified God on account of him. (Gal. 1:21-24) If our calculations are correct, it was now about A.D. 39 (see above), and Saul was to spend about four years of his ministry among the inhabitants of Syria and Cilicia. Our approximation of the number of years spent by Saul in his ministry among these people is arrived at in this way: Saul had been in Antioch a year or more (yet future at this time) when the prophet Agabus made the prediction of a great famine throughout the world. (Acts 11:26-28) The passage cited tells us that the famine "came to pass in the days of Claudius Caesar." Claudius began his rule in A.D. 41, which means that the famine came after that time. Apparently the famine must have been at its height when Saul and Barnabas, after giving aid to the Saints, returned from Jerusalem to Antioch after or about the time of the death of Herod Agrippa, which occurred in A.D. 44. (Acts 11:29-

[2]See p. 9.

30; 12:21-25) Josephus, the great Jewish historian, tells us specifically that the famine occurred under the procurators Cuspius Fadus and Tiberius Alexander, A.D. 44 and 48. This fact gives us another check on our estimates. We can assume, then, that Saul preached in Syria and Cilicia from about A.D. 39 to 43.

That the Lord did not forget Saul during this period of his ministry near Tarsus is shown in his Second Epistle to the Corinthians, which was written about A.D. 55 or 57. Revelations of surpassing grandeur were given to him, as these words attest:

> It is not expedient for me doubtless to glory. I will come to visions and revelations of the Lord. I knew a man in Christ above fourteen years ago [about A.D. 41 or 43], (whether in the body, I cannot tell; or whether out of the body, I cannot tell: God knoweth;) such an one caught up to the third heaven. And I knew such a man, (whether in the body, or out of the body, I cannot tell: God knoweth;) how that he was caught up into paradise, and heard unspeakable words, which it is not lawful for a man to utter. (2 Cor. 12:1-4)

All during his sojourn in his native province, Saul must have grown wonderfully through his missionary experiences and his direct contact with the heavens. This growth and spiritual discipline were to prove of glorious worth to the Church in its expansion of later years.

Barnabas Seeks Saul and Brings Him to Antioch.— Luke tells us that the persecution "that arose about Stephen" (in which Saul had taken a part) had scattered the Church membership as far as Phoenicia, Cyprus, and Antioch, and some of the fugitives preached only to Jews in these places. (Acts 11:19) Others, however, men of Cyprus and Cyrene in Africa, when they came to Antioch, preached the Lord Jesus to the "Grecians" (Grecian Jews) or "Greeks," depending on which text of Acts 11:20 one uses. Such was the success of these fugitive missionaries that, with God's help, great numbers believed and turned to the Lord. (Acts 11:21) Tidings of the great successes in conversion led to the Authorities' sending Barnabas, a trusted emissary, to investigate. It is not at all improbable that the number of Gentiles who joined the Church caused the Church Authorities a little uneasiness at first. Their choice of Barnabas to look into matters was a happy one, because he was not only a "good man, and full of the Holy Ghost and of faith" (Acts 11:24), but also a broad-gauged judge of the characteristics of the Gentile element in the region, having originally come from Cyprus. His magnetic presence and personality would also give him prestige among the regular members and converts of the Church in Antioch. Barnabas quickly ascertained the true state of affairs and was glad of God's grace to the converts, whom he exhorted to cleave to the Lord with fixed resolve. (Acts 11:23) Not only was Barnabas delighted with the converts, both Jews and Greeks, but he felt that he needed someone to help him carry on the good work in Antioch. He thought immediately of Saul, whom he had met in Jerusalem, and whose fame in the ministry round about Tarsus had reached to other regions. So he left for Tarsus, and having found Saul, "brought him to Antioch." (Acts 11:25-26) Saul was doubtless glad for the opportunity to labor in this, the third ranking city of the Roman Empire. Only Rome and Alexandria surpassed her in greatness. Antioch was the Greek metropolis of Syria. Native Syrians made up the greater number of the population, followed by the Greeks and a large colony of Jews. The city had a reputation for learning and culture as well as for its licentiousness. It is also significant that "the disciples were called Christians first in Antioch." (Acts 11:26)

Saul would be a mighty help in working with the Gentile Greeks, because they were his special mission, but we can also be sure that his great Jewish learning would be often called into play. "And it came to pass, that a whole year they [Barnabas and Saul] assembled themselves with the Church, and taught much people." (*Ibid.*)

Barnabas and Saul Bring Relief to the Saints in Jerusalem.—When Saul had spent a year in Antioch, he suddenly found himself (approximately A. D. 44) in a new role, along with Barnabas his distinguished companion. It appears that certain prophets came from Jerusalem to Antioch, among them Agabus, who "signified by the Spirit" that there would be a great famine throughout the world. (Acts 11:27-28) The disciples in Antioch, each according to his means, determined to send relief to the Saints in Jerusalem, for the famine did break out as predicted, and the people of Judea seem to have been heavy-hit. Josephus tells of the famine in these words:

> ... Claudius was emperor of the Romans, and Israel was our high priest, ... when so great a famine was come upon us, that one tenth deal [of wheat] was sold for four drachmae, ...[3]

We know that great numbers also perished.

Barnabas and Saul were sent from Antioch with whatever form the relief took, whether cash or commodities or both. The relief was duly delivered by them to the "Elders" in Jerusalem and, we trust, was wisely distributed to the needy Saints. (Acts 11:30)[4] When Barnabas and Saul had completed their mission, they returned to Jerusalem, bringing with them John Mark, a cousin of Barnabas (Col. 4:10) and son of Mary, to whose home Peter had hastened when he had been miraculously released from prison. (Acts 12:16-17) Peter later referred to Mark as his spiritual "son" (1 Peter 5:13), which doubtless meant that he had converted and baptized him. Mark was to become famous as the author of the Gospel by his name. Both Barnabas and Saul must have been impressed with Mark as a potential missionary companion and helper.

[3] *Ant.* iii, 15, 3.

[4] The author cannot believe with Sir Wm. Ramsay, *St. Paul the Traveller*, p. 51, that Barnabas and Saul "acted as administrators (diakonoi) of the relief." The Church Authorities in Jerusalem would probably be in charge of the distribution. The machinery of the distribution was already in existence. (Acts 4:32-37; 6:1-6) We need not deny that Barnabas and Saul helped the local brethren, the "Elders," in their work.

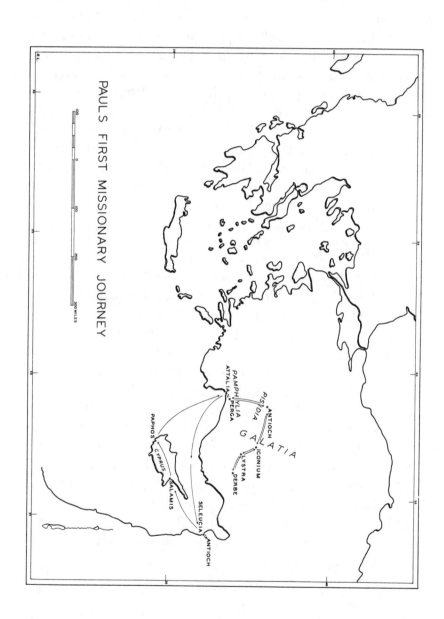

PAUL'S FIRST MISSIONARY JOURNEY

100   0   100   200   300 MILES

GALATIA

PISIDIA
ANTIOCH
ICONIUM
LYSTRA
DERBE

PAMPHYLIA
ATTALIA
PERGA

PAPHOS
CYPRUS
SALAMIS

SELEUCIA
ANTIOCH

R.L.

Chapter 6

THE FIRST MISSIONARY JOURNEY
AND THE SOJOURN IN ANTIOCH

Saul and Barnabas Are Set Apart to Preach to the Gentiles.—The call to preach in all the world had been given by the Savior at least three times following His resurrection. First, Peter had learned quite convincingly, through the Cornelius episode (Acts 10:1-11:18), that the Gentiles could receive the Gospel as well as the Jews. We have already seen how at Antioch the Gentiles (Greeks) also received the Gospel and were administered to by Barnabas, Saul, and others. Now we are to see how Barnabas and Saul together received a formal call to make a missionary tour to the Gentiles. This and succeeding tours were to make world history.

Luke tells us of certain prophets and teachers in Antioch. Agabus seems to have departed, but Barnabas, Simeon that was called Niger, Lucius of Cyrene, Manaen (a former courtier of Herod Antipas), and Saul were still in the city. (Acts 13:1)

When on a certain occasion these brethren ministered to the Lord and fasted, the Holy Ghost moved them and said, "Separate me Barnabas and Saul for the work whereunto I have called them." (Acts 13:2) Then, after fasting and prayer, the companions of Barnabas and Saul laid their hands upon them and set them apart to their new mission. The general field of service was probably known to them and had doubtless been discussed at length, for Barnabas and Saul seem to have felt no uncertainty as to where they were to go. Barnabas appears to have been the

older man of the two, and was a senior to Saul also in
point of service. It will be remembered, after Saul had left
Damascus and had come to Jerusalem especially to see
Peter, that Barnabas, already well known to the Church
Authorities, was the one who introduced him to them. (Acts
19:26-27) In the call of the Holy Ghost to the two missionaries, notice the order in which Acts speaks of them: "Separate me Barnabas and Saul." (13:2) Later the order was
to change. In connection with the call of Barnabas and
Saul there is an interesting question that may as well be
brought up now as later.

Was Saul an Apostle at This Time?—If Saul was at
this time an Apostle, why does he appear as a junior to
Barnabas?—unless Barnabas was also an Apostle. And, in
fact, both men are called Apostles (Greek: *apostoloi*) in Acts
14:4, 14. But does this title mean that they had been formally ordained as such, or does it have the common meaning of "one sent" or "missionary"? And if Barnabas and
Saul were formal Apostles in the sense that they were special
witnesses of the Christ and regarded as our Apostles are in
the Church today, why was it necessary for them to be set
apart for their missionary journey by men of inferior rank?
Surely Simeon called Niger, Lucius of Cyrene, and Manaen
(Acts 13:1), although inspired men, were not Apostles. Even
if Barnabas and Saul were true Apostles at this time, it may
well be taken for granted that they were never formal
members of the Twelve. The history of New Testament
times offers little or no proof that they ever were. In fact,
there is no proof that any other man was ever ordained to
take the place of any of the original Twelve as they died
except Matthias, who took the place of Judas the traitor.
(Acts 1:23-26) None of us doubts that Saul became an
Apostle; he repeatedly asserted that he was one (I Cor.1:1;
2 Cor. 1:1; Gal.1:1; Eph. 1:1; I Tim. 1:1; 2 Tim. 1:1; Tit.
1:1), but there is no record that he was ever ordained by

Peter or any other member of the Twelve. And when Saul says that he was an Apostle, he emphasizes the fact that his doctrine and holy office came not by man, but by Jesus Christ; at least, that is the clear import of Gal. 1:1-24. Some authorities hold that Saul became an Apostle at the time of his conversion;[1] others believe that he received the sacred office at the time of his vision in the Temple at Jerusalem.[2] (Acts 22:17-21) Still others hold to another time. The author feels that it is difficult to believe that Saul was even yet, at the beginning of the First Missionary Journey, an Apostle. But just when he became one is difficult to say. However, Sir William Ramsay is very sure that both Barnabas and Saul were Apostles before their call to the First Missionary Journey as recorded in Acts 13:1-4:

> What was the effect of the public ceremony described in v. 3? The high authority of Lightfoot answers that it constituted Barnabas and Saul as Apostles. He acknowledges that Saul's 'conversion may indeed be said in some sense to have been his call to the Apostleship. But the actual investiture, the completion of his call, took place some years later at Antioch (*Acts* XIII 2).' He considers that Barnabas and Saul were only prophets before this, and did not become Apostles until they were elevated to that rank by their 'consecration to the office' at Antioch (*Ed. Galat.* p. 96).
>
> Our view, on the contrary, is that Barnabas and Saul were Apostles before this. The Apostle was always appointed by God and not by the Church. The proof of Apostleship lay in the possession of apostolic message and powers, conversion of others and performance of signs. It is an historical anachronism to attribute to this period such belief in the efficacy of a Church-ceremony. Moreover, in XXII 17, 21, and XXVI 17, Paul claims to have been an Apostle from his conversion, and represents his work in Cilicia and Syria as an Apostolate. In *Gal.* I he declares that his message came direct from God at his conversion. Further, there is no sign XIII 2, 3, that this 'consecration' by the Church was more efficacious than the original Divine call: the ceremony merely blessed Barnabas and Saul

---

[1]E.g., A. T. Robertson, *Epochs in the Life of Paul*, p. 58; J. E. Steinmueller, *A Companion to Scripture Studies*, Vol. III, p. 231.

[2]See David Smith, *The Life and Letters of St. Paul*, p. 77.

for a special work, which was definitely completed in the next three years.[3]

Despite some insights provided by Sir William, the author can not believe that his arguments and citations prove his point. Pure scholarship alone can not determine the problem of when Paul became an Apostle. This is a problem which is better solved by spiritual insight than by scholarship, however great. Perhaps it will be better to drop the matter at this point and revive it as the situation proves favorable.

Barnabas and Saul Set Forth for Cyprus.—It was possibly during the Spring of A.D. 45 when the Church at Antioch bade Barnabas and Saul farewell on their missionary labors. So these great men, "being sent forth by the Holy Ghost," set forth to Seleucia, the seaport of Antioch, sixteen miles down the Orontes River, from whence they sailed to Cyprus. (Acts 13:4) Cyprus, as the name indicates, was famous for its copper. It was an island about 160 miles long by 30 to 50 or 60 in breadth in its more compact part; its mountains could be seen on a clear day from the coast from whence Barnabas and Saul sailed, some 70 miles distant. Probably Cyprus was chosen for their first missionary labors on this tour by Barnabas and Saul because (1) the former had lived on the island, had friends there, and knew it well; and (2) some of the scattered Saints who had been persecuted in Judea (Acts 11:19-20) had come to the islands and had doubtless made converts. Possibly the situation in Antioch had been repeated on a smaller scale on Cyprus.

It should be noticed that John Mark was taken along by the missionaries as a servant or attendant. (Acts 13:5) He probably acted as a secretary and reader to Barnabas and Saul, performed baptisms, and went ahead of his more famous colleagues to schedule appointments for them and

[3]*St. Paul the Traveller*, p. 66f.

fill appointments which they might perchance be unable to take care of. (See D. & C. 84:107-8.)

On reaching the port of Salamis (a salt-mining center) many hours after leaving Seleucia, the little party "preached the word of God in the synagogues of the Jews." (Acts 13:5) A large number of Jews had been on Cyprus for long years past, and more especially after Augustus had sold rights to Herod the Great to mine the copper on the island.[4] It should be noticed that Saul, though his mission was to the Gentiles, usually gave the Jews their chance to receive the Gospel first. Only when they turned away and rejected their true Master did Saul turn to the Gentiles. (See Acts 13:46; 28:17-18)

We are not told by Luke what success, if any, was enjoyed by the missionaries in their labors at Salamis. Probably little. Presently they made their way in methodical fashion through the island, evangelizing (such seems to be the meaning of the Greek) the towns north and south as they steadily proceeded westward to Paphos on its southwest extremity. They seem to have been kindly treated as they advanced through the country with its grain fields, vineyards, and olive orchards. In Saul's time Cyprus was a Senatorial Province governed by a proconsul, who ruled the island from Paphos, a seaport and the Roman capital. It was while they were at Paphos that the first signal triumph was achieved by Barnabas and Saul in their labors upon the island. Apparently Sergius Paulus, the Proconsul, a man with a good knowledge of practical affairs, had advance knowledge of the preaching of Barnabas and Saul. His curiosity led him to summon the missionaries before him, and he "desired to hear the word of God" from their lips. (Acts 13:7) That the Proconsul was impressed and heard them gladly we may take for granted, because of an unusual incident that now took place. The Proconsul, like

[4]Josephus, *Ant.* XVI. iv. 5.

so many rulers of his age, had an astrologer by his side whose business it was to tell fortunes and predict future events by means of the stars. This man was probably used to predict the course of the Roman Empire and help decide questions of local policy. His name was Bar-jesus, and his title was Elymas, "the Wizard." The Authorized Version refers to him as a "sorcerer," "a false prophet," and a "Jew." (Acts 13:6) When this charlatan realized that his master was deeply impressed by the sacred message of Barnabas and Saul, he took alarm and sought to turn away the Proconsul from the faith. (Acts 13:8) No wonder, for his title and easy living were at stake. He made such a nuisance of himself, it appears, that Saul could stand his impudence no longer.

> Then Saul, (who also is called Paul,) filled with the Holy Ghost, set his eyes on him, and said, O full of all subtilty and all mischief, thou child of the devil, thou enemy of all righteousness, wilt thou not cease to pervert the right ways of the Lord? And now, behold, the hand of the Lord is upon thee, and thou shalt be blind, not seeing the sun for a season. (Acts 13:9-11)

In accordance with Saul's prediction, the man became blind, and "he went about seeking some to lead him by the hand." (Acts 13:11) So powerful and convincing was this miracle, together with the doctrines preached by the missionaries, that Sergius Paulus "believed" in them. (Acts 13:12)

If Barnabas and Saul had converted only the Proconsul, they could count their mission on Cyprus as being a very successful one. A man of his stature and influence would find it possible to help the Christian cause in ways available only to one of high rank.

Paul and Barnabas Depart for Southern Galatia.— Paul and Barnabas had now spent a considerable time preaching the Gospel in Cyprus—just how long we do not know, but it must have consumed many months. It will be noticed at this point that Luke in his account in the Acts speaks of Paul rather than Saul, giving him his Roman name instead of his Jewish one. (Cf. Acts 13:9; 13:13). Not only that, but Paul is usually, though not always, mentioned first in the narrative. It is now Paul and his company (Acts 13:13), Paul and Barnabas (Acts 13:43, 46), and the like. After the incident involving Sergius Paulus in Paphos, the leadership of the missionary party suddenly seems to have passed to Paul. Paul now evidently thinks it more fitting to use his Roman name in dealing with the Gentiles, because his mission is mostly to them. In dealing with the Romans, particularly their officials, it would be far more prudent for him to use his Roman name than his Jewish one. (See I Cor. 9:20-21.) At any rate, we notice these changes in the narrative of Luke and wonder what happened upon the island that is not expressly told by him. Did the Lord, for example, give a special revelation to the missionaries, directing Paul to take the lead? Of this we cannot be sure, but it seems passing strange that Barnabas should leave Antioch as the leader of the missionary group, and that Paul should lead it after leaving Cyprus. Perhaps such an arrangement was agreed upon at the first, but this seems improbable.

When Paul and his company "loosed from Paphos, they came to Perga in Pamphylia." (Acts 13:13) Their vessel would take a course north and west of Paphos and sail into Attaleia, the port on the Cestrus river about seven miles below Perga. The Cestrus was navigable to this latter city, the capital of Pamphylia. The ancient geographer Strabo tells us that Perga was graced by a Temple of Artemis on a height adjacent to the city. Scholars generally associate the metropolis with Greek rather than with Roman civilization. Paul and his companions probably came into Pamphylia in the middle of the summer. Although the country was beautiful with the back-drop of the Taurus mountains, its enervating climate in midsummer must have

weakened Paul severely. Not only that, but there is a good
probability that he contracted malaria, whose recurring
attacks may have been the "thorn in the flesh," "the messenger of Satan," that caused him so much affliction throughout the remainder of his life. (2 Cor. 12:7) All sorts of
guesses have been made concerning the nature of Paul's
ailment, but malaria seems to the author to be as reasonable an explanation as any. At any rate, the victim referred to his difficulty as an "infirmity of the flesh." (See Gal.
4:13-14.)

John Mark Deserts the Party.—During their stay
(probably short) in Perga a most unfortunate incident was
to add to the troubles of Paul and his companion. The Acts
refers to it in the simple reading, "John departing from
them returned to Jerusalem." (13:13) No explanation is
forthcoming; only the fact is given. Apparently Luke wanted
to spare John Mark, particularly in view of his later record.
But at that time Paul took John's desertion hard, as is proved
by the fact that when the Second Missionary Journey was
proposed, he refused to fellowship with him:

> And Barnabas determined to take with them John, whose sur-
> name was Mark. But Paul thought not good to take him with
> them, who departed from them from Pamphylia, and went not
> with them to the work. (Acts 15:37-38)

There are doubtless two sides to the story. To leave
him while he was ill was regrettable, but for John to desert
when his services could be so valuable to the missionaries
(see p. 38) was even more so in the eyes of the zealous
Paul. On the other hand, it is reasonable to suppose that
John Mark was suffering from plain homesickness. Nearly
every young missionary has experienced that uncomfortable
malady. Then we must in fairness suspect that Paul was
such a tireless worker that he had about worn out the
younger man during the long months of the missionary cam-
paign in Cyprus. Every experienced mission president knows

only too well how in many instances an older missionary has worn out a youngster in the field. Then, too, the prospects of facing the dangerous trip over the mountains into Pisidia may have somewhat unnerved John Mark. Finding a vessel leaving Perga at the time of his longing for the comforts and joys of his good home in Jerusalem, he boarded her and decamped.

We are overjoyed to know that in his later years Paul forgave John Mark. He did not hold any permanent grudge against him. During Paul's Roman imprisonment, he commends John Mark to the Colossian Saints (Col. 4:10); and before his death he writes that "Mark, . . . is profitable to me for the ministry." (2 Tim. 4:11) John Mark was made of good stuff, as the great Apostle willingly admitted.

Paul and Barnabas Proceed to Antioch in Pisidia.— With John Mark gone, Paul and Barnabas proceeded over the mountains, almost directly north, to Antioch in Pisidia. Despite the steep and dangerous passes of the Taurus, not to mention the robbers and brigands who infested the rugged territory (cf. 2 Cor. 11:26), Luke disposes of the journey in less than a line:

> But when they departed from Perga, they came to Antioch in Pisidia, and went into the synagogue on the sabbath day, and sat down. (Acts 13:14)

At least we cannot accuse Luke of not getting things done!

Antioch had an elevation of about 3600 feet and must have been a much more healthful city than Perga. It was situated in the southern part of the Roman province of Galatia, in the Phrygian District, near the borders of Pisidia, and was for that reason designated "Antioch toward Pisidia" and "Pisidian Antioch" to distinguish it from Antioch in Syria and Antioch on the Maeander. The city was the center used by the Romans for the civil and military administration of the southern part of the province. The city, when originally founded by Seleucus Nicator (312-280 B.C.), was

Greek, with native Phrygians on its borders, but Seleucus granted certain rights of citizenship to the Jews. Paul and Barnabas thus found a Jewish community with a synagogue in the city.

Paul and Barnabas Rejected by the Jews, Turn to the Gentiles.—One Sabbath morning shortly after their arrival in Antioch, Paul and Barnabas entered into the synagogue and sat down (Acts 13:14), presumably among the regular worshippers, composed both of Jews and prose-lytes ("God-fearers", Acts 13:16) to Judaism. The service proceeded as usual until after the reading of the Scripture —lessons from the Law and the Prophets. Then the leaders of the synagogue sent word to the two visitors to come forward and speak. "Ye men and brethren, if ye have any word of exhortation for the people, say on." (Acts 13:15) It was the custom among the Jews in that day to extend such an invitation to visitors who might prove interesting to a congregation. There can be little doubt that the presence of Paul and Barnabas in the city was already well known, and the people were eager to hear from them. Paul took immediate advantage of the invitation and stood up (Greek fashion), gesturing with his hand as he began to talk. He took advantage of the Scripture-lessons which had been read from Isaiah and Deuteronomy, as a study of the sermon shows, and plunged into a discourse on certain high lights of Hebrew history from the time of Israel's bondage in Egypt to the time of Christ. In the course of his talk Paul spoke of John, who as a forerunner heralded the advent of a Savior—Jesus—from the seed of David, the son of Jesse. Then he dwelt upon the cruel death of Jesus at the hands of the people of Jerusalem and their rulers in fulfilment of the predictions of the Prophets. Without finding Him guilty of any capital offense they had urged Pilate to put Him to death. When all of that had been carried out, they had taken Him off the cross and placed Him in a tomb.

Then Paul spoke at length and with emphasis upon the resurrection of Jesus from the dead, which subject seemed to be the heart of his unusual message.

In the last part of his sermon Paul gave his audience to understand that through Jesus forgiveness of sins could come to them; in Him every believer could be absolved (justified) from all offenses (things) from which they could not be absolved (justified) under the law of Moses. Certain of the narrow-minded Jews in the congregation must have had some anger in their hearts when Paul closed with these words, part of which are from Habakkuk 1:5:

> Beware therefore, lest that come upon you, which is spoken in the prophets: "Behold, ye despisers, and wonder, and perish: for I work a work in your days, a work which ye shall in no wise believe, though a man declare it unto you." (Acts 13:40-41)

Many writers agree that Paul's sermon, the first we have from him, is masterfully handled and adapted to a rather difficult situation. Everyone should read it carefully. (Acts 13:16-41)

It is too much to expect that we have all of Paul's words which he spoke at the time, and it is possible that the report we do have is due to the fact that Luke himself was in the audience. There is also a good possibility that this illustrious physician treated Paul's infirmities when the missionaries reached Antioch. He became one of Paul's most beloved followers.

Paul's sermon in the synagogue roused such interest that the "Gentiles besought that these words might be preached to them the next Sabbath." (Acts 13:42) Many of the Jews and "God-fearers" apparently collected around Paul and Barnabas, still anxious to hear the "good news" from their lips. We can imagine that the two brethren were thrilled with the interest in them, and finally persuaded their new friends to "continue in the grace of God" (Acts 13:43)—that is, to keep up the spirit of inquiry and the interest that had whetted their souls.

We can readily imagine that Paul and Barnabas talked to many private persons during the week, and so followed up their initial success. It was the custom of the Jews to hold meetings on Monday and Thursday as well as on the Sabbath; doubtless the names of the missionaries were on all lips, for on the following Sabbath "came almost the whole city together to hear the word of God." (Acts 13:44) Paul and Barnabas were almost too successful, for when the "Jews saw the multitudes, they were filled with envy, and spake against those things which were spoken by Paul, contradicting and blaspheming." (Acts 13:45) It was probable that many of the Jews, even of those who had been favorably disposed, resented Paul's teaching that the Gentiles were to be given an opportunity with themselves. When Paul and Barnabas were interrupted by them and were forced to listen to blasphemy, they rightfully turned from them to the Gentiles.

> Then Paul and Barnabas waxed bold, and said, It was necessary that the word of God should first have been spoken to you: but seeing ye put it from you, and judge yourselves unworthy of everlasting life, lo, we turn to the Gentiles. For so hath the Lord commanded us, saying, I have set thee to be a light of the Gentiles, that thou shouldest be for salvation unto the ends of the earth. (Acts 13:46-47)

The Gentiles were delighted at the opportunity afforded them, "and glorified the word of the Lord." The verse adds these strange words, "and as many as were ordained to eternal life believed." (Acts 13:48) The prophet Joseph Smith points out that this clause should read, "and as many as believed were ordained unto eternal life." ("Inspired" revision)

Luke points out that the gracious tidings of Paul and Barnabas were "published throughout all the region,"— that is, the Phrygian District. (Acts 13:49)

We must conclude, then, that the preaching of the two missionaries had been remarkably successful, despite the opposition of the Jews. The success of Paul and Barnabas, however, led the enraged Jews to enlist the services of prominent women who worshipped in the synagogue, and of the leading men of the city, to aid them in stirring up persecution against the missionaries. They succeeded so well that the two servants of God were expelled from the District. (Acts 13:50) But Paul and Barnabas left many good friends and converts in the city, who were to be glad to see them again on their return trip.

The Missionaries Depart for Iconium.—Having shaken off the dust of their feet against their persecutors (cf. Mark 6:11), Paul and his companion, leaving their converts filled with joy and with the Holy Ghost, came to Iconium, capital of the Lycaonian District, about eighty miles east and slightly south of Antioch. Situated in a favorable spot in the high, waterless plain of Lycaonia, Iconium was already in Paul's day a city of extreme antiquity. In order to reach it, Paul and Barnabas would be obliged to travel over the Roman Royal Road, built in the days of Augustus, for about thirty-five miles, and then at a point some three miles beyond Misthia, turn off on an inferior road which led to their destination.

Once in the city, the two intrepid missionaries proceeded to re-enact almost the same story we have told concerning their work in Antioch. They proceeded to the local Jewish synagogue, and by their speaking were so convincing that a "great multitude both of the Jews and also of the Greeks believed." (Acts 14:1) Again, the unbelieving Jews made trouble, stirring up the Gentiles so as to embitter them against the brethren. Nevertheless, Paul and Barnabas remained a long time, speaking boldly "in the Lord," who gave testimony of His power and grace, by granting miracles and wonders to be performed under their hands. (Acts 14:3)

That the influence of the missionaries was great is shown by the fact that the population of the town became

divided, some taking sides with the Jews and others with
the "apostles" (here the term is used as "messengers", for
the men had apparently not been ordained. Acts 13:1-3).
But when both Gentiles and Jews conspired with their local
civil authorities (Archons?) to deal outrageously with and
to stone Paul and Barnabas, these brethren, aware of the
plot, fled from the town.

Paul and Barnabas Preach in Lystra.—Paul and
Barnabas fled to another town in the Lycaonian District
by the name of Lystra. Lystra, the terminus of the Roman
Royal Road, was situated about eighteen miles south and
a little west of Iconium. It contained a Roman military
colony for the control of brigands, but otherwise was of
little importance. The population of the town, aside from
the Roman garrison, was composed of native Lycaonians
who spoke their own aboriginal vernacular, but they could
also speak Greek and therefore understood Paul and Barnabas. Inasmuch as there was little business done in the town,
the missionaries found no convenient Jewish synagogue to
which they could repair and preach. We are not told where
they preached in the town, other than "there they preached
the Gospel." (Acts 14:7)

The native Lycaonians, like the Gentile Greeks, would
have to be preached to in a different manner than would
the Jews, because they had no knowledge of the Scriptures.
Apparently at first the missionaries had little or no success,
but one day as Paul preached, a congenital cripple, "who
never had walked," drew his interest and attention. Paul,
perceiving that the man had faith to be healed, cried with
a loud voice, "Stand upright on thy feet." (Acts 14:10)
The cripple not only sprang up but walked about, to the
astonishment of the crowd, for reverting to their native
Lycaonian, they cried aloud, "The gods are come down
to us in the likeness of men." (Acts 14:11) The pagan
populace took Barnabas for Jupiter (Zeus) and Paul for

Mercury (Hermes). (Acts 14:12) Barnabas was taken for the chief god because the heathen people had a myth about these two divine beings in which Mercury (Hermes) appeared as the prophet and spokesman of Jupiter (Zeus). Hence Paul, as the spokesman, was mistaken by the people for Mercury. From Luke's account of what followed it may be inferred, or at least it has been inferred, that Paul and Barnabas failed to understand the meaning of the shouts and speech of the Lycaonians, and so returned to their lodgings. We may digress at this point for a moment to say that some authorities believe the two missionaries may have lodged at the home of the one Jewish family in Lystra. The head of the home was a widow by the name of Eunice, whose Greek husband had apparently been long since dead and who had a young son by the name of Timothy. Lois, the aged mother of Eunice, resided with her. Whether or not Paul and Barnabas lived at the home of Eunice at this time and converted the household, we are not prepared to say, but we are certain that Paul knew them later as Christians. (See Acts 16:1-3; I Tim. 1:5; 3:15)

Meanwhile the excited crowd wished to celebrate the supposed appearance of the heavenly visitors who had performed a miracle before their very eyes. So they rushed to the Temple of Zeus outside the city, and "the priest of Jupiter [Zeus], which was before their city, brought oxen and garlands unto the gates, and would have done sacrifice with the people." (Acts 14:13)

Whether at their lodgings or still preaching elsewhere in the town, Paul and Barnabas, on hearing what the crowd were doing, rent their clothes in a typical oriental expression of disgust at the blasphemy, and, joining the multitude, protested to the people in these vigorous words:

> Sirs, why do ye these things? We also are men of like passions with you, and preach unto you that ye should turn from these vanities unto the living God, which made heaven, and earth,

and the sea, and all things that are therein: who in times past suffered all nations to walk in their own ways. Nevertheless He left not Himself without witness, in that he did good, and gave us rain from heaven, and fruitful seasons, filling our hearts with food and gladness. (Acts 14:15-17)

Paul is Stoned and Left for Dead.—Paul and Barnabas barely succeeded in restraining the people from sacrificing unto them. (Acts 14:18) In fact, from what was soon to happen, we may suspect that many in the crowd were somewhat resentful at the missionaries for appearing on the scene and testifying to the truth that, after all, they were only men and not gods. For in a short time we find Jews coming from Antioch and Iconium, probably a party of the old mobocrats, who proceeded to stir up the people against the servants of God. The disgruntled and angry crowd even went so far as to stone Paul, and supposing him dead, they carried his body out of the city (Acts 14:19; cf. 2 Cor. 11:25), presumably to escape Roman justice, which would come if their lawless deed were to be discovered.

We can only imagine the sorrow of Barnabas and the "disciples" (Acts 14:20) when they found the body of Paul where the mob had deposited it. The fact that disciples are mentioned indicates that the word of the missionaries had been fruitful, despite the actions of their enemies. As Paul's friends stood about his limp form, they must have been joyfully surprised when he became conscious, stood up, and came with them into the city. (*Ibid.*) And the toughness of Paul's constitution must have caused no end of wonder to those near him.

The Missionaries Proceed to Derbe.—The next day Paul had recovered sufficiently to accompany Barnabas out of Lystra and thence south-eastward about forty miles to Derbe, a military outpost near the frontier of the Province of Galatia. Here there was a customs house, with probably some few conveniences for travelers who might happen that way. The town was relatively unimportant,

but it afforded Paul and Barnabas an opportunity to rest and consider their future course of action. Nor was their preaching in the town unfruitful. The Greek text of Acts 14:21 suggests that they "evangelized that city, and won many disciples." Apparently one of these disciples was Gaius, who later was to accompany Paul on his last journey to Asia. (Acts 20:4)

Paul and Barnabas Revisit Their Converts and Return to Antioch.—Paul and Barnabas had now completed their mission and, if it had been feasible at the time, might have proceeded directly back to Syrian Antioch by way of the Cilician Gates through the Taurus Mountains. But they decided to return home by retracing their steps through the various cities where they had preached, those in Cyprus excepted. The two missionaries had doubtless given prayerful consideration to the over-all situation of their converts in the towns from whence they (the missionaries) had been driven, and decided that the various groups of believers needed further instruction, encouragement, and organization. Accordingly Paul and Barnabas "returned again to Lystra, and to Iconium, and Antioch, confirming the souls of the disciples, and exhorting them to continue in the faith, and that we[5] must through much tribulation enter into the kingdom of God." (Acts 14:21-22) And in respect to the organization of branches of the Church, the Authorized Version says that "when they had ordained them Elders in every church, and had prayed with fasting, they commended them to the Lord, on whom they believed." (Acts 14:23) The Greek word "cheirotoneo" in this passage means "to elect by a show of hands." What the Latter-day Saints would say happened in each branch of the Church is this: Paul and Barnabas would carefully select men who they felt were adequate leaders and present them to their respective congregations to be received

[5]Does "we" suggest a personal touch of Luke's?

by the principle of popular consent, which would be indicated by a show of hands. Only when the church membership had voted to sustain the men nominated by Paul and Barnabas would they be "ordained" Elders by the missionaries. (See D. & C. 20:63; 26:2.)

It is not necessary to believe, with Ramsay,[6] that Paul and Barnabas could return safely to Lystra, Iconium, and Antioch because new magistrates had come into office in these cities where they had been. In the first place, Paul and Barnabas were brave men, who did not hesitate to take reasonable chances in shepherding their flocks. Second, it is highly unlikely that new magistrates would be able to restrain the Jews in every city at this time; and third, the missionaries seem not to have made contact with the Jews or to have attempted to make new converts on their return trips to these cities. They quietly worked among the previous converts. In this way they avoided stirring up new trouble.

After finishing their work in Antioch, Paul and Barnabas proceeded south through the difficult mountain passes into the Province of Pamphylia, where they "preached the word in Perga." (Acts 14:25) They probably did not stay long in Perga, and how successful their preaching was we are not told by Luke.

In due time they went down to Attaleia and sailed from that port to Antioch. (Acts 14:25-26) Here they arrived, in all probability, sometime in the fall of A.D. 47 or 48.

Paul and Barnabas Report to the Church in Antioch. —When the missionaries arrived in Antioch, they gathered the Church members together and gave their report. Here is Luke's account:

> And when they were come, and had gathered the church together, they rehearsed all that God had done with them, and

---

[6]*St. Paul the Traveller*, p. 120.

how He had opened the door of faith unto the Gentiles. (Acts 14:27)

To this brief account of Luke's we should add this later account of Paul's to Timothy:

> But thou hast fully known my doctrine, manner of life, purpose, faith, long-suffering, charity, patience, persecutions, afflictions, which came unto me at Antioch, at Iconium, at Lystra; what persecutions I endured: but out of them all the Lord delivered me. (2 Tim. 3:10-11)

We are told by Luke that Paul and Barnabas abode with the disciples in Antioch for a considerable time. (Acts 14:28)

Chapter 7

THE GREAT JERUSALEM COUNCIL AND PAUL'S SOJOURN IN ANTIOCH

Certain Judaizers Arouse Contention in Antioch.— For a long time after the return of Paul and Barnabas from their mission, they must have continually borne witness of the fact that Gentiles could receive the Gospel without first becoming Jewish proselytes and obeying the Law of Moses. There seems to have been the freest fellowship between the Jewish members of the Church in Antioch and the Gentile converts; in fact, such communion must have been considered as a Gospel requirement and beyond controversy. But the quiet and peace among the Church membership in the city was now to be disrupted, as Luke reports.

> And certain men which came down from Judea taught the brethren, and said, Except ye be circumcised after the manner of Moses, ye cannot be saved. When therefore Paul and Barnabas had no small dissension and disputation with them, they determined that Paul and Barnabas, and certain other of them, should go up to Jerusalem unto the apostles and elders about this question. (Acts 15:1-2)

Paul and Barnabas and other Church authorities in Antioch must have been disturbed no little by the teachings of the Judean brethren. Such teachings could very well undo much of their hard work of the past years in the metropolis and prevent their preaching from being very effective in the immediate future, particularly among the Gentiles. The sympathies of most Christian readers are certainly with Paul, Barnabas, and the others as they read the account of the fundamental struggle of these men with the Judaizers, but we wonder whether Schaff is justified in saying this of the men of Judea:

> These men were Christians in name, but narrow-minded and narrow-hearted Jews in fact. They were scrupulous, pedantic, slavish formalists, ritualists, and traditionalists of the malignant type. Circumcision of the flesh was to them of more importance than circumcision of the heart, or at all events an indispensable condition of salvation. Such men could, of course, not understand and appreciate Paul, but hated and feared him as a dangerous radical and rebel. Envy and jealousy mixed with their religious prejudice. They got alarmed at the rapid progress of the gospel among the unclean Gentiles who threatened to soil the purity of the church. . .[1]

We sometimes forget that great struggles in institutions are more often than not between groups of very sincere and well-meaning men, however wrong one party may be. Who is to say that the men from Judea were pedantic and old reactionaries of the worst type? Actually they may have been very pleasant men who sincerely and honestly believed that Paul and Barnabas were leading the Church astray. Where is the evidence that they hated Paul? Christianity taught men not to hate, and it is entirely possible that these particular opponents of Paul's were in most respects good Church members. Only in their taking a wrong view of the Law of Moses and in coming to Antioch without authority do we have evidence on which to castigate them. And let us keep in mind the probability that they had come to Antioch at considerable personal sacrifice to oppose Paul and Barnabas.

We should also remember that Paul's struggle henceforth against the Judaizers was not against a large wing of evil and corrupt men in the Church. The Judaizers in the Early Church were simply a party of otherwise good men who needed a considerably broader and more accurate outlook on the teachings of Christianity. Most of them probably achieved it through the work of men like Peter, Paul, and Barnabas. In the end, only a relatively small

[1] *History of the Christian Church*, I, 338.

party of the irreconcilable die-hards were to give Paul a desperate battle in the years to come. And we shall probably find someday that these men were as much at odds with Peter and the other Church leaders as they were with Paul.[2]

Why There Were Judaizers in the Church.—It is the business of the historian not to resort to name-calling but to soberly present the facts and interpret them as intelligently as possible. How did it happen that many of the early Christians were Judaizers? Let us attempt, as far as possible, to look at the problem without prejudice. The first Christians were Jews. Of the hundreds and thousands who entered the Church, we should not expect many to be able to throw off at once all of their traditions, particularly those that had been ground into their souls respecting the Law of Moses. And circumcision was one of the oldest traditions in the Hebrew Church. It had been enjoined by God upon Abraham, his male children and his male slaves as an initiatory rite and as a symbol of the covenant entered into between the Father of the Faithful and himself. (See Gen. 17:1-10, 21.) And even foreigners who might desire to join themselves to the Hebrew commonwealth were required to submit to circumcision, whatever their age. (Gen. 34:14-17, 22; Exo. 12:48) The Hebrew people, by virtue of the covenant entered into by them with God, were a chosen and exclusive people, as the Old Testament clearly shows.[3] Not only were Gentiles required to be circumcised if they desired to come under the covenant and join the Hebrew commonwealth, but they were also required to observe the Mosaic Law. But strict as the Old Testament requirements were, before Paul's day certain compromises were often made with Gentiles, particularly in the matter of circumcision. However, sincere Jews who desired to be consistent in their religious observances

---

[2]Even our own Church has passed through a similar struggle in regard to the contents and interpretation of D. & C. 132. We still hear repercussions.
[3]Amos 3:2.

would earnestly deprecate such compromises with Gentiles. Is it any wonder, therefore, that many such Jews, when converted to Christianity, would insist that Gentiles should be circumcised and observe the Mosaic Law—in other words, become Jews—before joining the Church? They were the Christians who looked askance at the practice of Paul and Barnabas in admitting Gentiles to the Church without circumcision or other Mosaic observances. Nor should we forget what Fernand Prat observes:

> The . . . Church of Jerusalem still adhered so closely to the Synagogue that it might have passed for a Jewish sect. Distinctions between foods that were clean and foods that were unclean, visits to the Temple, sacrifices, legal purifications — all these almost identified, outwardly at least, the new disciples of Christ with devout Israelites. Their assiduous attendance at the Temple was exemplary;[4] Peter and John went there to pray at the ninth hour, according to the custom;[5] several years later, Peter had not yet touched any food forbidden by the law.[6] Even in 57 or 58 A.D. the brethren were still zealous observers of the Mosaic code, and it was in order not to scandalize them that Paul submitted to a ritual ceremony[7]. . .[8]

Thus we begin to see the magnitude and importance of the problem of Mosaic observance that faced the Early Church. It is a strange fact, in many ways, that the Nephite Church on the American Continent faced the problem much more clearly, speedily, and decisively, though not without some difficulty, than did the Church in Palestine and surrounding areas.[9] We must credit men like Paul and Barnabas with a clear understanding of the problem; without such men the infant Church in the Mediterranean region would have suffered severely.

Paul, Barnabas, and Others Face the Problem of the Judaizers in Jerusalem.—As we have already pointed out, the problem raised by the Judaizers in Antioch became so

[4]Acts 2:46.
[5]Acts 3:1.
[6]Acts 10:14. The Cornelius episode.
[7]Acts 21:20-26.
[8]*The Theology of St. Paul*, I, 45.
[9]3 Nephi 15:2-8.

acute that it was determined, or more probably agreed to by the people in the branch (possibly including the visiting Judaizers), that Paul, Barnabas, and others should take the question "to Jerusalem unto the apostles and elders." (Acts 15:2) If this visit to Jerusalem is the same one Paul mentions in Galatians 2:1-2, then Titus was taken along, and we find that Paul had had a revelation instructing him to go:

> Then fourteen years after [his conversion?] I went up again to Jerusalem with Barnabas, and took Titus with me also. And I went up by revelation, . . .

On the way to Jerusalem, the brethren visited the branches of the Church in "Phoenicia and Samaria, declaring the conversion of the Gentiles: and they caused great joy unto all the brethren." (Acts 15:3)

When the little party reached Jerusalem, "they were received of the Church, and of the Apostles and Elders, and they declared all things that God had done with them." (Acts 15:4) The Church Authorities must have been very glad to receive the personal reports of Paul, Barnabas, and the others concerning their work and the progress being made through their labors.

But Paul did not want his mission to Jerusalem to have been in vain, and so he sought out the Church Authorities privately in order to explain in detail the principles he was teaching to the Gentiles:

> I . . . communicated unto them that gospel which I preach among the Gentiles, but privately to them which were of reputation, lest by any means I should run, or had run, in vain. (Gal. 2:2)

It was well that the Apostles and others should know the details of Paul's views and acts before they came up for discussion in the general meetings and Councils of the Conference. Much was at stake. And indeed, in a public meeting which apparently followed, the question of circumcising the Gentiles and of commanding them to observe the Law of Moses was duly brought up by the Judaizers:

> But there rose up certain of the sect of the Pharisees which believed, saying, That it was needful to circumcise them, and to command them to keep the Law of Moses. (Acts 15:5)

Apparently Titus, the Greek companion of Paul, was mentioned as a test case by the Judaizers, who demanded that he be circumcised. (Gal. 2:3) And Paul and Barnabas must have argued with all the skill at their command, and with some heat, against the demands of their opponents. At any rate the facts were brought into the open and aired by both sides before the meeting dismissed. Then a formal meeting of the Church Authorities seems to have convened, in which a decision on the matter was finally reached after intense debate. The fact that even amongst the highest authorities there was "much disputing [discussion]" (Acts 15:7) should warn us against using intemperate language against the Judaizers. But what undoubtedly will surprise Latter-day Saints is that at this late date (A.D. 50) the question of whether or not the Early Church membership should observe the Law of Moses should even be brought up. But the question continued to be raised and, in our opinion, was one of the things that helped in the end to split the Church wide open and to bring about the "Great Apostasy." Now let us look at the Council meeting again:

> And the Apostles and Elders came together for to consider of this matter. And when there had been much disputing, Peter rose up, and said unto them, Men and brethren, ye know how that a good while ago God made choice among us, that the Gentiles by my mouth should hear the word of the Gospel, and believe. And God, which knoweth the hearts, bare them witness, giving them the Holy Ghost, even as He did unto us: and put no difference between us and them, purifying their hearts by faith. Now therefore why tempt ye God, to put a yoke upon the neck of the disciples, which neither our fathers nor we were able to bear? But we believe that through the grace of the Lord Jesus Christ we shall be saved, even as they. (Acts 15:6-11)

Peter's powerful words and influence must have given relief and comfort to Paul and Barnabas as they sat in what was one of the most important of the councils of the Early

Church. The two great missionaries were now given opportunity to speak to the audience, which they did, "declaring what miracles and wonders God had wrought among the Gentiles by them." (Acts 15:12) The wonderful personality of Barnabas, followed by the eloquence, learning, and vigor of Paul, must surely have impressed even the Judaizers. Undoubtedly many of them turned from their former beliefs at the missionaries' recital of how God had done wonders among the Gentiles.

Last of all came the speech of the influential James, "brother of the Lord" and traditionally "Bishop of Jerusalem,"[10] who seems to have conducted the Jerusalem Council, and who now handed down his opinion in these words:

> Men and brethren, hearken unto me: Simeon hath declared how God at the first did visit the Gentiles, to take out of them a people for his name. And to this agree the words of the prophets; as it is written, After this I will return, and will build again the tabernacle of David, which is fallen down; and I will build again the ruins thereof, and I will set it up: that the residue of men might seek after the Lord, and all the Gentiles, upon whom my name is called, saith the Lord, who doeth all these things. Known unto God are all his works from the beginning of the world. Wherefore my sentence is, that we trouble not them, which from among the Gentiles are turned to God: but that we write unto them, that they abstain from pollutions of idols, and from fornication, and from things strangled, and from blood. For Moses of old time hath in every city them that preach him, being read in the synagogues every Sabbath day. (Acts 15:13-21)

It was plain that Paul and Barnabas had won a clear-cut victory in their contention that the Gospel did not require Gentiles to be circumcised or to obey the Law of Moses in order to become members of the Church. And not only that, but the "Apostles and Elders, with the whole church" (including, we hope, most of the Judaizers), decided to send their own representatives back to Antioch with Paul and Barnabas bearing copies of an official letter giving the decision reached by the Council of Jerusalem.

---

[10]Early authorities believed that James was the first Bishop of Jerusalem. See Hegesippus as quoted by Eusebius ii. 23, iii. 32, iv. 22.

Judas Barsabas and Silas were selected to return with the two missionaries in this official capacity. (Acts 15:22-23)

Now here is the official letter, copies of which would be taken by Judas and Silas to be read in the Church branches where the Judaizers had operated or might operate to the discomfiture of Paul and Barnabas:

> The Apostles and Elders and brethren send greeting unto the brethren which are of the Gentiles in Antioch and Syria and Cilicia: Forasmuch as we have heard, that certain which went out from us have troubled you with words, subverting your souls, saying, Ye must be circumcised, and keep the Law; to whom we gave no such commandment: it seemed good unto us, being assembled with one accord, to send chosen men unto you with our beloved Barnabas and Paul, men that have hazarded their lives for the name of our Lord Jesus Christ. We have sent therefore Judas and Silas, who shall also tell you the same things by mouth. For it seemed good to the Holy Ghost, and to us, to lay upon you no greater burden than these necessary things: that ye abstain from meats offered to idols, and from blood, and from things strangled, and from fornication; from which if ye keep yourselves, ye shall do well. Fare ye well. (Acts 15:23-29)

Paul would, of course, have no objection to the prohibitions added at the end of the letter, since they involved no important principles for which he had fought so hard. He doubtless heartily approved the inspiration and wisdom of the Church Authorities in adding them to the letter.

Paul's Version of the Jerusalem Council.—For the completeness of the record it is well for us to add Paul's account of the Council in Jerusalem as he relates it in his letter to the Galatians some years later:

> Then fourteen years after I went up again to Jerusalem with Barnabas, and took Titus with me also. And I went up by revelation, and communicated unto them that gospel which I preach among the Gentiles, but privately to them which were of reputation, lest by any means I should run, or had run, in vain. But neither Titus, who was with me, being a Greek, was compelled to be circumcised: and that because of false brethren unawares brought in, who came in privily to spy out our liberty which we have in Christ Jesus, that they might bring us into bondage: to whom we gave place by subjection, no, not for

an hour; that the truth of the Gospel might continue with you. But of these who seemed to be somewhat, (whatsoever they were, it maketh no matter to me: God accepteth no mans person:) for they who seemed to be somewhat in conference added nothing to me: but contrariwise, when they saw that the gospel of the uncircumcision was committed unto me, as the gospel of the circumcision was unto Peter; (for He that wrought effectually in Peter to the apostleship of the circumcision, the same was mighty in me toward the Gentiles:) and when James, Cephas, and John, who seemed to be pillars, perceived the grace that was given unto me, they gave to me and Barnabas the right hands of fellowship; that we should go unto the heathen, and they unto the circumcision. Only they would that we should remember the poor; the same which I also was forward [eager] to do. (Gal. 2:1-10)

It will be noticed from this letter of Paul that the Church Authorities fully recognized the hand of God in the special call given to him and to Barnabas in preaching to the Gentiles. As Latter-day Saints we should recall that these two men were not set apart by the Jerusalem Authorities when they went on their first missionary journey from Antioch; they were called by the Holy Ghost. (Acts 13:2-3) We should also notice that Paul was given a commission to remember the poor, a fact not mentioned in the other accounts of the Conference. Paul's victory in not being required to have Titus circumcised is another fact to be noticed with interest.

Paul and Barnabas Return to Antioch.—When the Jerusalem Conference had been dismissed, Paul and Barnabas and the remainder of their entourage, including Judas and Silas and probably John Mark, returned to Antioch. There "they [Judas and Silas] delivered the epistle" that had been prepared in Jerusalem by the Church Authorities. (Acts 15:30) The multitude of the people rejoiced at their words concerning the decision of the Jerusalem Conference. (Acts 15:31) Judas and Silas also exhorted their audiences and did what they could to heal the wounds caused by the Judaizers. Such would seem to be the plain meaning of Acts 15:32. Since the letter of the Council included the branches of the Church in Syria and Cilicia, it is more than probable that Judas and Silas made the necessary visits at this time and explained to the people who were involved the decisions made in Jerusalem. On their return to Antioch they were released, "let go in peace," from their mission, and were free to go back to "the Apostles" in Jerusalem. (Acts 15:33) Judas probably departed for Jerusalem, but Silas seems to have liked Antioch and the brethren he found there so well that he remained on. (Acts 15:34) This circumstance was later to prove very providential to Paul.

Peter Comes to Antioch and is Rebuked by Paul.— Although authorities are by no means agreed that Peter came to Antioch at this time, his visit, so it seems to the author, can fit in with the known facts just as well at this point as any other. We are indebted to Paul for what facts we have concerning Peter's visit. (Gal. 2:11-14) It is probable that, following the Jerusalem Conference, Peter decided to visit Antioch in order to see how matters were progressing with the brethren in their labors in this metropolis. The great leader, on arriving, ate "with the Gentiles" (Gal. 2:12) and got along famously with all concerned. But in the course of his sojourn, it appears that other visitors ("from James") appeared on the scene from Jerusalem, and these men were observers of the Law of Moses. (*Ibid.*) Let it be remembered that, although the Jerusalem Conference had decided that Gentiles were free from the observance of the Mosaic Law, there was apparently nothing said against the observance of the Law by a private individual if he desired to fulfill its demands. And Peter was now embarrassed by the presence of a delegation of keepers of the Law. Instead of being his true self and continuing to eat with whom he pleased, "he withdrew and separated himself, fearing them which were of the circumcision." (*Ibid.*) This act of Peter's had a very undesirable effect, because "the other Jews dissembled likewise with him; in-

somuch that Barnabas also was carried away by their dissimulation [Greek: "play-acting"]." (Gal. 2:13) Peter's
influence and example had such weight that Paul recognized if his action were to go unchallenged, it would have
repercussions all over the Church and undo most of what
the Jerusalem Conference had sought to correct. Righteously
indignant at Peter, Barnabas, and the other Jews for their
bad example, for "they walked not uprightly according to
the truth of the Gospel," Paul said unto Peter before the
entire assemblage, "If thou, being a Jew, livest after the
manner of Gentiles, and not as do the Jews, why compellest
thou the Gentiles to live as do the Jews?" (Gal. 2:14) This
criticism of Paul's must have been very painful to Peter,
but he doubtless recognized the justice and moral rightness
of the fiery Tarsian's reproof. It will be noticed in the recital
of this incident that Paul does not challenge the Jews who
came from Jerusalem; it was their own business if they
wanted to keep the requirements of the Law of Moses as
Christians.

Looking at this incident from a distance in point of
time, we may suggest that Peter's action at the coming of
the "circumcision" from Jerusalem was really meant to be
a conciliatory one. He may have recognized in the party
certain weak persons whose faith would be hurt if they discovered their great leader's close and continued association
with the Gentiles. If so, "the spirit of conciliation," as Fernand Prat observes, "led him too far. His conduct was really
dissimulation, as St. Paul was soon to tell him reproachfully,
since he was acting contrary to his closest convictions, and
appeared to accept an obligation the need of which he did
not admit in conscience."[11]

Many writers have made much of this incident as showing an open rupture and a very fundamental disagreement
between Paul and Peter. Actually these two men were too

---

[11]*Op. cit.*, I, 52.

great to let the incident make for personal estrangement. As J. G. Machen, like Prat, rightly points out, Paul was not condemning Peter for his principles; he was rebuking him for concealing his correct principles for fear of men.[12]

[12]*The Origin of Paul's Religion*, p. 102.

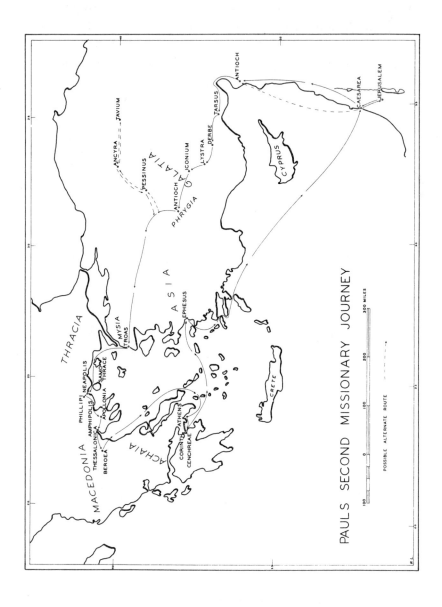

PAUL'S SECOND MISSIONARY JOURNEY

POSSIBLE ALTERNATE ROUTE — — — —

100   0   100   200   300 MILES

Chapter 8

PAUL'S SECOND MISSIONARY JOURNEY

Paul and Barnabas Disagree Over Taking John Mark.—After the recent exciting events had taken place, Paul and Barnabas continued their work in Antioch, "teaching and preaching the word of the Lord, with many others also." (Acts 15:35) These two men had now labored about three years in Antioch following their first mission. The missionary-minded Paul began to feel the urge to get in the field again and proposed to Barnabas, "Let us go again and visit our brethren in every city where we have preached the word of the Lord, and see how they do." (Acts 15:36) Barnabas was willing, but purposed to take John Mark, his kinsman, with them. He doubtless felt that the young fellow should be given another chance to make good, following his desertion of the missionaries on their last journey. Barnabas was forgiving and generous-minded in his attitude, but Paul was bitter and thought it "not good to take him with them, who departed [apostanta, "played the apostate"] from them from Pamphylia, and went not with them to the work." (Acts 15:38) We are told that the "contention" which arose between Paul and Barnabas over John Mark was "so sharp . . . , that they departed asunder one from the other." (Acts 15:39) Barnabas was like Paul in this respect: when he thought he was right he held his ground; and time did prove he was in the right, as Paul was not loathe to admit, in effect, in later years. (Col. 4:10; 2 Tim. 4:11) It was unfortunate that these two great men should have such a falling out that it resulted in their never seeing each other again. Such seems to be the case, for "Bar-

nabas took Mark, and sailed unto Cyprus" (Acts 15:39)
where he appears to have labored for several years, and
where, if the tradition is true, he died a martyr's death. It
is said that the Jews burned him at the stake near Salamis
and would have thrown his remains in the sea except for
the fact that Mark and other disciples stole them away and
buried them in a cave. We should not suppose that Paul
and Barnabas left each other as implacable enemies; for
two great Christian missionaries, that would be unthinkable. Besides, in writing to the Corinthians in later years
Paul makes a reference to Barnabas that can only be inter-
preted as kindly meant. (I Cor. 9:6)

**Paul Chooses Silas to Accompany Him on His
Second Mission.**—It had probably been the design of Paul
and Barnabas, when the question of their second mission
came up, to visit Cyprus as well as the towns in Southern
Galatia. But their falling out on the question of John Mark
doubtless brought about a meeting between the two in
which it was decided that Barnabas should take Cyprus,
his old home, as his field of labor, and Paul would keep to
the mainland. After the departure of Barnabas and John
Mark, Paul cast about for a suitable companion to accompany him on his latest venture. There were probably many
good men in Antioch who would gladly have gone with
him, but Paul seems to have singled out a man who was
ideal for the purpose. This man was Silas, who was yet
residing in Antioch. His spiritual qualities were recognized,
for he is spoken of as a prophet. (Acts 15:32) Then, too,
the fact that he was known and respected by the Church
Authorities in Jerusalem was shown when he was chosen
as one of two to deliver the letter that was formulated at
the Council so recently held. The fact that he was a Jew,
with no leanings toward the Judaizers, and the further fact
that he was a Roman citizen (Acts 16:37), with the dignity
and privileges accorded such a one in Roman territory, con-

vinced Paul that here was the man of the hour for him. And so Silas, whose Roman name was Silvanus, was chosen to be his companion.

Paul and Silas Traverse Syria, Cilicia, Galatia, Phrygia, and Mysia to Troas.—Paul and Silas possibly left Antioch in the Spring of the year A.D. 51 on their way north. We are told by Luke. that they were "recommended by the brethren unto the grace of God." (Acts 15:40) It is to be noticed that the missionaries were not "set apart" by the laying on of hands of the brethren in Antioch as had happened when Paul and Barnabas went on their first mission. (Acts 13:3) At least nothing is said about it. Nor is anything said about their being called of the Holy Ghost, as in the first instance. (Acts 13:2, 4) The problem is raised simply as an interesting difficulty concerning Church government and custom. The mission is one which seems to have been undertaken simply on Paul's suggestion, without any call from higher authority. (Acts 15:36) Perhaps Paul felt that he had never been released as a missionary and needed no special call. If he were at this time an Apostle in the unusual sense of the term, we could understand his right to go, but there is no record of his having been ordained as one since his first mission. Nor do Paul and Barnabas seem to have been regarded as Apostles at the Jerusalem Conference. (See Acts 15:22-23.) The first solution, that Paul had never been released as a missionary, seems preferable, and we shall leave it at that.

The brethren proceeded north, "confirming [Greek: 'propping up,' 'supporting'] the churches" that had been organized in Syria and Cilicia. (Acts 15:41) Paul had had much to do with the organizing and building up of many of these branches of the Church. Luke says nothing about their work in Syria and Cilicia, but one can imagine the joy with which Paul's old friends must have received them. And surely Paul must have tarried at some length in Tarsus, his old home. But not a word do we get concerning Paul's parents. From Tarsus the missionaries would probably proceed north through the famous "Cilician Gates" in the Taurus range. Through this pass had come Xenophon and the Ten Thousand some four and a half centuries before to fight in a Persian civil war. Passing west and some south from the Cilician Gates through the Kingdom of Antiochus, Paul and Silas reached Derbe, on the border of South Galatia. (Acts 16:1) Here the brethren began to retrace the steps made by Paul and Barnabas on the First Missionary Journey. Paul, at least, was on familiar ground. After greeting the members of the local branch of the Church, Paul and Silas read and explained to them the decrees of the Council of Jerusalem. This they did in all the branches they visited, not only in Derbe, but in Lystra, Iconium, and Antioch. "And as they went through the cities, they delivered them the decrees for to keep, that were ordained of the Apostles and Elders which were at Jerusalem." (Acts 16:4) This information encouraged the Gentiles, who now understood that salvation came not by the Law of Moses, but by observance of the Gospel of Jesus Christ. Nor would a Jew be offended. He could observe certain requirements of the Law of Moses if he so desired, but it was not necessary to do so. Paul doubtless explained to his Jewish friends that the Law of Moses as given in the Old Testament was truly divine and authoritative, but it was a temporary expedient, a schoolmaster to bring the Hebrew people to Christ. (See the Epistle to the Romans.) He might have explained as did Abinadi of Book of Mormon fame:

> And now I say unto you that it was expedient that there should be a law given to the children of Israel, yea, even a very strict law; for they were a stiffnecked people, quick to do iniquity, and slow to remember the Lord their God; therefore there was a law given them, yea, a law of performances and of ordinances, a law which they were to observe strictly from day to day, to keep them in remembrance of God and their duty towards him. But behold, I say unto you, that all these things were types of things to come. (Mosiah 13:29-31)

With the coming of Christ the law that was given to Moses was fulfilled, Paul would explain, and therefore had an end.

When Paul and Silas reached Lystra, they found Eunice, the Jewish widow, still there, together with her mother Lois and her son Timothy. Assuming the possibility that Paul and Barnabas had converted these good folk, Paul found them still true to the faith they had been taught on his first visit to them. Timothy had won the confidence not only of the brethren in Lystra, but also of those in Iconium (Acts 16:2), whose branch of the Church he must have visited from time to time. In this lad, Paul believed, was the answer to the need he and Silas felt for such a helper as John Mark had been on the first mission until he deserted at Perga. Young Timothy was probably eager to go, so Paul circumcised him, "because of the Jews which were in those quarters: for they knew all that his father was a Greek." (Acts 16:3) Paul has been much criticized for this action, in view of the fact that he had stood adamant against the circumcision of Titus at the Council of Jerusalem. (Cf. Acts 15:5; Gal. 2:3-5.) Paul was probably indifferent to circumcision himself, but he must have felt that there was no point in wounding Jewish feelings or needlessly trying their faith in the matter. As to Titus, Paul had fought his being circumcised, because he was a Gentile and doubtless because it had been held that his salvation depended on it.

Timothy was destined to become one of Paul's most favored companions. He appears from time to time in the Acts or in Paul's Epistles.

As the little missionary party moved on, they were rewarded in their labors, for Luke tells us that "the churches were established in the faith, and increased in number daily." (Acts 16:5)

When the missionaries reached Antioch in Pisidia (not mentioned in the narrative), they may have been joined by Luke the physician, so some authorities believe.[1] If Luke didn't join them at Antioch, he probably did so at Troas, judging from the beginning of the "we" passages of Acts in 16:10.

The movements of Paul's party after leaving Pisidian Antioch are a subject of much dispute among the best authorities. The account in Acts simply says this:

> Now when they had gone throughout Phrygia and the region of Galatia, and were forbidden of the Holy Ghost to preach the word in Asia, after they were come to Mysia, they assayed to go into Bithynia: and the Spirit suffered them not. And they passing by Mysia came down to Troas [on the coast of the Aegean Sea]. (Acts 16:6-8)

Sir William Ramsay and those of his school of thought believe that after Paul's party left Pisidian Antioch, they went north through the Roman Province of Asia, in which they were forbidden to preach, until they came to Mysia; from here they would have gone into Bithynia, but were again forbidden; then, turning west, they either skirted Mysia or passed through it to Troas.[2] The other—and more common—view is that after leaving Pisidian Antioch, the party went northeast into Galatia proper and founded, during a sickness of Paul's, the "churches of Galatia." (Gal. 1:2; 4:13-15) They went northeast in order to obey the command of the Spirit not to preach in Asia. When Paul had finished preaching in Galatia proper, he would have entered Bithynia, but was prevented; and so, as in Ramsay's theory, he turned west through or skirted the territory of Mysia to Troas.

Luke gives such a brief account of this part of the journey that we judge he was more eager to tell about Paul's European mission, with which he was personally familiar. Either that, or he was not with Paul in Galatia and was told little about the party's experiences there.

[1]E.g., David Smith, *The Life and Letters of Paul*, p. 121.
[2]See A. D. Nock, *St. Paul*, pp. 119f., who opposes this theory.

Paul's Vision and Call to Macedonia.—Paul and his party were now in an interesting seaport town. Troas got its name from the Greek, the Troad, the region around Troy of fame in Greek literature. Troas in Paul's day was a Roman colony, whose renown had been such that Julius Caesar, according to Suetonius,[3] had once contemplated the transfer there of the seat of his imperial government. The town was not far from Ionian cities whose contribution to Hellenistic literature and civilization rivalled the fame of Greece itself. We may notice that the antiquity and distinction of these cities, every one of which—Ephesus, Colossae, Laodicea, Hierapolis, Philadelphia, Sardis, Thyatira, Pergamum, Smyrna, Miletus—would in a few years become centers of Christianity.[4]

Although Paul may have thought somewhat of the fame of the region in which he found himself, and of its Greek associations, it is probable that he and his party were more interested in how they could reach and heal the souls of men. If they were intent on where to preach next, the answer was soon to come, for in a vision of the night Paul saw a Macedonian entreating him and saying, "Come over into Macedonia, and help us." (Acts 16:9) The little band of missionaries, confidently inferring from Paul's vision that God had called them to the new European field of labor, sought immediate passage to Macedonia. (Acts 16:10)

The taking of the Gospel to Europe from Asia was an historic occasion. Paul and the members of his party may not have thought of it in that way, but as we look back upon it, it certainly was. There were doubtless some Jewish and even Gentile members of the Church who had preceded him to Europe and who had made a few converts in local centers; but no one made the impression that Paul did, or performed missionary work on the scale that the man of Tarsus performed it.

[3]Roman historian, A.D. 70?—140?
[4]See Goodspeed, *Paul*, p. 70f.

On the way north and a little west of Troas, the ship upon which Paul, Silas, Timothy, and Luke sailed put in at the island of Samothrace after the first day's voyage. (Acts 16:11) This island has an area of approximately 30 square miles, and there is a mountain upon it about 5,000 feet high. Those who have been fortunate enough to visit the Louvre in Paris will remember well the famous statue of Victory and associate it with the island of Samothrace, where it was found in 1863. Samothrace is in the archipelago off the coast of Thrace, hence the name (Greek, Samos of Thrace).

The next day, after sailing about 80 miles west and a little north from Samothrace, the ship put in at Neapolis, the port of Philippi. The missionaries landed and made their way, by road or up the Gangites River, about ten miles northwest to Philippi. Luke says in his record that "Philippi, . . . is the chief city of that part of Macedonia, and a colony: and we were in that city abiding certain days." (Acts 16:12) The fact is well known that the city got its name from Philip of Macedon, the father of Alexander the Great. Rich gold and silver mines in the vicinity helped Philip to carry out his unusual projects. In later years, when the Romans had long been in possession of the territory, Augustus Caesar with understandable interest sent a Roman colony to Philippi, which was close to the battlefield where he and Antony had won decisive battles over Brutus and Cassius, leading assassins of Caesar. (42 B.C.) As Luke records, Philippi was the chief city of the district but was not the capital, which honor fell to Amphipolis. And to be sure Philippi was an important city, in respect both to its position near the sea and also to its situation upon the wonderful Egnatian Road, which reached from Dyrrhachium on the Adriatic coast to the Hellespont. It should be noted that the road also passed through Neapolis. The city was populated mainly by the native Macedonians, by an important group of Roman colonists, and by a mixed group of Orientals, including a very few Jews. Such was the character of the first city in which Paul preached in Europe.

Paul and His Party Preach in Philippi.—As was his custom, Paul first attempted to carry his "good news" to the Jewish population of the city, but there were so few that they could not maintain a synagogue; instead they had a place for prayer by the riverside outside the city. There the missionary party went on the Sabbath following their arrival and talked with the women-folk who had assembled. Among these was a certain business woman, who belonged to the city of Thyatira in Lydia on the Asiatic side of the Aegean Sea. Lydia—that was her name—may well have been the Philippian representative of a firm of purple-dyers from Thyatira, for this city was famous for its purple-dyeing. At any rate Luke mentions her as a "seller of purple" and a worshipper of God. (Acts 16:14) She seems to have been a "God-fearer," that is, not a Jewish proselyte, but a woman receptive to the Scriptures and moral teachings of the Jews. Paul and the members of his party talked earnestly to her, and the Lord opened her heart to the Gospel. Finally, she and her household were baptized. Her hospitality and Christian spirit were shown when she said, "If ye have judged me to be faithful to the Lord, come into my house, and abide there." (Acts 16:15) Indeed, she pressed or "constrained" them, as Luke recites the incident. (*Ibid.*) Apparently she had become well-to-do in her business ventures, and had ample quarters in her home for the Lord's servants, whom she wanted to help. Her generosity seems to have set the example in the Church branch in Philippi, for Paul had occasion, years later, to refer to it. (Phil. 4:15-17) Lydia's home must have become from that time forward the headquarters of the missionaries and a place where meetings could be held.

Paul Casts Out an Evil Spirit.—However, the missionaries did not cease going regularly to the Jewish "place of prayer," where they hoped to make other converts. One day as they went, a certain girl possessed, so we are told, "with a spirit of divination" met them and cried out, saying, "These men are the servants of the most high God, which shew unto us the way of salvation." (Acts 16:16-17) This same girl met them "many days" and cried out each time the same words. The "spirit of divination" possessed by her, in the Greek, *pneuma puthonos*, has been explained by most commentators as referring to her ability as a ventrilo-quist, then regarded as a form of possession. This ability she used to bring "her masters"—apparently she was a slave girl —much money. (*Ibid.*) Despite the commentators, members of our Church today will clearly recognize that the un-fortunate girl was possessed of an evil spirit, for finally, "Paul, being grieved, turned and said to the spirit, I command thee in the name of Jesus Christ to come out of her. And he came out the same hour." (Acts 16:18) Ser-vants of the Lord do not take away from a person his or her ability as a ventriloquist, but they do cast out evil spirits. The evil spirit having been cast out of the girl by Paul, she could no longer be of use to her masters. These men, now touched in their purses, where it hurt them most, took hold of Paul and Silas and literally dragged them into the market-place before the magistrates (properly "duumvirs," who had probably assumed the high rank of "praetors"). (Acts 16:19)

Paul and Silas are Scourged and Jailed.—On bring-ing them before the praetors, the unscrupulous masters of the girl, knowing that their financial losses would not be considered, cleverly proceeded to accuse Paul and Silas, as Jews, of creating a disturbance in the city and of teach-ing customs which Romans were not permitted to adopt or practice. (Acts 16:20-21) The rabble in the place also joined in the outcry against the two men. (Acts 16:22) Rioters and Jews would get little consideration here. It was bad enough to break the Roman law, let alone be a Jew, for shortly before this time the Emperor Claudius had expelled Jews from Rome. (Acts 18:2) The praetors, without any preliminaries, ordered their lictors to strip off the prisoners' tunics and scourge them—a terrible form of punishment—a completely illegal procedure when perpetrated upon Roman citizens, which Paul and Silas were. When they had been severely beaten, they were cast into jail, and the jailer was bidden to keep them safely, which he proceeded to do by thrusting them into the inner prison and securing their feet in the stocks. (Acts 16:22-24) Wounded, bleeding, and humiliated as Roman citizens, not to mention being held in the filth of a vermin-infested prison, Paul and Silas suffered in silence until midnight. Then the courageous stuff of which these men were made, together with the knowledge that they were suffering in the service of the God of Heaven, caused them to pray and to sing praises to the Almighty. Even the prisoners heard them. (Acts 16:25) Their God heard their cries, for there can be little doubt that they prayed for deliverance, and "suddenly there was a great earthquake, so that the foundations of the prison were shaken: and immediately all the doors were opened, and every one's bands were loosed." (Acts 16:26) Rationalists may explain away the miracle by pointing out that earthquakes are not uncommon in that region, which is true enough, but how can they explain the loosing of all the bands of the prisoners? Besides, what a convenient earthquake, just when Paul and Silas needed it! But the Lord had deeper things in mind when He loosed the prisoners, as we shall now see.

The Jailer and His Household Converted.—When the jailer was awakened by the earthquake and perceived that the prison doors were open, he drew his sword and would have killed himself, because he knew the Roman law would bring him disgrace, possibly even death, in the event that prisoners in his charge escaped. But Paul was alert to the situation and cried to the jailer in a loud voice, "Do thyself no harm: for we are all here." (Acts 16:28) Calling for a light, the jailer "came trembling, and fell down before Paul and Silas, and brought them out, and said, Sirs, what must I do to be saved?" (Acts 16:29-30) There is obviously more to the story than Luke has left us, because the jailer must have been deeply impressed with Paul and Silas before they were put in prison. Possibly he had even heard them preach, or someone had told him about their message. Be that as it may, the two missionaries now bore testimony to the honest-hearted warden, "Believe on the Lord Jesus Christ, and thou shalt be saved, and thy house." (Acts 16:31) Not only did Paul and Silas preach to the jailer; they also explained the Gospel to all who were in his house. The joyful warden now took the pain-wracked missionaries and washed their stripes. Not only that, but he and all his household were baptized at once and proceeded to set food before Paul and his companion. The Gospel made a happy family, as Luke testifies. (Acts 16:33-34)

Paul Makes a Point with the Praetors.—The next morning after their stay in jail, the praetors sent their lictors to the jailer with an order to release the prisoners. So the jailer came to Paul, told him what had transpired, and said that he and Silas could go their way in peace. (Acts 16:35-36) But Paul was determined that he and his companion, dignified Roman citizens, were not going to be dealt with as common hoboes or transients and be let go on a "floater." It was well to teach these magistrates a lesson concerning their ill-advised methods of handing out justice, if such it could be called. So Paul said to the lictors:

> They have beaten us openly uncondemned, being Romans, and have cast us into prison; and now do they thrust us out privily [secretly]? nay verily; but let them come themselves and fetch us out. (Acts 16:37)

When the lictors reported Paul's answer to the praetors, they were thoroughly alarmed, because not until now were they aware that the men they had grossly abused and detained were Roman citizens. If such news were bruited about, it could have very grave consequences for themselves, for Roman justice was not to be taken lightly. Therefore they came at once to the prison, and made their peace with Paul as best they could. Not only that, but they personally conducted Paul and Silas out of the prison and petitioned them to leave the city. (Acts 16:38-39) In this affair Paul was solicitous not only that he and Silas be accorded their rights as Roman citizens, but also that hereafter missionaries and members of the Church be treated in a manner befitting their high station as ambassadors and representatives of Christ.

Paul and Silas, despite the painful treatment they had received, probably left the prison in high spirits, because they had brought a whole household to Christ, whose representatives they were. They returned to the gracious home of Lydia, their generous hostess, where they rejoined Luke and Timothy.

The Missionaries Leave Philippi and Proceed to Thessalonica.—After comforting the "brethren" at Lydia's home, and doubtless the household there, Paul, Silas, and Timothy took leave of their kind friends and departed. Luke, so some believe, remained in Philippi, for no more "we" passages are found in the narrative of Acts until 20:5. I find it hard to believe that Paul left Philippi with anything but a cheerful heart, for in the few months they had been in the town the missionaries had set up a rather strong branch of the Church and were leaving it in good hands. The conversion of Lydia alone would have made their stay in Philippi successful, because of her vigorous and generous spirit, not to mention the fact that she was a good manager and woman of affairs. She doubtless attract-

ed many other substantial people into the Church as years
passed on.

Paul and his companions set forth upon the Egnatian
Road from Philippi, traveling southwestward through
Amphipolis (about thirty miles) the capital of the district,
thence to Apollonia (another thirty miles), and finally,
after another trek of about thirty-five miles west and a little
north, to Thessalonica, at the north end of the Thermaic
Gulf, now called the Gulf of Salonika. For some reason
Paul didn't preach in Amphipolis and Apollonia, but we
may suspect that he felt that the Gospel could be spread
faster in the larger population centers, and besides, there
were no Jewish synagogues in those two cities, so we judge
from Acts 17:1.

Paul and Silas Preach in Thessalonica.—The missionaries had now traversed a distance of about one hundred
miles since leaving Philippi, probably walking most of the
way in about six days. Thessalonica was the capital of the
Second District of Macedonia, of which there were four,
and was named after Alexander the Great's half-sister, the
wife of Cassander, who founded the city in 315 B.C. Thessalonica, an important military and commercial station on
the Egnatian Road, had been made a free city, a self-
governing democracy, in 42 B.C. The civil magistrates of
the city were designated Politarchs. There appears to have
been a good sized community of Jews in the city, because
it could boast the presence of a synagogue.

According to his custom, Paul entered into the synagogue and for three successive Sabbaths reasoned with the
Jews and "God-fearers," of whom there seem to have been
a goodly number, out of the Scriptures, showing that Christ
must needs suffer and rise from the dead. "This Jesus," said
Paul, "whom I preach unto you, is Christ." (Acts 17:3)
Paul and his companions created an extraordinary interest
in and response to their preaching. "And some of them

believed, and consorted with Paul and Silas; and of the devout [worshipping] Greeks a great multitude, . . ." (Acts 17:4) Not only were men attracted by the glad tidings, but a not inconsiderable number of the foremost women of the city were drawn to the missionaries. (*Ibid.*) So gratified was Paul with the response to their efforts that months later he could write back to the Thessalonians these words:

> And ye became followers of us, and of the Lord, having received the word in much affliction, with joy of the Holy Ghost: *so that ye were ensamples to all that believe in Macedonia and Achaia. For from you sounded out the word of the Lord not only in Macedonia and Achaia, but also in every place your faith to God-ward is spread abroad: so that we need not to speak any thing.* (I Thess. 1:6-8; italics ours.)

The work of Paul and his friends was spread abroad, as these words indicate, to a great audience far beyond Thessalonica. Christianity became known throughout all the region.

But as Paul knew only too well, success usually brings with it the envy of some, and unusual difficulties arise to block the spread of it. And Thessalonica was no exception, for as Luke records:

> The Jews which believed not, moved with envy, took unto them certain lewd fellows of the baser sort [Greek: certain evil men of the market-loungers], and gathered a company, and set all the city on an uproar. (Acts 17:5)

Not only did it set up a riot in the city, but the mob overran the house of Jason who had befriended the missionaries and had taken them into his home. The rioters had hoped to bring out Paul and Silas to be manhandled by the rabble, but luckily they were out, so instead they dragged Jason and "certain brethren" before the politarchs and charged their missionary friends with raising a tumult throughout the Empire, and all of them with setting the decrees of Caesar at naught by declaring that there is another King—one known as Jesus. (Acts 17:5-7) The practical-minded Roman magistrates probably recognized the trumped-up charges for what they really were, but they could not lightly disregard the charge of treason. So they cleverly disposed of all the charges by putting Jason and the others under bail and letting them go. (Acts 17:9) The evil effect of this simple but effective decision was to compel Paul and his companions to leave town for fear that Jason and his friends would lose their worldly possessions in case of another Jewish outbreak, which would be sure to come. Luke tells us that "the brethren immediately sent away Paul and Silas by night unto Beroea." (Acts 17:10)

Chapter 9

PAUL'S SECOND MISSIONARY JOURNEY
(Continued)

Paul and Silas Preach to the Beroeans.—On leaving
Thessalonica, Paul and Silas not only were forced to depart
from friends and converts but were obliged suddenly to
give up the work by which they had sustained themselves.
Luke says nothing about their manual labor while they
were in Thessalonica, but months later, when he writes
back to the Church branch there, Paul reminds us of it in
these words:

> For ye remember, brethren, our labor and travail: for laboring
> night and day, because we would not be chargeable unto any
> of you, we preached unto you the gospel of God. I Thess.
> 2:9; cf. 2 Thess. 3:8-10.)

Paul doubtless labored at his trade as a tent-maker,
and Silas may have helped him, but on this point we cannot be certain. It is also of interest to us to learn that
although Paul would receive no help from the Thessalonians, yet he did accept assistance from the Philippian
saints, possibly because he knew them better and also because they may have been more well-to-do. Notice these
words in Paul's Epistle to the Philippians:

> For even in Thessalonica ye sent once and again unto my neces-
> sity. (Phil. 4:16)

Paul must have felt sad to leave his very successful
labors in Thessalonica, but he and his companions could
cheer themselves at the thought that they had left behind
them a fine nucleus of converts who would carry on success-
fully after their departure. The missionaries had to retreat;

nevertheless, they had the satisfaction of victory even in withdrawal.

Paul, Silas, and Timothy made their way, possibly for a short distance to begin with, upon the Egnatian Road, some forty-five miles west and south of Thessalonica to Beroea, one of the most populated cities in Macedonia. The journey must have taken at least two days.

On their arrival, according to Luke, they "went into the synagogue of the Jews." (Acts 17:10) Paul never failed to give the Jews their opportunity to receive the gospel, and this was no exception. But the missionaries found the Jews and Greeks in Beroea to be unusually open-minded and amenable to their preaching:

> These were more noble than those in Thessalonica, in that they received the word with all readiness of mind, and searched the Scriptures daily, whether those things were so. Therefore many of them believed: also of honorable women which were Greeks, and of men, not a few. (Acts 17:11-12)

Paul had come in contact with so many persons having closed minds and lean intellects (what missionary hasn't?) that the Beroeans must have seemed to him like beings from a better world. An open-minded man may not be the greatest of the creations of God, but he is certainly among the greatest. Luke says that not only did these people receive the word with "all readiness of mind," but they also "searched the Scriptures daily" in order to verify for themselves the truth of what was told them. (*Ibid.*) No wonder the author of the Acts brands the Beroeans as "noble"! We call the attention of all Latter-day Saints, particularly the younger generation, to the emphasis placed here upon the Scriptures as a basic spiritual source. The Beroeans used it to test Paul and his companions. So we ought to test the truth of the various doctrines of our day.

The missionaries converted not only Jews but also prominent Greeks, who had been previously attracted to the high moral teachings of the Jews and to their Scriptures. We ought never to forget how indebted were the early Christian missionaries, men like Paul, Barnabas, and Silas, to the presence of Jewish centers of worship in the great centers of Asia and Europe. In these centers were converted to the Church many Jews and Gentiles.

How long the missionaries continued their successful ministry under ideal conditions we do not know, but it must have been relatively short, possibly two or three months at the most. Word of Paul's success reached Thessalonica in due time, either by Jews from Beroea or by Jews who came from Thessalonica and saw for themselves. In any event, angry Jews from the synagogue in Thessalonica made haste to Beroea and repeated the infamous tactics that had proved so successful against the missionaries in their own city. (Acts 17:13) It appears that Paul was the special object of their fury, because "the brethren" found it possible to engineer his escape only by employing a ruse: an escort of them made as if to send him away by sea and, when clear of the city, seem to have changed their course southward and accompanied him all the way to Athens. (Acts 17:14-15) Silas and Timothy were left in Beroea for the time being.

Paul Faces the Philosophers in Athens.—When Paul's friends had seen him safely in Athens, they returned bearing a message from him to Silas and Timothy to join him as speedily as they possibly could. (Acts 17:15) While waiting for them, Paul had ample opportunity to observe Athens and her people at close range. We have no reason to believe that he was insensible to the greatness of the city as the chief center of culture in the world of that day. It was true that her golden age was now long past, but she had a great university, and learned men from all over the Mediterranean flocked there. And Romans often sent their sons there to visit and be educated. The Greeks were the

intellectual elite of the day. A great tradition of art, architecture, literature, and philosophy still hovered over the
city in spite of its decadence. The mute evidence in stone
of a great talent in sculpture and architecture was all about
Paul. Everywhere he looked were to be seen glorious statues
and buildings. Here was the Jew eyeing the Greek and
taking stock.

While on visits to the Acropolis, the author has often
wondered what Paul's thoughts of the Greeks were. As one
wanders through the Parthenon and other ruins, one cannot help but marvel and wonder at the genius of the Greeks
and their sense of beauty. Nor should we Westerners forget
the great debt which our civilization owes to the Greeks.

Paul the Jew was doubtless impressed by the outward
evidence of Greek talent, but spiritually he was roused to
anger within himself for, as Luke reports, "his spirit was
stirred [Greek: roused to anger] in him, when he saw the
city wholly given to idolatry." (Acts 17:16) What the
people of this city desperately needed, he had to give, the
"good news" of the Gospel of Jesus Christ. So he repaired
to the synagogue, where he reasoned with the Jews and the
"God-fearers" who were in the congregation.

In the meantime, Silas and Timothy seem to have
joined Paul in Athens. These two brethren had doubtless
labored hard, but quietly, to put the work in Beroea on a
firmer foundation after Paul's flight. But Paul was concerned
with the branches that had been raised up in Macedonia.
He concluded that it was wiser to send Silas and Timothy
back, rather than to labor with them in Athens, where
the prospects of establishing a healthy branch of the Church
were slim. So young Timothy, inexperienced as he was, was
sent to Thessalonica:

> Wherefore when we could no longer forbear, we thought it good
> to be left at Athens alone; and sent Timotheus, our brother,
> and minister of God, and our fellow-laborer in the Gospel of

> Christ, to establish you [Greek: buttress, or strengthen you], and to comfort you concerning your faith. (I Thess. 3:1-2)

These words of Paul, months later, do not tell us where Silas was sent, but it is highly probable that he was sent to Philippi, because in due time contributions seem to have reached Paul from there. (Phil. 4:15)

Once more left alone in Athens, Paul continued his labors with members of the synagogue; and to the market-place, day after day he resorted and struck up discussions with any and all whom he happened to meet there. It was the custom of the day for philosophers to frequent the market-place and discourse to the public. Paul simply imitated them so as to get an audience, but he had something far more valuable to give to his audience than philosophic jargon. During his rounds in the market-place Paul encountered some Epicurean and Stoic philosophers who, in their intellectual conceit, asked, "What has this *spermologos* [i.e., seed-picker, or retailer of second-hand information] to say?" (Acts 17:18) Others answered on this wise, somewhat literally translated, "He seems to be a reporter of foreign demons [evil-spirits]." (*Ibid.*) They said this because he had announced to them the glad tidings of Jesus and the Resurrection. (*Ibid.*) The Greek word *Anastasis* (Resurrection) they took for a goddess and supposed that when Paul was speaking of "Jesus and Anastasis," he was referring to two foreign divinities. The philosophers then led Paul to the Areopagus, "Mars' Hill," before the Council of the Areopagus, saying:

> May we know what this new doctrine [teaching] whereof thou speakest, is? For thou bringest certain strange things to our ears: we would know therefore what these things mean. (Acts 17:19-20)

It is supposed by some authorities that Paul had to have his competency as a religious lecturer passed on by the Council at this time, but such is doubtful, in view of Luke's amusing comment on the above passage:

For all the Athenians and strangers which were there spent
their time in nothing else, but either to tell, or to hear some
new thing. (Acts 17:21)

It is more than likely that the Council, such as it was,
was more interested in hearing novel points of view in
Paul's teaching, and in amusing themselves at the expense
of this foreign "hay-seed," than in trying to prove his competency.

Paul was too sensitive and intelligent a person not to
recognize the spirit that moved his audience, but he determined, if possible, to penetrate the callousness and conde-
scension of its members and appeal to any latent spirituality
that they might possess. It was his duty to appeal to the
honest in heart, if there was but one such person in the
crowd. Paul had never had such an audience as this, and
never did he need to marshal all of his spiritual and intellectual resources as with this mixed array of curious spectators.
He was in a sense on trial before the Greek philosophers
and intellectuals, not to mention a possible scattering of
strangers from various parts of the Mediterranean world.

Paul's address, as far as he was able to proceed with it,
was a masterpiece and eloquently delivered. It dealt with
the true nature of God, the greatest of all the themes known
to man. The theme was tactfully introduced and developed
in such a way as to appeal to the Greek yearning after God.
In the words of A. T. Robertson:

> He [Paul] waves aside the worship of idols by an argument from
> nature and represents God as near those who are groping in
> the dark toward him (cf. in Rom. 1 and 2, the other side, the
> heathen going away from God). He presents God, the living
> God, as the centre of life and the Father of all men, as spirit
> and to be worshipped in spirit. This God commands repent-
> ance from sin and will judge all by the man whom he has sent
> and raised from the dead.[1]

[1]*Epochs in the Life of Paul*, p. 161, Charles Scribner's Sons, New York. Used by permission.

With this brief introduction, the reader is urged to consider the address in detail:

> Then Paul stood in the midst of Mars' Hill, and said, Ye men of Athens, I perceive that in all things ye are too superstitious. For as I passed by, and beheld your devotions, I found an altar with this inscription, TO THE UNKNOWN GOD. Whom therefore ye ignorantly worship, him declare I unto you. God that made the world and all things therein, seeing that he is Lord of heaven and earth, dwelleth not in temples made with hands; neither is worshipped with men's hands, as though he needed any thing, seeing he giveth to all life, and breath, and all things; and hath made of one blood all nations of men for to dwell on all the face of the earth, and hath determined the times before appointed, and the bounds of their habitation; that they should seek the Lord, if haply they might feel after him, and find him, though he be not far from every one of us: For in him we live, and move, and have our being; as certain also of your own poets have said, For we are also his offspring. Forasmuch then as we are the offspring of God, we ought not to think that the Godhead is like unto gold, or silver, or stone, graven by art and man's device. And the times of this ignorance God winked at; but now commandeth all men every where to repent: because he hath appointed a day, in the which he will judge the world in righteousness by that man whom he hath ordained; whereof he hath given assurance unto all men, in that he hath raised him from the dead. (Acts 17:22-31)

This was as far as Paul got in his address. He was about to proclaim the heart of the Christian message, Christ and Him crucified, but his mention of *anastasis*, resurrection, was more than his audience could bear, and some mocked at him either by word or gesture. Still others, more polite but none the less bored by his talk, turned to him and said, "We will hear thee again of this." (Acts 17:32) So the proceedings broke up, to what would have been Paul's complete humiliation, had not a few persons attached themselves to him, "and believed: among the which was Dionysius the Areopagite [a member of the Council], and a woman named Damaris, and others with them." (Acts 17:34) Perhaps one of the "others" was Stephanas of Corinth, who must have been visiting in Athens at the time. He is prominently mentioned by Paul in his letter

to the Corinthians as the "first-fruits of Achaia." (I Cor.
16:15-17)

Paul's experiences with the philosophers and intellectuals in Athens taught him what so many of God's servants have found out, that when men are smug in their
intellectual conceit, the word of God cannot touch them.
"But to be learned is good," said Jacob, a Book of Mormon
prophet, "if they hearken unto the counsels of God." (2
Nephi 9:29)

Paul now determined to leave Athens, and it is by no
means impossible that Stephanas persuaded him to go to
Corinth.

Paul Departs From Athens and Proceeds to Corinth.
—Paul could have traveled overland on foot to Corinth,
but it is highly probable that he took the much more direct
and convenient water route through the Saronic Gulf and
landed at Cenchreae, a port about eight miles east and a
little south of Corinth. Burned to ashes in 146 B.C., Corinth
was rebuilt in 44 B.C. by Julius Caesar and became the
political and commercial capital of the Roman Province
of Achaia. The town was built around the Acro-Corinthus,
a rocky hill, whose summit served as a citadel and as a
temple site. The strategic commercial position that Corinth
held on the narrow isthmus between the Gulf of Corinth
and the Aegean can best be realized from an airplane, as
the writer can attest, and today a great canal connects
these two bodies of water. But in Paul's day, goods had to
be unloaded from ships, hauled across the isthmus, and
reloaded in order to avoid the long and dangerous voyage
around the Peloponnesus. The commerce through Corinth
was so great that the city was possibly the richest in Greece.
Not only that, but the famous Isthmian games attracted
great crowds and considerably enlarged the city's income.
Paul may well have attended these games, to judge from
one of his letters to the Corinthians. (I Cor. 9:24) It should

be noticed that Corinth was not unknown as an intellectual center, and her art was especially prized.

But vice often attends great wealth and prosperity, and Corinth was in the throes of Aphrodite worship, with all its licentiousness and vicious immoral practices. So widespread and brazen was the immorality of the city that it gave birth and meaning to a verb, "to corinthianize."

Despite the wickedness of Corinth, Paul's ministry there was to prove far more successful than the one at Athens, where the arrogant philosophers were so disdainful of spiritual matters.

Paul Works at His Trade with Aquila and Priscilla. —On coming to Corinth, Paul had become acquainted with a Jewish couple, Aquila (native of Pontus) and Priscilla, and because he plied the same trade as they—that of tent-making—he lodged at their home and worked with them. (Acts 18:1-3) Apparently Aquila and Priscilla were already members of the Church, for no mention is made of Paul's converting them. They had but recently come from Italy because of Claudius's edict banishing all the Jews from Rome. This edict had been issued about A.D. 50, and it is quite possible that Aquila and Priscilla had been converted in Rome and were members of the Church there when the order of expulsion came. The Romans would look upon the Christians as merely members of a Jewish sect. The names of this prominent Christian couple (Acts 18:18-19; I Cor. 16:19; Rom. 16:3; 2 Tim. 4:19), Jews though they were, are Roman, because it was common and understandable for Jews living outside Palestine to assume such names. Because of the fact that the New Testament several times mentions Priscilla's name before that of her husband, it has been conjectured that she was originally a woman of high station, who became a proselyte and afterward married Aquila.

Paul Preaches to Jews and Greeks.—Sabbath after Sabbath, following his tent-making during the week, Paul entered the Jewish synagogue in Corinth and preached earnestly, seeking to persuade both Jews and Greeks. (Acts 18:4)

After a time Silas and Timothy arrived from Macedonia. In this book we are assuming that this is the second time that these brethren joined Paul from that field of labor, the other time being while he was in Athens. Many writers on Paul believe this to be his first meeting with Silas and Timothy after leaving Beroea. The author finds it somewhat difficult to believe that Paul would ask his friends, who had accompanied him to Athens, to return and send Silas and Timothy "with all speed" (Acts 17:15) and then be able to countermand the order in time to prevent their coming to him. He could possibly have done it in some way, but we should keep in mind that the sending of mail was not the simple and speedy affair then that it is now. Furthermore, it is more than likely that his friends would have nearly reached their homes before Paul came to the conclusion to remain in Athens alone. (I Thess. 3:1) The friends would have Silas and Timothy well on their way to join him, before Paul could countermand the previous order and direct them instead to proceed to Thessalonica and Philippi.

But whatever the truth may be regarding a previous meeting in Athens, the fact remains that Silas and Timothy had now reached Corinth in time to find Paul "pressed in the spirit" and giving solemn evidence that Jesus was the Christ. (Acts 18:5) Silas had probably left Philippi with several of his brethren and a generous contribution to give Paul (cf. 2 Cor. 11:9), and, by pre-arrangement, met Timothy in Thessalonica, from whence all came on to Corinth together. The coming of the brethren tended to relieve Paul's anxieties respecting the Church branches in Macedonia, for although there had been persecution, severe enough at least in Thessalonica to match the difficulties in Judea, still the people had remained firm and steadfast in the faith. (I Thess. 2:14-16) But after hearing Timothy's report, Paul was aware that the Thessalonians needed some advice and counsel by letter from him.

Chapter 10

PAUL'S SECOND MISSIONARY JOURNEY
(Concluded)

THE FIRST EPISTLE TO THE THESSALONIANS

Purpose of the Epistle.—Paul's Epistle to the Thessalonians, in which he was joined by Silas and Timothy, was probably written some time in A.D. 52. As we have already indicated, Timothy's report to Paul concerning the Thessalonians was generally favorable, but Paul felt that steps should be taken to correct certain abuses and misconceptions that were prevalent among them. Among these were the following: (1) The purity of the missionaries' motives and conduct while among them seems to have been questioned by some. (I Thess. 2:1-12) (2) Some appeared liable to relapse into their old pagan vices and seemed lacking in brotherly love and the willingness to do honest work. (I Thess. 4:1-12) (3) Still others seem to have been troubled or worried about the fate of loved ones who died prior to Christ's Second Advent, thinking they would be at a disadvantage compared with those who lived. (I Thess. 4:13-18) (4) Certain Church members were apparently speculating about the date of Christ's Advent, and their personal habits were becoming objectionable. (I Thess. 5:1-11) (5) There seems to have been some lack of respect for brethren in presiding positions, which would tend toward disorder and lack of peace. (I Thess. 5:12-15)

These problems and difficulties can be sensed in and between the lines as one reads the Epistle.

Outline of the Epistle.—The Epistle may be logically divided into four parts, an introduction, an historical-apologetical section, a moral section, and a conclusion.

I. The introduction (1:1-10).

    A. The greeting of Paul, Silvanus and Timothy (1:1).

    B. Paul gives thanks to God for the good spiritual condition of the Church members (1:2-4).

    C. The Gospel came in power with the Holy Ghost to the Thessalonians, who received it in much affliction and joy (1:5-6).

    D. The members were such good examples and sent out "the word" with such effect that the missionaries needed not "to speak anything" (1:7-8).

    E. People report of their own accord Paul's visit to the Thessalonians and how they turned from idols to God, to await the return from heaven of His Son, whom He raised from the dead (1:9-10).

II. The historical-apologetical[1] section (2:1-3:13).

    A. Paul tells of the establishment of the Church in Thessalonica (2:1-16).

        1. The Apostle discusses the errand and conduct of the missionaries among the Thessalonians (2:1-12).

        2. He expresses thanks for the fidelity and steadfastness of the members amidst persecution (2:13-16).

    B. Paul speaks freely about his feelings and hopes during his absence from the Thessalonians (2:17-3:13).

[1]This word is used in its theological sense, which deals with the defensive facts and proofs of Christianity.

1. His attempts to return to Thessalonica were
   twice frustrated by Satan (2:17-20).

2. He sends Timothy back to Thessalonica
   from Athens to comfort and strengthen
   them (3:1-5).

3. Timothy returns to Paul with good tidings
   concerning their faith, charity and con-
   stancy (3:6-9).

4. Paul's prayer for an opportunity to visit
   them again and for an increase in their
   spiritual perfection (3:10-13).

III. The moral section (4:1-5:22).

   A. Paul's exhortations for the people to live so as
   to please God, to observe moral purity, to love
   one another, to mind own business and work
   with their hands (4:1-12).

   B. Explanations involving the Second Advent of
   the Lord (4:13-5:11).

      1. Those who are living at the time of the
         Lord's Advent are not to enjoy any prece-
         dence over those who shall have passed
         away (4:13-18).

      2. The exact time of Lord's Advent is un-
         known, for He is to come "as a thief in the
         night" (5:1-3).

      3. Counsel to observe a sober and vigilant
         life (5:4-11).

   C. Paul's miscellaneous exhortations: respect presiding officers, admonish the unruly, comfort
   the faint-hearted (not "feebleminded" as in
   A.V.), sustain the weak, be patient (not quick-
   tempered), not render evil for evil, aim to do
   good one to another, be joyful, pray unceas-
   ing, do not quench the Spirit, do not set pro-

phecies at naught, prove all things and hold
fast that which is good, hold yourselves aloof
from every form of evil (5:12-22).

IV. Conclusion: Final blessing and farewell (5:23-28).

Perhaps little needs to be added to the Epistle, by
way of explanation except to a part dealing with
the Lord's Second Advent (III, B, 1). Let us quote
the passage in question:

> But I would not have you to be ignorant, brethren,
> concerning them which are asleep [dead], that ye
> sorrow not, even as others which have no hope. For
> if we believe that Jesus died and rose again, even so
> them also which sleep in Jesus will God bring with
> him. For this we say unto you by the word of the
> Lord, that we which are alive and remain unto the
> coming of the Lord shall not prevent [Greek: "anti-
> cipate" or "precede"] them which are asleep. For
> the Lord himself shall descend from heaven with a
> shout, with the voice of the archangel, and with the
> trump of God: and the dead in Christ shall rise first:
> then we which are alive and remain shall be caught
> up together with them in the clouds, to meet the
> Lord in the air: and so shall we ever be with the
> Lord. Wherefore comfort one another with these
> words. (I Thess. 4:13-18)
>
> The "Inspired" revision by the prophet Joseph Smith
> reads differently from A.V. in verse 15: "For this we
> say unto you by the word of the Lord, that they who
> are alive at the coming of the Lord, shall not pre-
> vent [precede] them who remain unto the coming of
> the Lord, who are asleep."

When Paul introduced a subject of unusual importance,
he customarily said, "Now I would not have you to be ignorant, brethren, etc." In this instance he is correcting some
misapprehensions of the Thessalonians concerning his teaching about the Second Advent of Christ. They had supposed
that the Second Coming of our Lord would occur in their
own generation. Incidentally, many modern scholars are
also mistaken in supposing that Paul taught such a doctrine.
Having in their minds such a mistaken notion, the Thessa-

lonian saints, some of whose loved ones had recently passed
on, were very sorrowful, believing that these would thus
never witness or have any part in our Lord's glorious Advent. This idea Paul corrected by pointing out through
revelation, "by the word of the Lord," that at the Coming
of Christ, those who are then alive shall not have any advantage or precedence over those who shall have passed on.

Those who insist that Paul did teach the doctrine that
the Second Advent of our Lord was near at hand in his
day point to I Thess. 4:17 (see above quotation) as proof:
"Then we which are alive and remain shall be caught up
together with them in the clouds, etc." Offhand, the use of
the first person plural seems convincing, but it should be
pointed out that Paul was speaking rhetorically and is not
to be understood as including himself and his missionary
companions among those who were to witness the Second
Coming in mortality. That he had no intention of teaching
such doctrine is clear from what he says in I Thess. 5:2; 2
Thess. 2:1-3. Furthermore, it is not likely that he would be
at loggerheads with the Lord's own teaching (Matt. 24:27-
44; Acts 1:6-11).[2] No Latter-day Saint teacher is liable to
be guilty of holding that Paul taught such doctrine, in view
of the implications of several modern scriptures. (See D. &
C. 7:1-8; 3 Nephi 26:3; 28:6-8; D. & C. 1:12; 2:1; 5:19,
etc.)

The Authenticity of I Thessalonians.—In times past
some scholars have questioned the authenticity of I Thessalonians on purely internal grounds, but today we can report
that few critics dispute its Pauline authorship.

The external evidence in favor of Paul's authorship of
the Epistle is strong. The Apostolic Fathers, St. Ignatius
Martyr and the Shepherd of Hermas, by their allusions and
citations, seem to have made early use of it as Scripture.

---

[2]On this question it is interesting to read C. J. Callan, *The Epistles of St. Paul*, II, 219 f.,
who does not believe that Paul taught the imminent advent of Christ.

It is also included in Marcion's (A.D. 140) Pauline collection and in the Muratorian Fragment (A.D. 170).

Irenaeus seems to have been the first to quote from it, and the later allusions made to it by Tertullian and Clement of Alexandria make it clear that Paul's authorship was definitely accepted. Of importance also is the fact that the Epistle is contained in the Syriac and Old Latin Versions of the New Testament.

The internal evidence in favor of Paul's authorship is equally strong. The doctrine, language and style, not to mention the confident and affectionate tone of the Epistle, the wise combination of reproof and exhortation, and its vigorous style, are all characteristically Pauline.

Paul Continues His Preaching in Corinth.—In the intervals between his letter writing, Paul continued his preaching to Jews and Gentiles alike. But his solemn affirmation to the Jews that Jesus was the Christ brought about their opposition to him, and they used such scurrilous and abusive language that Paul shook the loose folds of his garments, a typical Oriental gesture signifying that he would have nothing more to do with them. (Acts 18:5-6) He then said to them, "Your blood be upon your own heads; I am clean; from henceforth I will go unto the Gentiles." Acts 18:6)

In accordance with his words, Paul quitted the synagogue, taking with him, among others, no less a personage than Crispus, "the chief ruler of the synagogue," and proceeded to hold services in the house of one Justus,[3] who lived next door. Crispus and his household, Gaius, the household of Stephanas, and many others were baptized (Acts 18:8; 1 Cor. 1:14-16; 16:15) Gaius seems to have been a man of substance and generosity, for in his Epistle to the Romans Paul speaks of him as "mine host, and of the whole church." (Rom. 16:23)

[3]Some mss. give his full name as Titius Justus.

Paul's activities adjacent to the synagogue must have aroused the anger of the Jews to such a pitch that he feared for his life. But in a vision by night the Lord spoke these words to him:

> Be not afraid, but speak, and hold not thy peace: for I am with thee, and no man shall set on thee to hurt thee: for I have much people in this city. (Acts 18:9-10)

Since Paul knew that the Lord is a majority in any company, he stayed right there "a year and six months, teaching the word of God among them." (Acts 18:11) The language in context seems to mean that the entire time Paul labored in Corinth was a year and six months.

Paul Before Gallio.—The Jews doubtless continued to harass Paul from time to time, but Roman justice must have kept them somewhat in check, for it was not until Gallio became proconsul of Achaia that the Jews unitedly rose against him and brought him before that Roman official. (Acts 18:12) As a senatorial province Achaia was governed by a proconsul, a new one taking office each year, usually about July 1. Gallio's real name was Annaeus Novatus, but after he had been adopted by the famous rhetorician Julius Gallio, he assumed his name. Gallio was the elder brother of the great Stoic philosopher Seneca and uncle of the poet Lucan. This proconsul seems to have been a real Roman gentleman, and his gracious qualities the Jews mistook for weakness. So on bringing Paul before Gallio they hoped to gain their evil ends. "This fellow," they said, "persuades men to worship God contrary to the law." (Acts 18: 13) But as Paul was ready to make his defense, Gallio showed himself to be a strong and discerning man, for he said to the Jewish mob:

> If it were a matter of wrong or wicked lewdness [Greek: "moral wrong" or "crime"], O ye Jews, reason would that I should bear with you: but if it be a question of words and names, and of your law, look ye to it; for I will be no judge of such matters. (Acts 18:14-15)

With these words Gallio drove the complainants out of court. (Acts 18:16) The Greek rabble in the courtroom then seized Sosthenes (the Synagogue Ruler, who possibly had succeeded Crispus and who had doubtless been foremost in the prosecution of Paul) and beat him in the very presence of Gallio. But the latter cared little for what the mob did, probably feeling that the Jews deserved the rough justice they received. (Acts 18:17) We cannot identify Sosthenes with the "brother" mentioned in I Cor. 1:1. If he should some day be proved so to be, we would have to conclude that he was brought into the Church subsequent to the trial, and under somewhat interesting circumstances.

Gallio's decision doubtless raised Paul's stock considerably in the Corinth community, and he was at liberty to preach without much opposition. This was a great blessing, for had the decision gone against him, he might have become subject to the Roman criminal law; or, as the Jews possibly hoped, he might have been delivered into their hands to be punished. His main recourse then would have been to appeal to Caesar, as a Roman citizen.

The upshot of the whole affair was that Paul "tarried there yet a good while" (Acts 18:18), possibly several months. Assuming that Gallio was Proconsul of Achaia beginning about July 1, A.D. 52, it is probable that Paul was brought before him in August or September of that year.[4]

THE SECOND EPISTLE TO THE THESSALONIANS

Purpose and Point of Origin of the Epistle.—Paul's First Epistle to the Thessalonians seems not to have had the kind of effect upon those people that he had desired. Apparently what he had written concerning the Lord's Second Advent (I Thess. 5:1 f.) had more than ever convinced some of the members that our Lord's Coming was

---

[4]See the discussion by Kirsopp Lake and Silva Lake, *An Introduction to the New Testament*, p. 249. I think their date given for Paul's reaching Corinth is too early.

at hand. (2 Thess. 2:2) However, a careful reading of this last reference gives the impression that some person might have forged a letter purporting to come from Paul, which gave faulty information to the Thessalonians and caused them to be shaken in mind and considerably troubled. Moreover, Paul had heard of disorderly members (2 Thess. 3:6), and some of them were idling away their time and becoming busybodies. (2 Thess. 3:7, 11) These reports from Macedonia together with accounts of continued persecution, convinced the great missionary that he ought to write the Thessalonian Saints another letter, encourage them, and clear up any and all misunderstandings they might have. This he did at once. That this letter was also written from Corinth and shortly (some months) after the First Epistle is shown by these facts: (1) Silas and Timothy are still with Paul (2 Thess. 1:1), whereas Silas is never again mentioned by Luke after Paul's departure from Corinth; (2) Paul speaks of his labors among the Thessalonians as if but a short time removed (2 Thess. 3:7-9); and (3) Paul's allusions in 2 Thess. 3:2 (cf. Acts 18:5 f.) seem to be to his troubles in Corinth.

The Epistle may have been written late in A.D. 52 or early in 53.

Outline of the Epistle.—The Second Epistle to the Thessalonians contains but three short chapters and may be divided into an introduction, a section dealing with the Second Advent, a moral section, and a conclusion.

I. The introduction (1:1-12).
   A. The greeting of Paul, Silvanus and Timothy (1:1-2).
   B. Paul's gratitude and thanksgiving for their faith, love, and patience amidst persecution and tribulation (1:3-4).
   C. God will reward and vindicate the Thessa-

lonian worthies with His rest at His coming
and take vengeance on those who afflict them
and do not acknowledge Him (1:5-10).

D. The Apostle's prayer that God will count them
worthy of His call, by His power accomplish
every desire for goodness and every work of
faith, in order that the name of the Lord may
be glorified in them, and they in Him (1:11-
12).

II. The Lord's Second Advent (2:1-17).

A. The Lord's Second Coming not at hand (2:1-
12). We shall analyze this as in Joseph Smith's
"Inspired" revision.

1. The saints are not to be shaken in mind,
or troubled by letter, unless from Paul;
neither by spirit, or by word, "as that the
day of Christ is at hand" (2:1-2).

2. The Second Advent is not to come until
(1) there comes a falling away [Greek:
"apostasy"] first, and (2) the man of sin be
revealed, the son of perdition (i.e., Satan),
who works and will continue to work, as
Christ suffers him, until the Lord takes
him out of the way with the brightness of
His coming. Satan will work with power,
signs, and lying wonders, to deceive those
who love not truth and believe in lies (2:3-
12).

B. Paul thanks God because He has from the beginning chosen the Thessalonians to salvation
through sanctification of the Spirit and belief
of the truth; whereby He called them by the
Gospel to the obtaining of the glory of the
Lord Jesus Christ (2:13-14); he exhorts them

to stand fast and hold to the truths taught
them. He prays the Lord to comfort their
hearts and buttress them in every good word
and work (2:16-17).

III. The moral section (3:1-15).

    A. Paul requests the prayers of the brethren that
the Lord's word may have a free course and
be glorified, even as with them; and that he
be delivered from unreasonable (perverse) and
wicked men. The Lord is faithful; he will make
the brethren steadfast and guard them from
the evil one. Paul has confidence in the Lord
that they will do as he commands. His prayer
that the Lord will direct their hearts into love
of God, and into steadfast endurance of Christ
(3:1-5).

    B. Paul's strong rebuke against disorderly breth-
ren, that is, brethren living on other people
and not according to the example he and his
companions set them. (Note: these brethren
did this, probably because they mistakenly
looked for the early Advent of the Lord.)
Saints had been taught that if they would not
work, they should not eat. Thessalonians are
told of the duty of quiet, honest work. They
are admonished not to associate intimately
with those who do not obey his written word,
in order to shame them. However, they are
not to regard such as enemies, but are to warn
them (3:6-15).

IV. Conclusion: Paul's final blessing and salutation
(3:16-18).

It should be noticed in the salutation that Paul says,
"The salutation of Paul with mine own hand, which is the

token in every epistle; so I write." (3:17) Paul probably dictated most of his letters, but in this one and some others he writes a greeting toward the end in his own distinctive handwriting, to give a warm personal touch and also to prevent forgery, for a false letter, purporting to be from him (see above) seems to have been circulated. (See 2 Thess. 2:2.)

Inasmuch as the Authorized Version rendition of 2 Thess. 2:1-12 dealing with Paul's views on the Great Apostasy differs considerably from its parallel in the prophet Joseph Smith's "Inspired" revision, we shall print the latter herewith.

> Now we beseech you, brethren, by the coming of our Lord Jesus Christ, and by our gathering together unto him, that ye be not soon shaken in mind, or be troubled by letter, except ye receive it from us; neither by spirit, or by word, as that the day of Christ is at hand. Let no man deceive you by any means; for there shall come a falling away first, and that man of sin be revealed, the son of perdition; who opposeth and exalteth himself above all that is called God, or that is worshipped; so that he as God sitteth in the temple of God, showing himself that he is God. Remember ye not, that, when I was yet with you, I told you these things? And now ye know what withholdeth that he might be revealed in his time. For the mystery of iniquity doth already work, and he it is who now worketh, and Christ suffereth him to work, until the time is fulfilled that he shall be taken out of the way. And then shall that wicked one be revealed, whom the Lord shall consume with the spirit of his mouth, and shall destroy with the brightness of his coming. Yea, the Lord, even Jesus, whose coming is not until after there cometh a falling away, by the working of Satan with all power, and signs and lying wonders, and with all deceivableness of unrighteousness in them that perish; because they received not the love of the truth, that they might be saved. And for this cause God shall send them strong delusion, that they should believe a lie; that they all might be damned who believed not the truth, but had pleasure in unrighteousness.

After Paul had finished his Second Epistle to the Thessalonians, he doubtless dispatched it by Timothy, who, on his return, could advise him concerning its effects and report to him again on the condition of the Church in Macedonia.

**Authenticity of the Second Epistle to the Thessa-
lonians.**—The external evidence for the authenticity of
Second Thessalonians is just as strong as that for First Thessalonians, if not stronger. The versions, Mss., and canonical
lists give the same testimony for both epistles, and the testimony of the Apostolic Fathers, Apologists and other Fathers
is even more clear and explicit regarding this letter. We
cite Polycarp, St. Ignatius Martyr, Irenaeus, Clement of
Alexandria, and Tertullian as proof.

As far as the internal evidence for the Epistle is concerned, we point to the fact that, as in the First Epistle, the
language, style, and teaching are typically Pauline. The
style, structure, and vocabulary of both epistles are very
similar. Certain critics have, in fact, questioned the authenticity of the Second Epistle on the grounds that its similarity
to the First suggests a copyist, but this objection may be
easily answered if it be assumed that Paul re-read his First
Epistle before dictating the Second.

Perhaps the greatest objection that has been raised
against the authenticity of the Second Epistle is based upon
the supposed difference of its teaching concerning the Lord's
Second Advent. Many of the rationalistic critics hold that
First Thessalonians definitely teaches the near Advent of
our Lord, whereas the Second Epistle (2:2-12) makes it far
away. We definitely cannot agree with such critics. It is
true that in the First Epistle Paul teaches the suddenness
of Christ's Coming as well as its unexpectedness, but these
teachings do not prove the imminence of His coming. In
fact Paul definitely points out that the exact date of our
Lord's Coming is unknown. (I Thess. 5:1-5) And if it be
held that he taught the doctrine that the Lord might come
at any time (I Thess. 4:15), we simply point to the fact
that Paul was speaking rhetorically. (See above.)

Paul Leaves Corinth and Returns Home.—Paul had
now been in Corinth a long time, and his restless spirit

decreed that he should leave for home and other fields of labor. So he took leave of "the brethren," and taking with him Aquila and Priscilla, he repaired to Cenchrea, the eastern seaport of Corinth. It is strange that no mention is made of Silas and Timothy, and many authorities assume that they accompanied him. While in Cenchrea, so the text says, Paul had "shorn his head: for he had a vow." (Acts 18:18) Some believe this refers to Aquila, but more likely Luke is speaking of Paul. What kind of a vow would Paul make that would require him to shear off the hair of his head? It has been supposed that he had at some time made a Nazirite vow (see Num. 6:13-21), which had only now reached its fulfillment, in token of which he cut off his hair. Others believe that Paul was ill when he reached Cenchrea and bound himself with a vow, which Jews often took, for deliverance. When he recovered from the illness, he sheared off his hair. Whatever he did, the text makes us pause and wonder over a Jewish custom strange to us. If Paul was indeed ill at Cenchrea, it can be pointed out that a certain sister, Phoebe by name, may have taken care of him, for in his letter to the Romans he says:

> I commend unto you Phoebe our sister, which is a servant of the Church which is at Cenchrea; that ye receive her in the Lord, as becometh saints, and that ye assist her in whatsoever business she hath need of you; for she hath been a succourer [Greek: "protectress" or "patroness"] of many, *and of myself also.* (Rom. 16:1-2; italics ours.)

So possibly in the autumn of A.D. 53, Paul set sail for Syria. Apparently Aquila and Priscilla, his close friends and companions, were transferring their business to Ephesus, which city the ship, after a voyage of two hundred and fifty miles, finally reached. Here Paul temporarily left his friends, but inasmuch as his ship had both to load and unload cargo, he found a little time to repair to the local synagogue and reason with the Jews. As in other places, the Jews were enthralled by his words and bade him to stay longer with them, but he did not consent, because of the coming feast in Jerusalem (Feast of Tabernacles?) which he desired to attend. However, he promised that he would return if he could. (Acts 18:19-21) Thereupon Paul sailed south and east to the port of Caesarea. The text says, "And when he had landed at Caesarea, and gone up, and saluted the Church, he went down to Antioch." (Acts 18:22) Some authorities reason that by this is meant that he disembarked and went into the town, not Jerusalem, but Caesarea. But in view of what is said in Acts 18:21, it is more natural to assume that Jerusalem is meant. No mention is made of what Paul did in the capital city. Apparently his stay there was short. Doubtless he greeted the Church Authorities and gave a report of his missionary activities, after which he left for Antioch.

Paul had now been gone for about two and one-half years, possibly three, and there must have been a great welcome home for him in Antioch on the part of missionary friends, converts, and other Church members, who would listen with a thrill to his report of missionary successes in Macedonia and Greece.

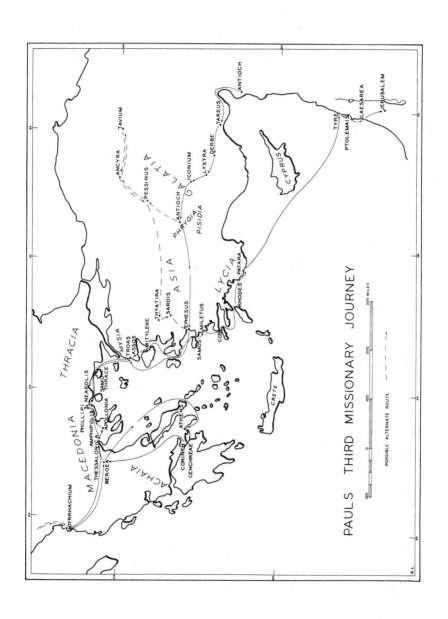

PAUL'S THIRD MISSIONARY JOURNEY

POSSIBLE ALTERNATE ROUTE

100   0   100   200   300 MILES

Chapter 11

PAUL'S THIRD MISSIONARY JOURNEY

Paul Revisits Galatia and Phrygia.—After returning to Antioch from his second mission, Paul was doubtless fatigued and required rest from his strenuous activities. And indeed Luke tells us that he "spent some time there." (Acts 18:23) If he arrived home in the autumn of A.D. 53, the chances are good that he did not depart again until the spring of 54, when weather conditions would be favorable for travel through the mountain passes to the north. We are not told who his companion or companions were when he left Antioch on the Third Missionary Journey, but the chances are that Timothy was along, whoever else may have accompanied him. We are simply told in the Acts 18:23 that Paul "departed, and went over all the country of Galatia and Phrygia in order [familiar ground to him], strengthening all the disciples." We may not know too accurately all of the geography implied in the terms "Galatia" and "Phrygia," but we can take it for granted that the zealous and kindly Paul would do a thorough job through these regions, whatever the areas or distances involved.

Paul Comes to Ephesus.—It must have been the early summer of 54 when Paul, having finished his work in Galatia and Phrygia, came to Ephesus by way of the northern roads [Greek: "having passed through the upper region"]. (Acts 19:1) This passage also says that Paul came to Ephesus while a certain Apollos was in Corinth. This man, a brilliant, powerful, and learned Alexandrian Jew, had come to Ephesus before Paul's arrival and had begun to preach zealously concerning the Lord, although he seems to have been acquainted only with the baptism of John. But Aquila and Priscilla, after listening to him, took him aside and gave him more accurate instruction concerning the "way of God." He must have joined the Church, for a short time later, in Corinth, where the members had been advised to give him a kindly welcome, he gave valuable assistance to them by overcoming the Jews in argument and by proving from the Scriptures that Jesus was the Christ. (Acts 18:24-28).

The city of Ephesus, to which Paul had now come in fulfillment of his promise to the Jews when he briefly stopped there on his way home from his Second Mission (Acts 18: 21), was on the west coast of Asia, at the mouth of the Cayster River, about midway between Smyrna on the north and Miletus on the south. It was located at the junction of natural trade routes, and the main route from Rome to the East passed through the city. In Paul's time, Ephesus was the capital of the Roman Province of Asia, and Pliny in his *Natural History* (V. 31) speaks of her as "the Light of Asia." Here was the seat of the Roman imperial Proconsul; the seaport city was prosperous and most influential in Asia Minor. Ephesus was most famous for her pagan Temple of Artemis, one of the Seven Wonders of the World, but was also noted for literature and art. The philosopher Heracleitos and his friend Hermodorus; the poet Hipponax; the painters Parrhasios and Appeles; and Alexander, statesman, orator, poet, historian, geographer, and astronomer, are all persons to be reckoned with in the history of the city.[1] The ruins of the famous theater of Ephesus still remain. Its auditorium was semicircular, 495 feet in diameter, the orchestra was 110 feet in diameter, and the stage was 22 feet wide. There were 66 rows of seats, which accommodated an audience of about 24,500 persons. This city was strategic

[1] See Smith, *The Life and Letters of St. Paul*, p. 226.

in every way, and it was fitting that the Church should have one of its principal headquarters here. The branch of the Church in Ephesus was one of the seven addressed in the Revelation of John (1:11; 2:1-7) toward the turn of the First Century. Tradition has it that the Apostle John spent several years of his life here.

Paul Preaches to Twelve Followers of John's Baptism.—On coming to Ephesus, Paul may well have lodged with Aquila and Priscilla—some mss. have it that way—as he did in Corinth, and continued to ply his old trade of tent making. (Acts 20:33-35; 1 Cor. 4:11-12) When he started to preach in the city, one of the first incidents mentioned by Luke that happened to him was his meeting a group of twelve "disciples." How Paul came across them we are not told, but he asked them, "Have ye received the Holy Ghost since ye believed?" To which they answered, "We have not so much as heard whether there be any Holy Ghost." (Acts 19:1-2) By this answer Paul knew, as any true member of the Church would, that these men, if instructed at all, had not been accurately taught the principles of the Gospel. He therefore questioned them further by asking, "Unto what then were ye baptized?" To which they answered, "Unto John's baptism." (Acts 19:3) The little group of twelve may , indeed, have heard of Jesus and his mission as John had taught these things, but were unaware of the Resurrection and of the coming of the Holy Ghost upon the Apostles and other disciples at Pentecost. So Paul explained the facts which they needed to know:

> John verily baptized with the baptism of repentance, saying unto the people, that they should believe on him which should come after him, that is, on Christ Jesus. (Acts 19:4)

Paul, of course, instructed them fully in words that Luke does not report, but the net result was as the Evangelist says:

When they heard this, they were baptized in the name of the Lord Jesus. And when Paul had laid his hands upon them, the Holy Ghost came on them; and they spake with tongues, and prophesied. And all the men were about twelve. (Acts 19:5-7)

Paul Preaches in the Synagogue and the School of Tyrannus.—In accordance with his usual custom, Paul entered into the Jewish synagogue at Ephesus, "disputing and persuading the things concerning the kingdom of God." (Acts 19:8) But unfortunately, as had so often happened to Paul, his eloquence, knowledge, and ability to overcome the arguments of his opponents, though drawing many to his side, also resulted in others openly fighting him and his cause. For "divers were hardened, and believed not, but spake evil of that way before the multitude." (Acts 19:9) Luke does not tell us how much Paul may have suffered at this time and later during his sojourn in the city, but his Epistles tell us something about it, how he fought with wild beasts (1 Cor. 15:32; metaphorical?) despaired of his life (2 Cor. 1:8), and doubtless received beatings and prison sentences. (2 Cor. 11:23) He and the disciples he had made separated themselves from the synagogue and removed to the school of one Tyrannus, whose lectures (as a rhetorician?) were delivered in the mornings, leaving his hall free in the afternoons. Codex Bezae on Acts 19:9 (and we take the text for what it is worth) indicates that Paul used the hall from the fifth hour to the tenth, that is, from 11:00 a.m. to 4:00 p.m. We don't know whether Tyrannus was a close friend or disciple of Paul's and so proffered the use of the hall free, or whether Paul had to hire it; probably the latter. But here Paul "disputed daily" for two years, and with such power and influence that "all they which dwelt in Asia heard the word of the Lord Jesus, both Jews and Greeks." (Acts 19:10-11) Paul directly or indirectly must have had much to do either with the setting up or building up of the "Seven Churches" mentioned in the Book of Revelation, which included in addition to Ephesus, the

branches at Smyrna, Pergamum, Thyatira, Sardis, Philadelphia, and Laodicea. (Rev. 1:11) His influence in Asia
was immense. Branches of the Church not hitherto mentioned, such as at Colossae, Hierapolis, Magnesia, Tralles,
and Miletus, would also be benefited by the spiritual power
and message of Paul.

As evidence of Paul's spiritual power, Luke cites these
facts:

> And God wrought special miracles by the hands of Paul; so
> that from his body were brought unto the sick handkerchiefs
> or aprons, and the diseases departed from them, and the evil
> spirits went out of them. (Acts 19:11-12)

This use of handkerchiefs and other articles that had
touched Paul's skin for bringing about miraculous cures
reminds one of remarkable cures wrought in the same way
by the prophet Joseph Smith in this dispensation.

The Sons of Sceva and the Evil Spirit.—Luke tells
of certain "vagabond Jews," exorcists, who attempted to cast
out evil spirits by calling on the name of "Jesus whom Paul
preacheth." (Acts 19:13) They had evidently seen Paul
cast out evil spirits in the name of his Master, and were
attempting to imitate him. Seven practitioners of their
black art, sons of Sceva, a Jew, are specifically mentioned
by Luke in an incident which he tells about. They were
attempting to cast out the evil spirit from a man in the
manner mentioned, when the evil spirit, speaking through
the man, said, "Jesus I know, and Paul I know; but who
are ye?" (Acts 19:15) Then the man, actuated by the evil
spirit, fell upon these imitators of God's servant, "and over-
came them, and prevailed against them, so that they fled
out of that house naked and wounded." (Acts 19:16) The
incident caused a sensation among the Jews and Greeks
living in Ephesus, and fear fell upon all of them. In this
way the name of the Savior was magnified; many who
believed in Him came and made confession and declaration

of their deeds. And many of those who had practiced magic arts brought their books together and burnt them in the presence of everybody. The value of these was reckoned to be fifty thousand pieces of silver ($10,000?). (Acts 19:17-19) Luke adds this significant line to his description:

> So mightily grew the word of God and prevailed. (Acts 19:20)

One who believes in the Scriptures and reads of the incident concerning the sons of Sceva must be impressed with the fact that the power to operate in God's name is confined to a relatively few of His servants. The Lord does not give His power to anyone who takes it upon himself to minister in His name. He is a God of order and operates through the appointed spiritual channels of His Church. Paul had the appropriate Priesthood and authority to act in God's name; the sons of Sceva did not. One hears slighting remarks these days about an "authoritarian" church, but the fact remains that God always acts through His one true Church; He does not work through sectarian channels. The sons of Sceva found that to be true in Paul's day. The same is true today.

Paul's Flying Visit to Corinth.—Although the matter is disputed, it would appear that Paul, while at Ephesus, made a quick visit to Corinth. Luke makes no reference to such a visit, and for our knowledge of his trip we are dependent on allusions which Paul makes in his Epistles. It will be remembered that Paul made his first visit to Corinth on his second missionary journey. According to Luke, the visit of Paul to Greece, during which time he would visit Corinth (Acts 20:2-3), was his second visit to that city. But in two passages from 2 Corinthians (12:14; 13:1), which was written prior to his departure for Greece as mentioned in Acts 20:2-3, Paul speaks of coming a *third* time. So what Luke would speak of as Paul's second visit, Paul himself speaks of as his third. And if the visit which the great missionary made after leaving Ephesus was his third, then it stands to reason that there must have been a second visit to Corinth before it. This second visit would logically take place during his long sojourn in Ephesus.[2] This hurried second visit of Paul's doubtless took place because he had received bad news concerning the conduct of the Corinthians. He speaks of it as a painful one (2 Cor. 2:1); it brought him humiliation because of the heinous sins of his own converts (2 Cor. 12:21); later he tells the people of his mourning over those who had dishonored Christ's name by "the uncleanness and fornication and lasciviousness which they have committed." *(Ibid.)*

Paul's Lost Letter to the Corinthians.—It is supposed that some time after Paul's hurried visit to the Corinthians he wrote them a letter which became lost. This theory is based on I Cor. 5:9, which reads: "I wrote unto you in an [lit. "the"] epistle not to company with fornicators." Fragments of this missing letter have, so certain scholars believe, been incorporated in Paul's two Corinthian letters that have come down to us. The fragments are supposed to be I Cor. 6:12-20 and 2 Cor. 6:14-7:1; they can be examined at leisure by the reader, and independent conclusions may be reached. The author can see no objection to the belief that Paul did write a letter to the Corinthians that was lost, but that the references given above indicate true fragments of the lost letter is something else again, though clever arguments are advanced in favor of the hypothesis.[3]

Paul's Plans to Pass Through Macedonia and Achaia, to Jerusalem and Rome.—Paul's ministry in Ephesus was rapidly drawing to a close. It was now early in A.D. 57, and he "purposed in the spirit," as Luke says, "when he

[2]Conybeare & Howson, *Life and Epistles of St. Paul*, p. 375, are in favor of the view given here, but also give some of the arguments against. F. J. Goodwin, *A Harmony of the Life of St. Paul*, pp. 94, 209 f., also favors the view adopted here.

[3]See Smith, *The Life and Letters of St. Paul*, p. 654. Other fragments in addition to those mentioned are held to by some scholars. See T. Henshaw, *New Testament Literature*, pp. 242-244.

had passed through Macedonia and Achaia, to go to Jerusalem, saying, After I have been there, I must also see Rome." (Acts 19:21). This is in essential agreement with what he says in 2 Cor. 1:16, but this plan had been abandoned when he wrote his first Epistle to the Corinthians, which we will deal with shortly, for he says, "I will not see you now by the way [Greek: 'in passing'], but I trust to tarry a while with you, if the Lord permit. But I will tarry at Ephesus until Pentecost [May]." (I Cor. 16:7-8) He trusts, however, that he may "abide" and "winter" with them, and hopes that they will speed him forward after that "whithersoever I go." (I Cor. 16:6) So Paul for the time being dropped his plan, "for a great door and effectual is opened unto me, and there are many adversaries," (I Cor. 16:9) but eventually he adopted it. In the meantime he sent two of his assistants, Timothy and Erastus, to Macedonia, and he himself remained for a while in Roman Asia. (Acts 19:22) In his First Epistle to the Corinthians, Paul exhorts the Church members to receive Timothy kindly; his companion, Erastus, may have been the person of that name who was "the treasurer of the city" (Rom. 16:23; 2 Tim. 4:20) and needed no introduction.

> For this cause have I sent unto you Timotheus, who is my beloved son, and faithful in the Lord, who shall bring you into remembrance of my ways which be in Christ, as I teach every where in every church. (I Cor. 4:17)

*   *   *

> Now if Timotheus come, see that he may be with you without fear: for he worketh the work of the Lord, as I also do. Let no man therefore despise him: but conduct him forth in peace, that he may come unto me: for I look for him with the brethren. (I Cor. 16:10-11)

Paul's words in I Cor. 16:10, "Now if Timotheus come," would seem to imply that Timothy had already left Ephesus before Paul wrote the Epistle.

THE FIRST EPISTLE TO THE CORINTHIANS

Purpose of the Epistle.—Paul had good reason to be disturbed concerning the welfare of the branch of the Church at Corinth, because disquieting reports had reached him from several sources concerning the actions of its members. From people connected with the household of a woman by the name of Chloe, who seems to have had connections in both Corinth and Ephesus, he received word concerning cliques and factions that had formed in the branch. (I Cor. 1:11) Possibly from Apollos, who was back in Ephesus (I Cor. 16:12), or from Stephanas, Fortunatus, and Achaicus, who were visiting in Ephesus (I Cor. 16:17), he learned of serious moral laxity among the Corinthians. (See I Cor. 5:1-3) Church members were also allowing pagan courts to decide their differences instead of settling them among themselves. (I Cor. 6:1) The Corinthians had sent Paul a letter (I Cor. 7:1) asking important questions which, too, needed answering. All of these facts and others unmentioned caused Paul to write the Corinthians the letter we know as I Corinthians.

Outline of the Epistle.—The Epistle contains three parts: an introduction, a body containing two sections, and a conclusion. We shall give a fairly condensed outline of this important epistle and follow it with a more detailed discussion of several of its most interesting teachings.

    I. Introduction (1:1-9).

        A. A greeting from Paul (who now acknowledges himself "an Apostle") and "brother" Sosthenes to the Church in Corinth and to all who invoke the name of Jesus Christ (1:1-3).

        B. Expression of thanksgiving for the fact that the Corinthians have been enriched with readiness of speech and with knowledge, so that they are not behind in any gift. Christ will confirm them to the end so that they will be free from reproach in the day of the Lord Jesus Christ (1:4-9).

II. The body of the epistle (1:10-15:58).
    A. Corinthian weaknesses and vices (1:10-6:20).
        1. Party cliques and factions (1:10-4:21).
            a. The Apostle entreats the Corinthians to avoid disputes and divisions and be in harmony in their minds and judgments. Their breaking up into cliques as followers of Paul, Apollos, Cephas and Christ is condemned, because all of them received the same baptism and Christ is not divided (1:10-16).
            b. Paul is sent to preach the Gospel in simplicity, not with clever words or according to human conceptions, "because the foolishness of God is wiser than men; and the weakness of God is stronger than men" (1:17-25).
            c. God has chosen to prevent mortal man from boasting before Him, by choosing the foolish things of the world in order to shame its wise men; and He has chosen the weak things of the world in order to shame what is strong. No man to be able to attribute his justification and salvation to his own wisdom, noble birth, or power, but to God's goodness and mercy only (1:26-31). For this reason Paul preached in Corinth in weakness, fear and trepidation; not with persuasive words of wisdom, but with the convincing power of the Spirit

Thus their trust would not rest on man's wisdom, but on God's power (2:1-5).

d. Yet the Gospel contains God's wisdom in a mystery, which worldly leaders have not learned. But to us God has revealed them by His Spirit. No man knows the things of God unless he has the Spirit of God. We have not received the spirit of the world, but the Spirit which is of God (2:6-12). Mysteries of God are perceived only by spiritual men (2:13-16). The spiritually immature Corinthians are not able to receive advanced doctrine; their strife and factious spirit demonstrates that (3:1-4).

e. Corinthian dissension is to be condemned, because preachers of the Gospel are mere instruments in God's hands and have to render an account of their ministry. Men are the Temple of God's Spirit, and should not defile themselves (3:5-17).

f. Mere human wisdom is of little worth; therefore the Corinthians should not prefer one missionary over another, for God alone is the judge of His servants (3:18-4:5).

g. The Corinthians and the leaders of their factions are advised [with keen irony] to imitate the humility and unpretentiousness of the Apostle, who entreats them and advises that he has sent Timothy to them (who will remind them of Paul's conduct as a Christian teacher), and will himself visit them in a short time. He asks whether he should come with a rod or in a loving and tender spirit (4:6-21).

2. Moral laxity and evils of litigation before pagan tribunals (5:1-6:20).

    a. The Corinthians are not to boast or be complacent because they have been tolerating, despite previous warning, an incestuous man; they are to remove him from among them, and are warned not to associate with immoral brethren (5:1-13).

    b. Disputes among Corinthian Saints are not to be judged in lawsuits before pagan courts. The Saints are to judge the world and should be able to adjudicate their own differences. Righteous living is indispensable (6:1-11).

    c. The freedom of Christianity is no excuse for licentiousness. Bodies of the Saints are members of Christ and are not members of a harlot. The body is the temple of the Holy Ghost, which is of God, and is the property of the divine tenant (6:12-20).

B. Replies to questions and doubts raised by the Corinthians in a letter to the Apostle (7:1-15:58).

    1. Answers concerning marriage and single state ("Inspired" revision 7:1-40).

        a. To avoid fornication, men and women should be married. They are to yield

to reasonable desires of each other, so
that Satan will not tempt them (7:1-5);
by permission (of Lord) Paul wishes
that unmarried and widows would
abide as he is (unmarried at the time),
but it is better to marry than to sin
(7:6-9).

b. A wife should not leave her husband,
   but if she does she should remain unmarried or be reconciled to him; the
   husband is not to put away his wife; it
   is Paul's advice, not the Lord's, that if
   either a husband or wife has an unbelieving mate, they are not to leave each
   other, for an unbelieving mate is sanctified by the others; else their children
   were unclean; but now they are holy.
   If the unbelieving mate decides to depart, let him depart, i.e., the believing
   mate may then remarry (see below);
   but if they stay together, the believing
   mate may be the means of saving the
   other (7:10-16; for explanation of vs.
   14 see D. & C. 74:1-7).

c. Whether or not a man is circumcised
   before conversion means nothing; the
   only thing that counts for salvation is
   keeping God's commandments; it is not
   necessary to change a respectable manner of life after conversion (7:17-20);
   whether a slave or freedman, let every
   convert continue in the honest and upright state in which the faith found him;
   the slave when converted becomes the
   Lord's freeman, and likewise, when a

freeman is converted, he becomes the Christ's bondman (7:21-24).

d. Concerning unmarried young women (virgins) and men: because of present distress (necessity, compulsion), Paul gives his opinion that it is well for a person to remain in his present situation (presumably unmarried); if bound to a wife, seek not to be released; if unattached to a woman, do not seek a wife; but if either a man or virgin marry, he or she does not sin, but will have sorrows in the flesh (7:25-28); but the Apostle gives this advice to those who are called on missions ("unto the ministry"), for the time is but short when they will be called, and even if they have wives, they should be as if they had none; for they are chosen to do the Lord's work. The unmarried under these conditions will think of the Lord's work and not, as the married, of how to please husbands. This advice is given for their own profit, that they may attend to the Lord's work without distraction (7:29-35; compare with Authorized Version.) Anyone who thinks he is not acting honorably to a virgin whom he has espoused does not sin if he marries her because he feels she is passing the bloom of youth. But if he stands fast and does not marry her, he does well (7:36-38). A wife is bound by the law as long as her husband lives; if he is dead, she may remarry, "in the Lord";

but in Paul's judgment she will be happier if she remains the way she is; and the Apostle thinks he has the Spirit of God (7:39-40).

2. Subject of food offered to idols (8:1-11:1).

    a. In principle, it is permissible to eat foods offered to idols, because an idol is nothing in itself and cannot defile food (8:1-8); but in actual practice the saints should not eat such foods if it scandalizes their weaker brethren (8:9-13).

    b. Paul gives himself as an example of self-restraint, and the conversion of the Corinthians is the seal on his Apostleship. As an Apostle he has the right to be supported and lead a wife around with him (9:1-14), but this right he has not used (9:15-18); Paul has given up his liberty and has become all things to all men, in order that he may save souls. All he does is for the Gospel's sake, that he may share in its blessings (9:19-23). The Apostle uses illustrations common in athletic circles to demonstrate the great efforts and sacrifices he makes in order to win the prize of eternal life. As a result of his example and others from Jewish history (the terrible fate that befell the Jews of the Exodus), the Corinthians must not be too confident of their salvation, but should put forth every effort to resist temptation and obtain it (9:24-10:13).

    c. Paul again deals with offerings to idols

and warns the Corinthians to take no part in the sacrificial banquets given in public by the pagans. Saints cannot be partakers both of the Lord's table and that of devils (10:14-22a). Ordinarily the saints, if invited privately by unbelievers, should eat what is placed before them, but should abstain from such if it scandalizes weaker brethren (10:22b-11:1).

3. Conduct at religious gatherings (11:2-34).

    a. Men praying or prophesying with head covered dishonor their heads. [Grecian slaves came with their heads covered before their masters.] Women who appear in church without a veil dishonor their heads. [The Romans shaved the heads of dancing women, who were generally harlots, and the Greeks treated their female slaves in the same manner.] A man ought to cover his head, because he is the image and glory of God; but the woman is the glory of man. Man is not of the woman, but the woman of man. The man was not created for the woman, but the woman for the man. Long hair is a glory to woman (11:2-16).

    b. The Apostle condemns the dissension and lack of order when the Corinthians come to worship and to partake of the Sacrament. Those who bring food eat it in private and leave none for the poor. Some drink to excess. Paul asks why, having homes in which to eat and drink, they show contempt for the Church

and shame the poor. [It appears that
at Corinth there was supposed to be a
common meal eaten before the Sacrament service. See vss. 21, 33, in which
Paul advises them to wait long enough
so that they can all eat together.] Paul
cites facts concerning origin of the Sacrament, its significance, and sacredness.
Many are ill among them because they
partake of the Sacrament unworthily
(11:17-34).

4. The spiritual gifts (12:1-14:40).

   a. The nature, origin and purpose of the
       gifts of the Spirit. These gifts, such as
       the word of wisdom, knowledge, faith,
       healing, working of miracles, prophecy,
       discerning of spirits, divers kinds of
       tongues, interpretation of tongues, etc.,
       are given to men by the Spirit to benefit
       each other (12:1-11; cf. Moroni 10:8-
       19; D. & C. 46:8-29).

   b. Paul illustrates the organic unity of the
       Church by comparison with the parts
       of the human body. As the human body
       is one, in spite of its various parts hav-
       ing greater or lesser importance, so the
       Church should have unity, making
       jealousy impossible. The unity of the
       Church should exclude pride and con-
       tempt among its members, for by
       analogy parts of the human body which
       seem somewhat feeble are nevertheless
       indispensable. Members of the Church
       who have been more especially favored
       by position or spiritual gifts must not

look down upon or despise brethren of lesser degree or talent. There is to be no schism in the body of the Church, for if one part suffers, every other part suffers, and vice versa. Unity obviously involves mutual dependence (12:1-31).

c. The Apostle advises the Corinthian saints that the greatest of all gifts is "charity," that it is the very foundation of all the others, and without which they are nothing (13:1-13). [The charity of which Paul speaks is more than simple love. It is the "pure love of Christ" which God bestows "upon all who are true followers of his Son, Jesus Christ." (Moroni 7:47-48) This and a question concerning the authorship of I Cor. 13 will be discussed below.]

d. Paul shows that of the spiritual gifts, prophecy is superior to and more edifying than the gift of tongues (14:1-6); that the gift of tongues is not profitable without the gift of interpretation (14: 7-20). Prophecy is of more value in dealing with unbelievers than the gift of tongues (14:21-45). Practical directions are given so as to bring about the orderly exercise of spiritual gifts. Women are not to speak publicly in the Church. They are not to rule, but to be subordinate, as the Law says (Gen. 3:16); if they wish to learn something, they may ask their husbands at home. It is a shame for women to rule in the Church. [It is man's function to preside in the

Church, inasmuch as he has the Priest-hood. This is doubtless what Paul im-plies.] The Corinthians are to conform to the discipline and practice of the Church. If anyone thinks he has the gift of prophecy or any other spiritual gift, he will recognize as the Lord's command what the Apostle is writing to them. All things are to be done de-cently and in order (14:26-40).

5. The resurrection of the dead (15:1-58; see "Inspired" revision.)

   a. The Apostle teaches of the resurrection of the dead by showing first through the Scriptures (Ps. 15:10; Isa. 53:10; Jonah 2:10, etc.) and other witnesses that Christ rose from the dead (15:1-11).

   b. If there is no resurrection from the dead, then our faith is vain and we are still in our sins (15:12-19).

   c. Christ is the first fruits of the resurrec-tion. Inasmuch as through Adam death comes to man, so through Christ shall all men be made alive. After Christ's resurrection follows that of other men in their order. Then the Christ delivers up the kingdom to God after having put down all rule, power and authority. Christ is to reign until all enemies, in-cluding death, are put under His feet. The Son is to be subject to God (15:20-28).

   d. If certain of the Corinthians do not be-lieve in the resurrection, why are they then baptized for the dead? (15:29) [This question will be discussed below.]

e. If there is no resurrection, there is no purpose or sense to the sufferings or persecutions endured by the Apostles and saints in this life (15:30-34).

f. By analogies to nature, Paul tells how the body will rise. All flesh is not the same; just as there is the flesh of birds, fishes and beasts, so there will be different resurrections among men of different calibers—celestial, terrestrial and telestial—depending on whether they rise in glory compared to the sun, moon, or stars (15:35-44). The change from an earthly body to a spiritual (resurrected) body is possible (15:45-49) and necessary. Death is to be swallowed up in victory when the resurrection comes. God gives the victory through Jesus Christ. The brethren are exhorted to be steadfast and unmovable, always abounding in the Lord's work (15:50-58).

III. Conclusion (16:1-24).

A. The Apostle orders the collection for the poor in Jerusalem (16:1-4).

B. Paul plans to come to Corinth (16:5-9), commends Timothy and others to the Corinthians (16:10-18).

C. Paul sends the greetings of the Church branches and especially of certain individuals in Asia (16:19-20), and then writes his personal salutation with his own hand (16:21-24).

A Discussion of Parts of the Epistle—(1) **Paul's Apostleship Again.**—In Chapter 6 we discussed the question of Paul's Apostleship. We came to the conclusion that at the time of the First Missionary Journey he was not an Apostle, and that it is difficult to tell when he did become one. In I Cor. 1:1 he does speak of himself for the first time as an Apostle. His testimony, which was given during his Third Missionary Journey, we of course accept. But we are still forced to say that there is no record of his being ordained to the high office, and there are few clues in the Scripture that can help us to determine within a few years' time when he became the Apostle of which he speaks. We call attention again to his language in the Epistle to the Galatians, "Paul, an Apostle, (not of men, neither by man, but by Jesus Christ, and God the Father, . . ." (Gal. 1:1) Doesn't this statement in effect mean that he received his commission directly from our Lord without the intervention of man? His mission, as we know, was a special one to the Gentiles, and was given directly by the Lord himself. (Acts 9:15; 22:15, 21, 26:16-18; Gal. 2:7-9) Paul received many revelations from the Lord (cf. 2 Cor. 12:1-7), and he could have received his special calling on any one of a number of occasions before A.D. 57 when he wrote I Corinthians. This conclusion will have to suffice us.

(2) **Paul's Marriage Status and His Views on Marriage.**—Before discussing the Apostle's views on marriage as given in I Cor. 7 ("Inspired" revision), it is well to point out again the probability that Paul was married during his early manhood. We discussed the problem in Chapter I of this book. But those who do not believe that Paul had ever married point to I Cor. 7:7-8, where the Apostle says this:

> For I would that all men were even as I myself. . . . I say therefore to the unmarried and widows, it is good for them if they abide even as I.

However, the Greek word translated "unmarried"

here is *agamos*, which has reference to a person in a state of wedlock, whether he or she has formerly been married or not. The word "unmarried" in the context above most certainly has reference to widowers, because it is masculine plural and also because Paul deals with virgins, male and female, in vss. 25, 26, 28. That is to say, the Apostle deals with widowers and widows in vss. 8, 9 and with those who have never been married in vss. 25, 26, 28. Paul's counsel in the passage quoted above simply means that widows and widowers should remain unmarried as he (a widower) had done.

But assuming that Paul had been married at one time, it may be difficult for many Latter-day Saints to reconcile his counsel that widows, widowers, and virgins, male and female, not marry with the Lord's express command that man should multiply and replenish the earth (Gen. 1:28) and with His saying that it is not good for man to be alone (Gen. 2:18). We should keep in mind that the great Apostle was very well aware, from both Scripture and common sense, that man should marry. Paul himself probably never re-married because he wanted to give his entire time to the business of bringing souls to Christ. (Cf. I Cor. 9:5, 6, 19-23). He doubtless also felt that many of the Corinthian saints, including widowers, widows, and virgins, could well afford to give much of their time to the Lord's service. During the period of time they were in the ministry, it would be better for them not to be married in order that there might be fewer distractions. The prophet Joseph Smith definitely points out that the present text of I Cor. 7 is faulty in places and hence fails to give the full truth which Paul meant to convey when he counseled the Corinthians on marriage. In the prophet's "Inspired" revision of the chapter, it appears that Paul's advice to many of the Corinthians to remain unmarried was so that they might do greater good, for they were definitely called to do missionary work. In the Prophet's revision Paul, among other things, says this:

> But I speak unto you who are called unto the ministry. For this I say, brethren, the time that remaineth is but short, that ye shall be sent forth unto the ministry. Even they who have wives, shall be as though they had none; for ye are called and chosen to do the Lord's work.(Verse 29)

What Paul really said gives a considerable twist to the whole problem of marriage as presented in the conventional text. The reader is advised to consult the whole chapter in the "Inspired" revision.

Verse 15 of Chapter 7 demands some special comment. The verse sets forth what the world calls the "Pauline Privilege," and has reference to mixed marriages, that is, of unbelievers to believers. The verse in question reads:

> But if the unbelieving depart, let him depart. A brother or a sister is not under bondage in such cases; but God has called us to peace.

This is usually taken to mean that if one of an unbelieving couple joins the Church and the other departs or separates himself so as to make cohabitation impossible, the Christian member of the marriage is bound no longer by the matrimonial tie and may remarry at his or her discretion. The Christian was to allow the separation inasmuch as there was no assurance that the unbeliever would finally join the Church. It would be better to let the unbeliever depart than to risk the discord and rancor that would otherwise result. God had called them to peace, not strife.

It should be kept in mind that Paul had to give his counsel and advice on marriage at a time when divorce and unchastity were rife among Jews and Gentiles alike. He wanted every member of the Church to guard himself scrupulously against acting wrongly.

(3) **The Apostle's Sermon on Charity as the Supreme Gift.**—The great sermon on charity, usually translated as "love" by modern scholars, as found in I Cor. 13, emphasizes that charity is the very root and soul of all other virtues

and that it endures forever. This virtue is not the ordinary "love" usually thought of as extended by man to man or man to woman, but is that supernatural virtue which the great Nephite prophet Mormon defines as the "pure love of Christ" that is bestowed by God "upon all who are true followers of his Son, Jesus Christ." (Moroni 7:47-48) Through it men may become the "sons of God" and "be like Him." (Vs. 48) Some of the qualities and fruits of "this pure love of Christ" are enumerated thus in I Cor. 13:4-7: it has *patience* (long suffering); *is kindly* (full of service to others); *is not envious* (not offended or jealous of the good or success of others); *does not vaunt itself* (is not boastful or pretentious in words and actions); *is not puffed up* (is not puffed up with anger or conceit); *does not behave itself unseemly* (does not behave amiss, unbecomingly, or dishonorably); *seeketh not her own* (not selfish or seeking own ends to the detriment of others); *is not easily provoked* (not easily aroused to anger); *thinketh no evil* (does not reckon or put down to the account of the evil-doer any harm or wrong suffered at his hands); *rejoiceth not in iniquity* (does not rejoice in the injustice or evil others do); *rejoiceth in the truth* (rejoices not only in the truth as spoken, but truth of idea, reality, sincerity, truth in the moral sphere, straightforwardness); *beareth all things* (keeps close, puts up with, endures patiently, bears up under the defects and faults of one's neighbor); *believes all things* (trustful of and believing only good things concerning one's neighbor); *hopes all things* (always hopes for the best concerning one's neighbor); *endureth all things* (bears up patiently under all the evils that come of the actions of men).

Just how good or Godlike we are may be judged in part from this list, which gives the characteristics and actual fruits of the "pure love of Christ," both negative and positive. Only as men take on these characteristics and produce the fruits mentioned do they tend toward perfection.

The Apostle Paul is usually credited with being the author of this great sermon or hymn concerning the "pure love of Christ." But inasmuch as Mormon, the great Nephite prophet and historian, quotes many of the same words, and in much the same order as Paul, we are justified in assuming that the sermon was accessible to both and came from the same source. (Cf. I Cor. 13:4-8 and Moroni 7:45-46) The author believes that this source was the Savior himself, who doubtless gave a sermon on charity while in mortality to His disciples in Palestine and also as a glorified, resurrected being to the Nephites on the American Continent.

(4)   **Paul's Reference to Baptism for the Dead.**—The reference of Paul in I Cor. 15:29 to baptism for the dead is to scholars one of the most vexing problems in the New Testament. Through modern revelation Latter-day Saints understand it thoroughly—that in the Temples of God men and women may enter and by proper authority delegated from God be baptized for and in behalf of their dead ancestors who had never heard of or had never had the opportunity to accept the Gospel and its ordinances in the flesh. (D. & C. 127:5-10; 128:1-25) Latter-day Saints believe that the ordinances of the Gospel are just as binding upon the dead as upon the living (John 3:3-5), and that inasmuch as baptism is an earthly ordinance which the dead cannot perform for themselves, it must be done for and in their behalf by their descendants in mortality. If the dead accept the Gospel in the spirit world, the ordinances performed in the Temples of God will become binding in their behalf. Paul the Apostle understood this fact and taught the doctrine to the Corinthians. He was therefore perplexed when some of them who were being baptized for their dead questioned the doctrine of the resurrection from the dead. He says to them in effect, "Why are you being baptized for your dead, if they do not rise from death?"

He assumes that baptism for the dead is useless if there is no resurrection, and in this he is correct. (See 2 Nephi 9:7-9.)

C. J. Callan, a reputable Catholic scholar, makes this commentary on I Cor. 15:29:[4]

> In the supposition that there is no resurrection of the dead, why, asks St. Paul, do some of the Corinthians receive Baptism for their friends and relatives who died without it? The Apostle is assuming that such a practice had in view the future resurrection of the body.
>
> What was this Baptism for the dead? Many widely different explanations have been given, but by far the most reasonable and the most common is the following: In the time of St. Paul, when a catechumen died without Baptism, it was customary for a friend or relative to have the ceremony performed upon himself on behalf of the dead person, thus publicly affirming, by a symbolic action, that his departed friend or relative had died in union with the Church and was awaiting a glorious resurrection. This is the explanation of Tertullian (*Adv. Marc.* v. 10; *De Resurr.* xxviii) and is adopted by the majority of modern exegetes, such as Bisping, Van Steenkiste, Le Camus, Cornely, MacRory, Rickaby, etc. The Apostle simply refers to this practice, which must have been well known to the Corinthians, without approving or condemning it. Although erroneous, it was perhaps tolerated in the early Church until heretics began to attribute to it the efficacy of real Baptism. Cf. Vacant, Bapteme des morts, in Dic. de la Bible; Cornely, h. 1.

A conservative Protestant scholar, gives this note on the various interpretations of the passage in question:[5]

> A much vexed passage. A mere enumeration of all the various interpretations would require, says Bengel, a dissertation. Cf. collection in Poole's *Synops. Crit.* occupying four folio pages. The clue to the Apostle's meaning lies in ver. 18: the hope of reunion in Heaven with their beloved dead who had 'gone to their rest in Christ,' had induced some, hitherto unbelieving, to profess faith and be baptised. Of other interpretations suffice it to indicate three which have had a long and wide vogue: 1. *Vicarium baptisma*, 'Vicarious Baptism' (Ambrstr., Grot.). Believers submitted themselves to the Sacrament in name of their

[4]Callan, Rev. Charles J., *The Epistles of St. Paul*, I, 424. By permission. Published by Joseph F. Wagner, Inc., New York, N.Y.

[5]Taken from footnote No. 1, found in *The Life and Letters of St. Paul*, by David Smith, p. 315. Used by permission of Harper & Brothers, Publishers. For more valuable material on baptism for the dead consult Hugh Nibley, *Improvement Era*, Vol. 52, Dec., 1948—June, 1949.

unbaptised dead, that these might rank as Christians and share
in the felicity of the Resurrection. The practice certainly prevailed in the time of Tertullian (cf. *De Resurr. Carn.* 48; *Adv.
Marc.* v. 10), but only, it would seem, among heretics—the
Marcionites (cf. Chrys.) and the Cerinthians (cf. Epiphan. Haer.
xxviii. 7). There is, however, no evidence that it was known at
Corinth, and it probably originated in a misunderstanding of
the text. After pouring scorn on that heretical practice Chrys.
propounds his own view. He explains the passage by the fashion
obtaining in his time at the administration of Baptism: the
catechumen repeated the article of the Creed 'I believe in the
Resurrection of the Dead,' and on the strength of this confession of his faith he was then immersed in token of his burial
and resurrection with Christ. Thus 'baptism for the dead' was
supposed to mean 'baptism on the ground of faith in the resurrection of the dead.' *Baptisma clinicorum,* 'Death-bed Baptism,'
administered on the approach of death to those who had postponed the observance of the Sacrament for fear of mortal sin
(Epiphan., Calv., Beng.). But (1) hyper ton nekron [original in
Greek type] cannot mean 'on the verge of death,' *jam morituri*;
and (2) it was not until a later period that the custom of delay-
ing Baptism arose (cf. Append. VI).

The Character and Authenticity of I Corinthians.—
None of Paul's Epistles is more noted than I Corinthians for
its clarity and simplicity or for the beauty and variety of its
figures of speech.[6] The great number of topics treated, particularly of a doctrinal nature, is not approached by any other
of Paul's Epistles. Its doctrinal value is unusually great.

The authenticity of I Corinthians is accepted by most
scholars; only a few minor objections have been raised by
certain Rationalists against the Epistle. Of the external
evidences we may note direct references to the Epistle in
St. Clement of Rome, Polycarp, the Muratorian Fragment,
Clement of Alexandria, and Tertullian. Allusions to the
Epistle are to be found in Ignatius of Antioch, the Didache,
and in the heretical writings of Basilides, Marcion, Ptolemy
and Heracleon.

The internal evidence fully supports the external evidence of the Epistle's authenticity. The historical facts cited

[6]Callan, *op. cit.,* p. 255. For a good account of the general characteristics of Paul's Letters one may consult F. Prat, *The Theology of Saint Paul,* I, 62-71.

and the dogmatic teaching, the peculiarities of language and style, and the harmony shown with the Acts and with the other writings of Paul make it impossible to believe that they are inventions or mere chance contacts. Callan also points out that the manner in which the Epistle refers to the Old Testament, the characteristic way in which arguments are developed, beginning with general principles and coming to particular conclusions, not to mention the personal touches which it shows on every page, point conclusively to Paul's authorship.[7]

[7]*Ibid.*

Chapter 12

PAUL'S THIRD MISSIONARY JOURNEY
(Continued)

The Apostle Sends Titus and a Companion to Corinth.—When Paul had finished I Corinthians it is quite probable that he dispatched the Epistle to Corinth by Stephanas, Fortunatus and Achaicus, who had been visiting Ephesus, as we have previously pointed out. And although at this point we are left to considerable conjecture, it would seem that in due time the Epistle reached Corinth and that Timothy returned to Ephesus with news for Paul concerning the manner in which it was received and the condition of the branch. Timothy's report was probably not altogether reassuring. At any rate, Paul doubtless sent Titus and a companion whose name is not given (2 Cor. 12:7-13, 18) to make further inquiries, give words of counsel and advice, and begin the kindly task of collecting money (2 Cor. 8:6) for the benefit of the saints in Jerusalem. The trip of Titus had important results, for together with his subsequent report and that of Timothy's (I Cor. 4:17; 16:10; 2 Cor. 7:6), Paul had occasion to write 2 Corinthians and to send Titus on his second mission to Corinth. (2 Cor. 8:6, 18, 23)

Demetrius the Silversmith Creates a Demonstration Against Paul.—We have previously pointed out that Paul had expected to remain in Ephesus until Pentecost (May, A.D. 57), but as Luke relates his "many adversaries" (I Cor. 16:9) now proved too strong for him. It will be recalled that Ephesus was famous for the great pagan Temple of Artemis (Roman "Diana"), the mother-goddess of Asia

Minor. Numerous worshippers came to Ephesus to take part in the festivities and solemn assemblies held in her honor. These worshippers usually desired to take home with them some memento or souvenir of their visit to the city, and a very brisk and lucrative business grew up of making silver models of the temple to supply the demand. Paul's preaching seems to have seriously cut into the business of the silversmiths, with these results, as told in Acts:

> For a certain man named Demetrius, a silversmith, which made silver shrines for Diana, brought no small gain unto the craftsmen; whom he called together with the workmen of like occupation, and said, Sirs, ye know that by this craft we have our wealth. Moreover ye see and hear, that not alone at Ephesus, but almost throughout all Asia, this Paul hath persuaded and turned away much people, saying that they be no gods, which are made with hands: so that not only this our craft is in danger to be set at nought; but also that the temple of the great goddess Diana should be despised, and her magnificence should be destroyed, whom all Asia and the world worshippeth. And when they heard these sayings, they were full of wrath, and cried out, saying, Great is Diana of the Ephesians. And the whole city was filled with confusion: and having caught Gaius and Aristarchus, men of Macedonia, Paul's companions in travel, they rushed with one accord into the theatre. And when Paul would have entered in unto the people, the disciples suffered him not. And certain of the chief of Asia, which were his friends, sent unto him, desiring him that he would not adventure himself into the theatre. Some therefore cried one thing, and some another: for the assembly was confused; and the more part knew not wherefore they were come together. And they drew Alexander out of the multitude, the Jews putting him forward. And Alexander beckoned with the hand, and would have made his defence unto the people. But when they knew that he was a Jew, all with one voice about the space of two hours cried out, Great is Diana of the Ephesians. And when the townclerk had appeased the people, he said, Ye men of Ephesus, what man is there that knoweth not how that the city of the Ephesians is a worshipper of the great goddess Diana, and of the image which fell down from Jupiter? Seeing then that these things cannot be spoken against, ye ought to be quiet, and to do nothing rashly. For ye have brought hither these men, which are neither robbers of churches, nor yet blasphemers of your goddess. Wherefore if Demetrius, and the craftsmen which are with him, have a matter against any man, the law is open and there are deputies: let them implead one another. But if ye inquire anything concerning other matters, it shall be determined in a lawful

assembly. For we are in danger to be called in question for this day's uproar, there being no cause whereby we may give an account of this concourse. (Acts 19:24-41)

The riot ended, but Paul knew that the commercial interests had temporarily triumphed over him. The Apostle realized that the hostility against him was bitter and inclined to such violence that his life and the lives of some of his friends were at stake. (See 2 Cor. 1:8-10). It was time to leave Ephesus, even if his previous plans of staying longer had to be altered. He called for his disciples, heartened them with an encouraging salutation, and made definite preparations to leave the metropolis. (Acts 20:1)

Paul Departs for Macedonia Via Troas.—In his original plans, the Apostle had purposed to visit Corinth twice by going directly from Ephesus to Corinth and thence into Macedonia and back to Corinth again, from whence he would set sail for Judea. (2 Cor. 1:15-16) This plan had been made before Paul had written I Corinthians, and his intentions had been made known to the saints at Corinth either by a messenger or through a Corinthian letter now lost to us. The Apostle would probably have never made any mention of his original plan had not his critics in Corinth charged him with being fickle. In defending himself against their accusations, he tells us about his first plan, which later underwent revision. In I Corinthians 16:5-6 he announced his revised plans, which were to go directly from Ephesus to Macedonia and from there to make his way to Corinth. This was the route which, as we have said earlier, he actually adopted.

Paul seems to have left Ephesus in the company of Timothy, Tychicus and Trophimus of Ephesus, Aristarchus of Thessalonica, and Gaius of Derbe. (2 Cor. 1:1; Acts 20:4) The party probably sailed for Troas, where the Apostle hoped to preach and also meet Titus, who would be on his journey homeward, and from whom he would be able

to get a report on conditions in Corinth. What actually
happened is told us in these words of Paul:

> Furthermore, when I came to Troas to preach Christ's gospel,
> and a door was opened unto me of the Lord, I had no rest
> Greek: ['relaxing' or 'relief'] in my spirit, because I found not
> Titus my brother: but taking my leave of them, I went from
> thence into Macedonia. (2 Cor. 2:12-13)

It would appear that because Paul had been obliged
to leave Ephesus earlier than expected, he arrived in Troas
before Titus could make the rendezvous. But so anxious
was the Apostle, and so troubled in spirit was he about the
Corinthians that, despite a good opportunity to preach the
Gospel in Troas, he hastened across the waters of the Aegean
Sea into Macedonia, the sooner to meet Titus. Doubtless
Paul sailed from Troas as he had done on his Second
Missionary Journey to Philippi via Samothrace and Nea-
polis.

Titus Brings Good News to Paul From Corinth.—
Paul's old friends in Philippi must have greeted him with
enthusiasm and affection when he arrived in the summer
of A.D. 57. Among these would probably be Luke, whom
he had left here in 51, some six years previously. While
waiting for Titus, the Apostle worked unceasingly in
Macedonia to build up the branches of the Church and to
allay the opposition, mainly Jewish, which troubled them.
(Acts 20:2; 2 Cor. 7:5) Not only that, but Paul was successful in getting the Macedonian Saints to contribute
most liberally for the benefit of the poor in Jerusalem.
(2 Cor. 8:1-5)

At length Titus arrived in the late summer—to Paul's
joy and satisfaction, for he came bearing news for which
the Apostle could hardly wait. It proved to be good news.
(2 Cor. 7:6) The Corinthians had about-faced and were
now mostly in harmony with him. Titus must have done
yeoman service in presenting Paul's views and in getting

the Corinthians to recognize his great contribution to their well being. Those who had broken up the Corinthian branch into cliques and factions had now come over to the Apostle's side again. They were now eager to regain his confidence and favor. They even wanted to punish the man who may have been chiefly responsible for leading the revolt against him. (2 Cor. 2:6-7) Traditional opinion is that this man was the incestuous person mentioned in I Cor. 5:1-8, but some recent interpreters believe it to be another offender of whom we know nothing outside of 2 Corinthians. It may be well here to spread before the reader Paul's own words concerning his joy at the coming of Titus and the news he brought:

> Nevertheless God, that comforteth those that are cast down, comforted us by the coming of Titus: and not by his coming only, but by the consolation wherewith he was comforted in you, when he told us your earnest desire, your mourning, your fervent mind toward me; so that I rejoiced the more. For though I made you sorry with a letter, I do not repent, though I did repent: for I perceive that the same epistle hath made you sorry, though it were but for a season. Now I rejoice, not that ye were made sorry, but that ye sorrowed to repentance: for ye were made sorry after a godly manner, that ye might receive damage by us in nothing. For godly sorrow worketh repentance to salvation not to be repented of: but the sorrow of the world worketh death. For behold this selfsame thing, that ye sorrowed after a godly sort, what carefulness it wrought in you, yea, what clearing of yourselves, yea, what indignation, yea, what fear, yea, what vehement desire, yea, what zeal, yea, what revenge! In all things ye have approved yourselves to be clear in this matter. Wherefore, though I wrote unto you, I did it not for his cause that had done the wrong, nor for his cause that suffered wrong, but that our care for you in the sight of God might appear unto you. Therefore we were comforted in your comfort: yea, and exceedingly the more joyed we for the joy of Titus, because his spirit was refreshed by you all. For if I have boasted any thing to him of you, I am not ashamed; but as we spake all things to you in truth, even so our boasting, which I made before Titus, is found a truth. And his inward affection is more abundant toward you, whilst he remembereth the obedience of you all, how with fear and trembling ye received him. I rejoice therefore that I have confidence in you in all things. (2 Cor. 7: 6-16)

It should be noticed that from Titus, the Apostle learned that his own change of plans for visiting Corinth had given cause for unfavorable criticism (2 Cor. 1:17), and that some injurious remarks on his character and manners had been disseminated. (2 Cor. 3:1; 5:11; 7:2-3; 10:10; 11:18-20) But, as we have seen, the effect of Paul's First Epistle to the Corinthians was generally favorable, for which fact the Apostle was grateful.

THE SECOND EPISTLE TO THE CORINTHIANS

Purpose and Origin of the Epistle.—We are not exactly sure where Titus found Paul in Macedonia when he returned from Corinth to report—whether at Philippi, Thessalonica or some other city. But his report was probably much better than the Apostle had expected. Paul determined to write the Corinthians again, for four main reasons: The first was to prepare their hearts for another of his visits, not an immediate one, but one in the not-too-distant future. The second was to express his approbation and appreciation for their penitent conduct and to give them additional counsel. The third was to stir them to action in collecting aid for the Jerusalem saints. And the fourth was his grief and concern with the continued opposition of a stubborn minority who accused him (1) of fickleness and vacillation (2 Cor. 1:15-17), (2) of commending himself when no one else would (2 Cor. 3:1-2), (3) of obscure and veiled meanings in his preaching (2 Cor. 4:2-3), (4) of grovelling humility when present, but being full of pride and arrogance when absent (2 Cor. 10:1-2), (5) of a weak and insignificant appearance (2 Cor. 10:10), (6) of acting like a fool, with little sense (2 Cor. 11:1, 16), (7) of being crafty and a deceiver full of guile (2 Cor. 12:16-18), and (8) of being conscious that he was a self-appointed, untimely Apostle (I Cor. 15:8-9; 2 Cor. 10:12-13).

That 2 Corinthians was written from Macedonia we are sure (2:13; 7:5-7; 8:1; 9:2-4), in fact, from the subscription (at very end) of the Epistle, which is early and possibly correct, the Epistle was probably written from Philippi, with Titus and Luke acting as amanuenses. It would have been written in the late summer or early autumn of A.D. 57.

Outline of the Epistle.—The Epistle may be divided into three parts: an introduction; the body, consisting of three sections; and a conclusion.

    I. Introduction (1:1-11).
        A. Greeting of Paul, "an Apostle . . . by the will of God," and Timothy to the Church at Corinth, with the saints in all Achaia (1:1-2).
        B. Thanksgiving to God for giving comfort in the midst of tribulation and sufferings, and for liberation from danger of death in Asia (1:3-11).

   II. The body of the Epistle (1:12-13:10).
        A. Personal defense of the Apostle against charges leveled at him (1:12-7:16).
            1. Reasons for his change of plans in not coming to Corinth (1:12-2:4).
                a. His motives have been disinterested and pure (1:12-14).
                b. He meant to give the Corinthians a twofold joy by visiting them twice, but fickleness is not the explanation of his change of plan, for as a faithful follower of Christ and preacher of the gospel, he is true to his promises. The real reason he didn't come to Corinth was that he wanted to spare them any severity on his part for their disorders and

sins. He wrote to them in deep affliction and anguish, not to pain them, but to show the abundant love he had for them (1:15-2:4).

   c. With a charitable spirit Paul urges the Corinthians to forgive and comfort a certain offender (2:5-11).

   d. Paul had good opportunity to preach in Troas, but having no relief of spirit on not finding Titus there, he went to Macedonia. He thanks God for Apostolic success in displaying everywhere the sweetness of the knowledge of Him. Does not corrupt or adulterate God's word, but with sincerity, before God, speaks in Christ (2:12-17).

2. Defense of his assurance or self-confidence (3:1-5:10).

   a. Against the charge of self-commendation and arrogance he points to the saints themselves as proof of his divine mission (3:1-3). His assurance and self-confidence is because his competence and ability comes from God (3:4-6).

   b. The new ministry and faith is superior to that of the Law of Moses. To this day when the Law is read a veil lies upon the heart of Israel, but when they return to the Lord the veil is withdrawn. Where the Spirit of the Lord is, there is freedom (3:7-18).

   c. Therefore Paul exercises his ministry clearly, openly, and without falsifying God's work. If the Gospel is veiled or hid, it is because of the blindness of unbelieving minds that shut out its light. He does not preach himself, but Jesus Christ as Lord; and he makes himself a servant of the Corinthians for the sake of Jesus (4:1-6).

d. His (Paul's) power comes from God, who makes use of weak, earthly instruments for His sublime mission. The Apostle continually surrenders himself to death for Jesus' sake, so that in his mortal nature the life of Jesus may be made manifest (4:7-12).

e. He has the Spirit of faith and knows that He who raised Jesus will raise him also and set him with the Corinthians in His presence. God's glory is promoted by his labors, and his light and transitory affliction will work for him a far more exceeding and eternal weight of glory. It is not the passing things of this world, but the lasting things, the things not seen with mortal eyes, that are eternal (4:13-18).

f. In his hope of a glorious resurrection, a spiritual and immortal body, Paul seeks only to please Christ, whether here in mortality, or in the future. All men must appear before Christ's judgment-seat in their true light, to receive an award for their actions in this life, whether good or bad (5:1-10).

3. The Apostle defends his sincerity (5:11-7:1).

a. Knowing the terror of the Lord, he per-

suades men. Paul writes this defense of himself, not to boast in his own behalf, but so that the Corinthians may have a ready reply to his detractors, who boast openly and insincerely. His labors have been only for God and the faithful (5:11-13).

b. The Apostle is moved and directed by the overmastering love of Christ in preaching the Gospel and in reconciling man to God (5:14-21).

c. The Corinthians are exhorted not to receive the grace (favor) of God in vain. The Apostle lists the ways in which he endeavors to give no cause for stumbling, lest he bring discredit to the ministry. He seeks to commend himself as God's servant by his Christ-like conduct. To the Corinthians he has freely opened his heart, and he requests in return that they open their hearts also (6:1-13).

d. The Apostle advises the Corinthians to avoid the vices and sins of pagan idolaters. They are told to avoid unsuitable connections with unbelievers. They are exhorted to cleanse themselves from all defilement of body and spirit, and attain holiness through the fear of God (6:14 -7:1).

4. Paul's defense of his previous letter (7:2-16).

a. He pleads for the Corinthians to show toward him the love which he has always displayed for them and for which, through Titus's timely arrival, he has

received relief in body and mind and
renewed hope. The report of Titus concerning their eager affection, grief, and
jealousy on his behalf (7:2-7).

b. Paul's severe letter to the Corinthian
saints brought them pain which led to
their repentance. This pain the Apostle
did not regret, for in it his hopes were
realized, and in addition he has been
filled with joy at the satisfaction which
Titus has received because of their conduct. Paul has complete confidence in
his Corinthian friends (7:8-16).

B. The collection at Corinth for the poor saints
in Jerusalem (8:1-9:15).

1. Paul appeals to the generosity of his Corinthian friends by citing the liberality of
the poor saints in Macedonia. Titus is to
be sent to complete the work of gathering
the fund which he commenced. They are
urged to give generously according to their
means, keeping in mind that Christ became
poor that they might become rich (8:1-15).

2. Titus comes of his own choice, and Paul,
to avoid any question of fraud, commends
him and two other brethren to collect the
funds. Paul urges a loving welcome for
them. The contributions of the Corinthians
were to be ready when Paul came lest he
be put to shame for boasting of them. He
who sows thinly will reap thinly. We shall
reap as we have sown. God will reward
their generosity with abundant blessings,
spiritual and temporal, because their gifts

will not only relieve the wants of the saints, but will also glorify Him (8:16-9:15).

C. Paul vindicates his Apostleship by directing an offensive against his inveterate enemies (10:1-13:10).

   1. The Apostle defends his authority (10:1-18).

      a. He requests his enemies to spare him the necessity of asserting his authority and spiritual powers when he comes (10:1-6).

      b. When Paul comes to Corinth, he will be prepared to act with boldness, if necessary, against his detractors who have underestimated his powers (10:7-11).

      c. Paul's boasting is not like that of his critics. He boasts and glories in the Lord, but keeps within the limits of the field which God has assigned, which field includes the Corinthians. If he glories concerning them, he is not boasting of other men's labors. He hopes his field of missionary activity may be enlarged until it goes beyond the Corinthians, thus having more converts in which to glory. It is not the man who commends himself that is accepted, but he whom the Lord commends (10:12-18).

   2. Paul enumerates his credentials as an Apostle (11:1-12:18).

      a. His folly of self-praise has been forced upon him; he asks the indulgence of the Corinthians for it, for he seeks only their good in that they are exposed to

the danger of being led into error. He
is not in any respect inferior to the
chiefest Apostles. He may be no orator,
but in knowledge he is not deficient
(11:1-6).

b. Paul contrasts himself with false teachers. Although he had a right to temporal support, he was a dead-weight
on no one for the sake of greater reward
and greater success in preaching. [The
Corinthians were providing a living for
the sham apostles.] To show his great
superiority to his detractors, Paul re-
calls the integrity of his life among the
Corinthians. He will continue to preach
the Gospel free of charge in Achaia and
thus cut the ground from under the
feet of the sham apostles, dishonest
workmen, who assume the garb of
Apostles of Christ (11:7-15).

c. Paul gives an ironical defense of his
own good sense. He is forced to boast
of himself because of the boasting of
others who have been tolerated by the
Corinthians. If others boast of being
Hebrews and descendants of Abraham,
so can he. If his adversaries claim to
be servants of Christ, so can he, and
exceeds them all in the greater sufferings, perils, and hardships he has gone
through for the Gospel's sake, and for
the Churches' (11:16-33).

d. In another particular Paul can boast of
a superiority over his detractors, and
that is in the greater spiritual gifts with

which God has blessed him. He glories in the visions and revelations given him, but it is more pleasing to glory in his humbling infirmities of the flesh. Satan's angel has given him a thorn in the flesh lest he be over-elated. [What this "thorn" was has been much debated, but most authorities agree that it was physical suffering of some kind.] The Apostle delights in insults, distresses, persecutions, and the like, for the Christ (12:1-10).

e. The Apostle did not like to boast, but he was compelled. The Corinthians should have vindicated him, because in no respect was he inferior to the pre-eminent Apostles. He gave all the signs of a true Apostle, and was no dead-weight upon them. He speaks of his intended visit to Corinth and of his love for them. His adversaries say Paul was cunning and entrapped the Corinthians, but he points out the unselfish motives of himself, Titus, and another brother (12:11-18).

3. Paul's warning to the rebellious members in Corinth (12:19-13:10).

a. In reality Paul is making no defense of himself to the Corinthians, but to God. Fears that he will not find the Corinthians as he wishes them, nor they him.

b. The Apostle tells of coming investigations and punishments. He will not spare them, since they want proof that

Christ speaks through him. Paul advises
the Corinthians to examine themselves
and test whether they are true believers
(13:1-6).

   c. He prays they may do nothing wrong,
and also prays for their perfection. He
writes the letter that they may repent
and thus make it unnecessary for him
to act severely when he comes (13:7-10).

III. The conclusion (13:11-13).

   A. The Apostle's exhortation to rejoice, be perfect, i.e., to correct faults, to be comforted, be
of one mind and live in peace. Then the God
of love and peace will be with them (13:11).

   B. Salutation: To greet each other with a "holy
kiss," i.e., as a sign of charity, a custom ex-
pressive of unity and charity that prevailed
among them. The saints where Paul wrote the
Epistle send their salutations (13:12).

   C. Paul's benediction (13:13).

The Character and Authenticity of 2 Corinthians.—
In 2 Corinthians we come nearer to the innermost soul of
Paul than in any of his other writings. It is by all means
the most personal of his Epistles. In no other letter are we
exposed to such a variety of his thoughts and feelings, as
Paul reveals his "joy and depression, anxiety and hope,
trust and resentment, anger and love." (Weizsacker as
quoted by Callan.) It is quite obvious that the Apostle did
not take as much care in composing the Epistle as he did
in writing the first letter. The Greek text is fairly rough.
The account and reasoning are frequently involved and
broken, and a lack of ease and smoothness is apparent
throughout. When Paul wrote the letter, he was evidently
in a great hurry and also under a greater tension than

when he wrote the first letter. Under these conditions we may understand the lack of polish, smoothness and orderly arrangement so apparent to the careful reader. It should be kept in mind also that in this letter Paul is more concerned with defending himself against his adversaries and in getting a good collection for the Jerusalem poor. We may look upon the letter as an open window through which we may look at and assess the personal character of the Apostle.

In respect to its authenticity, the Epistle is generally respected as being Pauline. Only a few Rationalists have denied the genuineness of it. The external evidence in favor of the Epistle is strong. It appears in the Muratorian Fragment and seems to have been familiar to Irenaeus, Tertullian, and Clement of Alexandria. Implicit references may be found to it in St. Clement of Rome and St. Polycarp. The early heretics, Marcion and Basilides, seem also to have used it.

The internal evidence is also very strong in its favor. The facts written in the Epistle are in agreement with those of I Corinthians and Acts. The grammatical constructions, expressions, and style of the Letter are typically Pauline. Also to be noted throughout is the dominant personality of the Apostle.

The Unity and Integrity of the Epistle.—Until comparatively recent times 2 Corinthians was generally accepted as being a unity. Now, however, scholars are prone to question the unity of the Epistle, and maintain that it is a composite work, consisting of portions of Paul's letters that were somehow preserved in the records of the Corinth branch of the Church and later brought together by an editor after the death of Paul. The author has not seen Dr. J. T. Dean's *St. Paul and Corinth,* but according to T. Henshaw, *New Testament Literature,* p. 244, Dean divides the contents of the letter in this way:

1. The Letter of Defence (2 Cor. 10-12; 2:14-6:13; 7:2-4; 13:1-10).
2. The Letter of Reconciliation (2 Cor. 1-2:13; 7:5-8:24; 13:11-14).
3. Sixth Letter (2 Cor. 9).
4. Fragment of Letter mentioned in I Cor. 5:9, and embodied in 2 Cor. 6:14-7:1).

Dean's analysis is fairly typical of the manner in which scholars today presume to question the unity of a letter which for centuries was never questioned. They do this in spite of the fact that there is no documentary evidence to support their claims of division in the Epistle. After reading the Letter many times, the author feels constrained to deny that it is composed of parts of several letters of Paul's which have been loosely strung together by some later "editor." There are no valid grounds, in fact, for denying the essential integrity of the Epistle because of the differences in tone and content that have been observed between its various parts. It would seem likely—at least the author is convinced —that an intelligent editor would be more inclined to produce a smooth, unified composition "than to strip letters of their introductory and concluding formulas and then string them loosely together."[1] The modern breakdown of 2 Corinthians is another typical case of what critics have done to so many books of the Old and New Testaments. Frankly, it is unnecessary.

Paul Sends Titus the Second Time to Corinth to Speed the Collection for Jerusalem's Poor and to Deliver His Second Epistle.—Having composed his Second Epistle to the Corinthians, Paul now sent it to them in the care of Titus and two companions (2 Cor. 8:18, 22), one of whom is supposed to have been Luke, the kindly physician and friend of the Apostle. Titus was not at all averse to returning

[1]See J. E. Steinmueller, *A Companion to Scripture Studies*, III, 290.

to Corinth again (2 Cor. 8:17), probably because of his previous success there and also because of his love for Paul. As we have already observed in the outline of 2 Corinthians, Titus and his companions were also to complete the collection for Jerusalem's poor which Titus had begun on his first visit. The Apostle strongly commended Titus and his companions to the kind care of the Corinthians and urged them (the Corinthians) to vindicate his boasting of them concerning their collecting of funds for the poor. (2 Cor. 8:24-9:5)

Chapter 13

PAUL'S THIRD MISSIONARY JOURNEY
(*Continued*)

Paul's Visit to Illyricum and His Plans to Go to Spain.—After Titus and his companions had departed for Corinth, probably in the early autumn of A.D. 57, Paul remained behind for some time, continuing his visits to the various communities in Macedonia where branches of the Church had been established. (Acts 20:1-2) It is also very probable that during this period the Apostle visited Illyricum, the country west and north of Macedonia; of this fact he later reports:

> So that from Jerusalem, and round about unto Illyricum, I have fully preached the gospel of Christ. Yea, so have I strived to preach the gospel, not where Christ was named, lest I should build upon another man's foundation. (Rom. 15:19-20)

His plans for visiting Spain must also have been fast crystallizing in his mind, for in the letter which he had but recently dispatched by Titus, he speaks not only of visiting his Corinthian friends but also of continuing on into the "regions beyond." (2 Cor. 10:16) The quotation has been confidently thought by certain scholars to have definite reference to Spain, for when Paul visited Corinth a little later he writes:

> Whensoever I take my journey into Spain, I will come to you [the Romans]: for I trust to see you in my journey, ... When therefore I have performed this, and have sealed to them this fruit [the collection for the Jerusalem poor], I will come by you into Spain. (Rom. 15:24, 28)

Paul's interest in Spain is noteworthy, and his words indicate the breadth of his thinking. He seems to have known well the speed at which Spain had developed under Augustus and Tiberius. Many people had migrated there, including a notable Greek population, who would be ripe to hear the Gospel. The missionary possibilities seem to have intrigued Paul, who was anxious to make fresh inroads for Christ in Europe, not building upon other men's foundations.

Paul Goes to Greece and Remains Three Months.— Paul labored long enough in Macedonia and Illyricum to afford the Corinthians ample time in which to finish making their collection for the Jerusalem poor before leaving for Greece. (Cf. 2 Cor. 9:1-5). It was possibly about the month of December in A.D. 57 when Paul left Macedonia in company with Sopater of Beroea, the son of Pyrrhus, Aristarchus and Secundus of Thessalonica, Gaius of Derbe, Timothy, and Tychicus and Trophimus of Asia. (Acts 20:4) It is generally assumed from Acts 20:2-3 that the Apostle and his party made the journey by land, but Dr. Goodspeed argues very effectively that the journey was made by ship in a series of coast journeys.[1] We are not told by Luke what cities in Greece Paul visited, but it may be assumed that most of the three months in Greece were spent at Corinth. Nor does the historian enlighten us on what happened in this, Paul's third visit (2 Cor. 12:14; 13:1) to that city. But it may be reasonably assumed that the Apostle went right to work straightening out the difficulties that had beset the Corinthians and himself. He would be the peacemaker, but if necessary we can be assured that Paul as an Apostle would set any recalcitrants in their place. From certain of Paul's Epistles we learn of some interesting facts. Paul's host in Corinth was his convert and friend, the generous-hearted Gaius, who probably made it possible for him to get some long-needed rest. (Rom. 16:23) The balmy winter in Corinth would be much appreciated by the great Apostle,

[1]*Paul*, p. 232 f.

who usually worked so strenuously. In addition to the members of the company who had come to Corinth with him, other friends of Paul's in or near the city with him were Phoebe, Lucius, Jason, Tertius, Gaius his host, Erastus, Quartus, Stephanas, Achaicus, and Fortunatus. (Rom. 16:1, 21, 22, 23; I Cor. 16:17)

THE EPISTLE TO THE GALATIANS

Some Facts About the Epistle.—In this book the author is assuming that Paul wrote the Epistle to the Galatians late in the year A.D. 57, possibly in December, while he was visiting Corinth. In so doing he is quite aware of the great differences of opinion among so-called authorities on the subject of the time and place of the Epistle's origin. In fact, from the early centuries of the Christian era opinions have been and still are sharply divided on the points involved. Many early writers and even a few recent scholars have insisted that the Epistle was written from Rome while Paul was a captive. Some have placed its composition before the Council of Jerusalem (A.D. 50), but others assign its writing to a time shortly after that Council. Still others would insist that it was written at Ephesus during the Third Missionary Journey. (A. D. 57?) Lagrange, the great Catholic scholar, thought it to have been written A.D. 54 at Ephesus. Ramsay and Weber put its composition at Antioch before the Jerusalem Council. Bleek and Lightfoot assumed that it was written at Corinth after Paul's three years of labor at Ephesus. In short, Rome, Ephesus, Antioch, and Corinth are the places mostly held to be the point of origin of the Epistle, and the dating of it, depending on the authority, may vary from A.D. 48 to 58. To be frank, this is a roundabout way of saying that we don't know when and where the Epistle was written.

It may be of interest to the reader to know that the name Galatia was originally given to the territory in north-central Asia Minor where certain invading Gauls settled in the third century B.C. and maintained an independent kingdom for a considerable period of time. During the first century before the Christian era, the Gallic population, which had been gradually absorbed into the other peoples living there, were allies of Rome. Amyntas, the last king of the Galatians, had augmented his territory by adding to Galatia Proper parts of Pontus, Lycaonia and Pamphylia, all of Pisidia, and finally, Phrygia, Isauria and Cilicia. But in 25 B.C. Amyntas was murdered, and his kingdom became the Roman Province of Galatia, the city of Ancyra becoming the official capital. In Paul's day the cities of Antioch in Pisidia, Iconium, Lystra and Derbe, all of which had been visited by him during his missionary journeys, belonged to the southern part of the Province. Under Roman rule, then, Galatia could mean Galatia as founded by the Gauls, or could refer to the whole Province, including Pisidian Antioch, Iconium, Lystra and Derbe.

The time and place of the writing of Galatians is closely related to two problems, one being geographical, the other chronological. The geographical problem concerns itself with the question as to whether the Epistle was addressed: (1) to the four branches of the Church (Pisidian Antioch, Iconium, Lystra, and Derbe) which Paul and Barnabas raised up on the First Missionary Journey in the southern part of Galatia; or (2) to the people converted in the northern part of Galatia, i.e., Galatia Proper, Ancyra being the capital; or (3) to all the organized branches of the Church and isolated members in the whole Roman Province of Galatia. The first hypothesis (1) is known as the South Galatian Theory; the second (2) the North Galatian Theory, and the third (3) the Mixed Theory.

The chronological part of the Galatian problem, closely connected with the geographical aspect, brings up the question as to whether the Epistle was written before or after the great Jerusalem Council, which we date in A.D. 50; and if after the Council, whether the Apostle composed it during the Second (A.D. 51-53) or Third (A.D. 54-58) Missionary Journey. The authorities who hold to the South Galatian Theory believe that the Epistle was composed at Antioch before the Jerusalem Council; those who adhere to the North Galatian Theory are generally of the opinion that it was written at Ephesus during the Third Missionary Journey; finally, the scholars who hold to the Mixed Theory mostly maintain that the Epistle was written during the Second Missionary Journey during Paul's sojourn in Corinth. Of the three theories the innocent reader may take his pick or modify one of them to suit himself. It should be said of the North and South Galatian theories that great authorities are aligned against each other and no clear-cut decision can be reached. Whenever or wherever the Epistle was written, Paul would obviously direct it to all the saints in Galatia who could be reached by the Judaizers, his implacable enemies. It would seem probable to the writer in view of the Apostle's great zeal to do missionary work, and further, from what is said in Acts 15:40-16:6; 18:23, that Paul went over most of the territory in Galatia, reaching many parts of it, both north and south, during both the Second and Third Missionary Journeys. We may assume with some reason that he was reasonably successful in North Galatia as well as in the South. In view of the relatively insoluble nature of the problem, the author will here simply make the assumption that Paul addressed the Epistle to the saints over all parts of Galatia, both North and South ,and that it was composed, as we have said before, late in the year A.D. 57, in Corinth. He has no favorite theory to defend; let us facetiously refer to the assumption above stated as the "Mixed Up" Theory. We may emphasize that no one is in possession of sufficient facts to clear up the problem.

Now let us look at the occasion and purpose of the Epistle. Here we are happily on firmer ground. From time to time Paul had evidently received notices that the Judaizers (see our Ch. 7) had come among the Galatians and were teaching, contrary to the doctrines taught and espoused by the Apostle, that in order to receive salvation it was necessary to be circumcised and conform to the Mosaic Law. (Gal. 3:1-4:31) The false teachers from Jerusalem, or perhaps Antioch, had invaded the branches of the Church in Galatia and, pretending to have the sanction of the Church Authorities, were busy controverting Paul's teaching and introducing another "gospel." (1:9) The Galatians were given to understand that the authority and commission of the original Twelve was everywhere admitted and understood, but as to Paul's Apostleship, it could well be doubted. If he had any authority, did it not come of men? (1:1, 12) True, he had had hands laid upon him at Antioch and had been sent out to preach (Acts 13:3), but he had been set apart by ordinary human beings, and his authority rested on his own testimony. (2:7-9) Furthermore, Paul's preaching had been opened to examination at the Jerusalem Council. (2:1-10) Peter had differences with him at Antioch (2:11-15), and he (Paul) was making a practice of pleasing all men for the sake of success. In his attempts to please men he had been guilty of inconsistency, teaching circumcision or uncircumcision as he found it expedient. (1:10; 5:11) Specious and unfair as their arguments were, the Judaizers appeared to the Galatians to be men of importance, and their flattery and fine talk so bewitched them that some of them were circumcised and began to "observe days, and months, and times, and years" (4:10), thus taking upon themselves the yoke and bondage of the Law with all of its burdens.

Naturally, the Apostle had great reason to be alarmed, because he saw clearly (1) that his authority and personal

influence might be almost completely undermined among
the Galatians, (2) that there might be a substitution by the
Judaizers of the doctrine of justification by the works of the
Law for the great doctrine which he had taught the Galatians, of justification by faith, and (3) that the destruction
of hopes that Christianity could become widespread among
the Gentiles. Inasmuch as he could not then visit the Galatians, Paul saw fit to write his Epistle to them in defense of
his Apostolic authority and the validity of his Gospel, to
point out to them the fatal results of cleaving to the doctrines
of the Judaizers, to call to their remembrance the gospel of
liberty which he had taught them, and to defend his
character against the allegations of his adversaries.

Outline of the Epistle.—We may analyze the Epistle
as consisting of an introduction, the body with three sections,
and a conclusion.

I. Introduction (1:1-10).
   A. Greeting of Paul, "an Apostle" (1:1-5).
   B. The Apostle upbraids the Galatians for accept-
      ing "another gospel" and rebukes the Juda-
      izers for distorting the Gospel of Christ. Paul
      gives the general theme of the Epistle: that
      the Gospel preached by him is unchangeable
      and divine, needing neither correction nor
      modification (1:6-10).

II. Paul vindicates his Apostolic authority, teaches
    justification by faith, and gives a practical exhor-
    tation: the effect of liberty (1:11-6:10).
    A. Paul vindicates his Apostolic authority (1:11-
       6:10).
       1. His Apostleship is not of human origin (1:
          11-24).
          a. His gospel is not of man; he received

or learned it by the revelation of Jesus Christ (1:11-12).

b. This he proves by his early career in Judaism—how he hated Christianity and persecuted the Church (1:13-14).

c. After his conversion he retired to Arabia and later returned to Damascus without conferring with the Apostles in Jerusalem or counseling with any human being (1:15-17).

d. As another proof that his Apostleship is not of human origin and that he had no need of learning his doctrine from the Apostles, Paul points out that only after three years' time did he visit Jerusalem after his conversion, that then he only spent fifteen days with Peter and saw none of the other Apostles except James, the Lord's brother (1:18-20).

e. After this short visit he preached in Syria and Cilicia, but was personally unknown to the Church branches in Judea. They only heard that their former persecutor was now preaching the faith (1:21-24).

2. Paul's teaching is shown to be in harmony with that of the other Apostles, as he proves by telling of two incidents (2:1-21).

a. Fourteen years after his conversion, the great Council in Jerusalem (A.D. 50) did not correct his teaching, nor did the Apostles give him any new suggestions, but recognized that he was entrusted with the preaching of the Gospel to the Gentiles, even as Peter had been with that to the Jews (2:1-10).

    b. Paul even rebukes Peter at Antioch, because until certain persons came from James, he did not hesitate to eat with Gentiles, but after their coming he acted inconsistently by withdrawing and separating himself for fear of the circumcision party. A man is justified, not by keeping the Law, but only through faith in Jesus Christ (2:11-21).

B. Paul teaches the doctrine of justification by faith (3:1-4:31).

    1. Paul berates the foolish Galatians and brings out that they received the Spirit and its gifts, not through the works of the Law, but through their faith in Christ. He asks them whether, having begun by the spiritual, they expect to reach perfection by the external (3:1-5).

    2. The Apostle's argument (3:6-18).

        a. By quoting Scripture (Genesis 15:6; 12:3; 18:18), Paul demonstrates that Abraham and his spiritual seed (including the Gentiles) are justified by faith, for those who rest on faith are blessed with believing Abraham (3:6-9).

        b. Those who depend on Law-performance or on obedience to the Law are under a curse (Deut. 27:26). No one can be made righteous or justified by the Law, for the righteous shall live by faith (Hab. 2:4). The Law has nothing to do with faith. Christ purchased our freedom by being cursed for us (Deut. 21:23). In Jesus Christ the blessing of Abraham comes upon the Gentiles. Through faith we receive the promise of the Spirit (3:10-14).

c. The Law, which was given 430 years after God's promise to Abraham because of his faith, did not invalidate or supplant that promise (3:15-18).

3. The purpose of the Law (3:19-4:31).

a. The Law was a divine institution and was not opposed to God's promises. It was given as a protection to the Jews and as a moral guide to make them sin-and-guilt-conscious, thus leading them to Christ (3:19-24).

b. When Christ came, there was no more need for a tutor (the Law), for it had filled its purpose. All are sons of God through faith in Christ Jesus. There cannot be Jews, Greeks, slaves, freemen, male and female, for all are one in Christ. If men are Christ's (i.e., baptized members of the Church of Jesus Christ), they are Abraham's offspring and are heirs in accordance with the promise (3:25-29; cf. Abr. 2:8-11; D. & C. 84:34. Note: these last two references are very important if Paul is to be rightly understood.).

c. Under the Law the Jews were, like minors, in no way different (legally) from slaves, under guardians and trustees; but the coming of Christ makes it possible for them to receive recognition as sons of God, having full rights of inheritance (4:1-7).

d. If the Galatians turn back as slaves to gods which are no gods, by showing observance to weak and worthless rudimentary notions, Paul feels that his labors among them will have been to no purpose. Mere external observances are worthless (4:8-11).

e. Paul reminds the Galatians of the time when he preached the Gospel to them having great physical infirmities, and of their love and tender solicitude for him. He pleads for them to rekindle their love for him and live the Gospel which he taught them. The Judaizers zealously pay court to them, but not honorably. Paul's anxiety for his children (the Galatians) and his perplexity over them (4:12-20).

f. The Apostle exhorts the Galatians to steadfastly maintain their freedom and remain as children of the promise. In the story of Sarah and Hagar he finds these wives of Abraham representing (allegorically) two covenants. Sarah represents the Church, because she was the mother of Isaac the freeborn; while Hagar represents Judaism, the mother of Ishmael the enslaved. The Church, like Sarah was long sterile, but is now fruitful and assured of blessings (Isa. 54:1). On the other hand, Judaism, a religion of fear, servitude, and observances, is to receive the same treatment which God gave to Ishmael, the son of Hagar the bondwoman; it is to be left out or excluded from the inheritance (Gen. 21:10). The Galatians, like Isaac, are the children of promise. Christ has made them free (4:21-31).

C. The Apostle gives a practical exhortation: the effect of liberty (5:1-6:10).

  1. Paul's general counsels (5:1-26).

    a. If the Galatians receive circumcision, their legalism leaves no room for Christ. If they seek acquittal by the Law, they have lost the good of union with Christ; they have fallen from grace. In Christ neither circumcision nor uncircumcision is of any avail; but only faith working through love. Christ makes us completely free (5:1-6).

    b. The Galatians were running the race nobly until someone stopped them from obeying the truth. Paul is convinced that they will not (permanently) adopt new views. The man who is troubling them will have to bear his sentence. If the Apostle still preaches circumcision, why does he still suffer persecution? Would that those who are unsettling them would mutilate themselves (i.e., emasculate themselves). [That is, the Apostle seems to hope (ironically) that the Judaizers would not only insist upon circumcision, but upon complete castration, if it pleased them better, in imitation of heathen fanatics who practiced these mutilations in honor of the goddess Cybele. One of the towns in Northern Galatia, Pessinus, was the center of such practices in the worship of Cybele.] (5:7-12)

c. The Galatians were called to freedom, but such was not to be an incentive to their lower natures. They were to serve one another in love (Lev. 19:18), and not bite and devour each other. Love is the spirit of the Law. If guided by the Spirit, they will not fulfil the cravings of their lower nature and will not be subject to the Law. Paul names the works of the flesh and warns them that those who practice the same will not inherit God's kingdom. The Spirit, in contrast, brings a harvest of love, joy, peace, long-suffering (forbearance), kindness, goodness, faith (integrity, loyalty), meekness, self-control. Against these things there is no law. Those who are Christ's have crucified the flesh with its passions and appetites. They are to shun glory and envy; they are not to provoke each other (5:13-26).

2. The Apostle's specific counsels (6:1-10).

a. If the Galatians discover misconduct, they who are spiritual are to restore and correct in a spirit of meekness. They are to carry each other's burdens, and so fulfil the law of Christ. Every man is to examine or put to the proof his own work or conduct (6:1-5).

      b. Those who receive instruction in the word are to share in all good things (temporal blessings? See 1 Cor. 9:14) with him who teaches the lesson. God is not mocked. Whatever a man sows, that will he also reap. He who sows for his lower nature will from that nature reap destruction; but he who sows for the Spirit will reap Life eternal. Men are not to lose heart in doing what is right; for in due time a harvest will be reaped, if they do not faint. As we have opportunity, we are exhorted to do good to all, and especially to the household of faith (6:6-10).

III. Paul's autographed conclusion (6:11-18).

    A. The Apostle writes with large letters in his own hand (6:11).

    B. Paul's enemies, who desire to make a good show outwardly, try to compel the Galatians to receive circumcision, in order that they themselves may escape being persecuted for the Cross of Christ. Those who would have the Galatians circumcised do not really keep the Law, but glory in their brethren being subjected to external rites (6:12-13).

    C. The Apostle glories only in the Cross of Christ. A new nature, not circumcision or uncircumcision, is the only thing of importance.

    D. The price of liberty is suffering. From henceforth he wants no one to trouble him (presumably about his doctrine or his Apostleship); for he bears on his body the brand-marks of Jesus (6:17).

    E. Paul's affectionate benediction (6:18).

The Authenticity, Importance, and Style of Galatians.
—Few writers today question the authenticity of the Epistle
to the Galatians. During the last century a few German
Rationalists questioned the genuineness of the Epistle, B.
Bauer and A. Pierson among them, but their objections
have been little heeded. The external evidence in favor of
the Epistle is strong, allusions to it being found in St.
Clement of Rome, St. Ignatius Martyr, St. Justin Martyr,
St. Polycarp and in the Epistle to Diognetus. St. Irenaeus,
Tertullian, Clement of Alexandria and the Muratorian
Fragment bear direct testimony to Paul's authorship. The
Epistle is also found in the Old Latin and Syriac versions
of the Bible, as well as in the oldest and best manuscripts
known to us.

The internal evidence of Paul's authorship is also very
strong. The casual reader must notice the marked similarity
between the subject-matter and style of the Epistle and
that found in Romans, which is universally acknowledged
to be by the hand of Paul. The vigorous style and emotional
manifestations point definitely to the great Apostle as the
author. The historical references in the Epistle also fit in
well with what we know of Paul's work.

The importance of the Epistle to the Galatians is
acknowledged by most theologians, both ancient and
modern. Paul's stress on the fundamental doctrine of justification by faith, his abrogation of the observances of the
Mosaic Law, and the emphasis placed upon the consequent
liberty of the Gospel are all noteworthy. Without the
personal biographical data furnished by Paul in the Epistle
we should be immeasurably poorer in our knowledge of
him and the early Church. He furnishes us with data concerning his preparation for the ministry that is given nowhere else, tells us how he obtained his knowledge of
Christianity, informs us of the source of his authority, and
reports how his doctrines conformed with those of the other

Apostles. The Epistle to the Galatians has been called the Magna Charta of Christian freedom. Martin Luther, the great reformer, said of it: "The Epistle to the Galatians is my Epistle. I have betrothed myself to it. It is my wife." At any rate, the Epistle seems to have furnished Luther with the inner strength necessary for him to plunge fearlessly into the great conflict with the Papistry and religious materialism of his day. A British writer, Dr. W. Graham Scroggie, has said, "Galatians was the battle axe which Luther brought down with terrific and telling force upon the helmets of his foes."

The style of Galatians is vehement and defensive. It is to be contrasted with the calm exposition one finds in Romans. Deeply filled with righteous indignation, Paul rushes on, as Callan notices, "like a mighty torrent, caring not for unfinished phrases, jolting omissions or grammatical mistakes, so long as he is able to give undoubted and unmistakable expression to his feelings . . . the sudden changes and transitions of thought and expression, the unexpected ruptures and unevenness of language, the bursts of anger towards his enemies, often swiftly alternating with tenderest words of sympathy for those that were well disposed,—all features so characteristic of St. Paul, make it impossible that anyone could have forged this letter by imitating any other of the Apostle's writings."[2]

The Doctrine of Justification by Faith.—Inasmuch as one of Paul's main themes, not only in Galatians but also in Romans, is that of justification by faith, we shall say a word about it here. It is a strange fact that we seldom if ever, hear the doctrine talked about or discussed in the Church, despite the fact that the great Apostle to the Gentiles expounded it often and with great force. Perhaps one reason why it is not dealt with is the fact that our problems are, in many respects, different from those he faced. Another

[2]*The Epistles of St. Paul*, I, 578. By permission of Joseph F. Wagner (Inc.), Publisher, New York.

and perhaps more potent reason is that the doctrine was for long years battled over by Protestants and Catholics. Not only that, but the doctrine was hard to understand. Paul Tillich, in his challenging book, *The Protestant Era,* says of it:

> Protestantism was born out of the struggle for the doctrine of justification by faith. This idea is strange to the man of today and even to Protestant people in the Churches; indeed, as I have over and over again had the opportunity to learn, it is so strange to the modern man that there is scarcely any way of making it intelligible to him. And yet this doctrine of justification by faith has divided the old unity of Christendom; has torn asunder Europe, and especially Germany; has made innumerable martyrs; has kindled the bloodiest and most terrible wars of the past; and has deeply affected European history and with it the history of humanity. This whole complex of ideas which for more than a century—not so very long ago—was discussed in every household and workshop, in every market and country inn of Germany, is now scarcely understandable even to our most intelligent scholars. We have here a breaking-down of tradition that has few parallels.[3]

Now that we understand the importance and difficulty of the doctrine of justification by faith, let us look at it directly. Unless we comprehend what is meant by the doctrine, the Epistle to the Galatians (not to mention that to the Romans) cannot be understood completely.

Now what is meant by "justification" and by "faith"? Let us deal with "justification" first. The Greek verb underlying the word means to *make righteous, defend the cause of, plead for the righteousness (innocence) of, acquit, justify;* hence, *to regard as righteous.* So it is defined by the great New Testament scholar, Alexander Souter. The great theological battle in years past between the Protestants and Catholics turned upon the meaning of "to justify" (Greek: *dikaioun*). The Protestants maintained that to justify, in spite of its causative form, meant to *declare* just, and not to *make* just, as was held possible by the Catholics. But aside from this

---

[3]Reprinted from *The Protestant Era*, p. 196, by Paul Tillich by permission of The University of Chicago Press. Copyright 1948 by the University of Chicago. All rights reserved.

theological struggle, by "justification" Paul seems to anticipate a favorable decision of "acquittal," or of regarding as
"righteous" the Christian convert who comes up before
God in judgment. (Rom. 5:9) Notice that the ordinary
person who lives a good life may not be regarded as being
justified, for the act of justification confers upon a man a
kind of supernatural life. It regenerates and renews him by
the Holy Spirit, which comes only as a result or fruit of
baptism. (Titus 3:5-7) The Holy Spirit is a "Spirit of life"
(Rom. 8:2) because it brings a life of grace or benevolence
in the person with whom it abides, or, as Paul indicates,
his spirit "has life because of righteousness [justification]."
(Rom. 8:10) Through baptism unto Christ we become
participants[4] in His life, a newness of life. (Rom. 6:3-5)
Our "old man" is indeed "crucified with Him" (Rom.
6:6), but at the same time we begin to live to the new. The
new man, Paul says, is "created according to God in justice
[righteousness] and sanctification [holiness]." (Eph. 4:24)
Justice and sanctity are, therefore, to Paul two nearly
equivalent ideas. In fact, he goes so far as to say that Christ
has become for us "justice, sanctification [holy, set apart],
and redemption." (I Cor. 1:30) Moreover, the Apostle also
told some of the Corinthian converts who had been adulterers, thieves, idolaters, and the like, this truth: "but ye are
washed, ye are sanctified, ye are justified in the name of
the Lord Jesus, and by the Spirit of our God." (I Cor. 6:11)
In other words, baptism by water and the Spirit lead to
purification, sanctification, and justification. It should be
observed that, aside from the Bible, the doctrine of justification is also found in Latter-day Scriptures. Notice this:

> And we knew that justification through the grace of our Lord
> and Savior Jesus Christ is just and true. (D & C. 20:30)

And the same may be said of the doctrine of sanctification. (D. & C. 20:31) In the Book of Mormon we are

[4]If we truly have been born of the Spirit. See Alma (5:14), who reminds us that we may
be baptized and not be born of God.

told by Lehi that "by the law [he does not here necessarily refer to the Law of Moses] no flesh is justified." (2 Nephi 2:5)

Paul teaches another important fact concerning justification, and that is that it is not dependent upon the merits (Rom. 3:27), wisdom, or the works of man to any degree; it is given as a free gift to man through God's grace or benevolence. Man cannot earn it or deserve it of himself. Neither descent from Abraham, nor the works and practice of the Law of Moses, nor the gifts and pursuit of human wisdom and philosophy give man title to it. King Benjamin long ago said:

> I say unto you that if ye should serve Him who has created you from the beginning, and is preserving you from day to day, by lending you breath, that ye may live and move and do according to your own will, and even supporting you from one moment to another—I say, *if ye should serve Him with all your whole souls yet ye would be unprofitable servants.* (Mosiah 2:21; italics the author's.)

In the words of Nephi, "for we know that it is by grace that we are saved, after all we can do." (2 Nephi 25:23; see also Alma 22:14)

The only assistance that the puny power of man can lend in obtaining justification before God is in having faith, and even that is a gift from Him. (Eph. 2:8) Now let us deal with "faith," the second important word in the phrase "justification by faith." That Paul taught the necessity of faith is proved by many passages from him. (See e.g., Rom. 1:16-17; 3:24-30; 4:1-25; 5:1-2.) The faith that the Apostle combines with justification has reference to an active faith in our Lord Jesus Christ, who redeemed us while we were yet sinners (Rom. 5:8) and enemies of God (Rom. 3:24-26; 4:24-25; 5:6-10, 15-21; 7:25; 8:29-30); for our very salvation is due to the sanctifying blood of Jesus Christ. (Rom. 8:32-39) The practical nature of the faith which, Paul taught, was necessary for justification is that firm belief or trust in God's word such as was displayed by Abraham. (Rom. 4:3, 9, 13-22; Gal. 3:6) The true Church member must have an unshaken trust in Christ as God, that he suffered for us, died and rose again in our behalf; "now if we be dead with Christ, we believe that we shall also live with Him: knowing that Christ being raised from the dead dieth no more." (Rom. 6:8-9) And again, "If thou shalt confess with thy mouth the Lord Jesus, and shalt believe in thine heart that God hath raised Him from the dead, thou shalt be saved." (Rom. 10:9) In the Apostle Paul's mind, Christianity was essentially and absolutely based on a belief in baptism, the reception of the Holy Ghost, the Divinity of Christ, the son of God, His Messiahship, the expiatory nature of His death and the like. Such is the nature of the faith that must form the basis of our trust in God. (Rom. 1:5; 3:3; 4:17-21; 6:16-19; 10:16; 15:18) The faith that justifies must, therefore, contain an intellectual devotion or adherence to the Gospel truths (Rom. 4:19-22; 10:8-17), and comply in a very practical way with the will of God as expressed therein. (Rom. 1:5; 10:3, 16; 11:30, 32; 2 Cor. 10:5; Eph. 2:2; 5:6-14) And so, though the works of the natural man or the observances of the Law of Moses are useless as far as sanctification is concerned, acts, such as repentance, fear, hope and the like, which express our intellectual devotion to the Gospel, are understood as necessary for justification.

It should be emphasized that the faith which Paul spoke of and taught as necessary for justification implied by its very nature the doing of good works; "Who will render to every man according to his deeds: to them who by patient continuance in well doing seek for glory and honor and immortality, eternal life: . . for not the hearers of the law are just before God, but the doers of the law shall be justified." (Rom 2:6, 7, 13; see also Gal. 5:6; Titus 3:8, 14)

Faith, indeed, is supported and accompanied by good

works, so that the man who is justified by it is not, as some have supposed, making a truce with Satan, or covering over his sins. A man who is justified by faith brings about an internal spiritual renovation in himself, endeavors to exclude all that separates himself from God (Rom. 1:1-3:20), and attempts to make himself totally dead to and free from sin, as the natural man dies to the sensible world about him. (Rom. 5:1-23; 8:1-5; 13:12-14)

As we have earlier pointed out, justification seems to anticipate for a Christian a decision of "acquittal" or of being regarded as "righteous" in a future Divine judgment. Can a member of the Church of Christ be regarded in the present time as being justified by faith? If he has truly been "born again" of the Spirit and continues in a newness of life, we may answer "yes." In anticipation of his continued observance of the requirements of God, he may be regarded as "acquitted" or as "righteous," and so is in Divine favor. A comparison may be made by reference to a man on an escalator. We anticipate that he will reach a given floor if he stays on the escalator. So a person will eventually be justified, but may be regarded as being so now, if he retains a remission of sins (Mosiah 4:26) and continually shows his faith in God. (See also Alma 34:16; 2 Nephi 31:19-20; important!)

Paul told the Galatians that the Law of Moses was a schoolmaster or tutor to bring Israel to Christ, "that we might be justified by faith." (3:24) But after the coming of Christ, the Law of Moses was no longer needed; in other words, "after faith is come, we are no longer under a schoolmaster." (3:25) By faith in Christ all men become children of God, understanding faith as explained above. (3:26) When men are baptized into Christ they put on Christ; that is to say, they assume His character, and clothe themselves with His dispositions and qualities. (3:27) Those who are thus united with the Christ in this most intimate union are no longer to be distinguished as Jew or Greek, bond or free, male or female; "all are one in Christ Jesus"; no differences, religious, national, or social, exist between them; they all form one moral and harmonious body with Christ as their head. (3:28) Under this situation they then become "Abraham's seed, and heirs according to the promise." (3:29) This last verse definitely demonstrates the fact that Paul understood the pact between God and Abraham much better than it is expressed in the Book of Genesis; in fact, he understood the covenant precisely as expressed and explained in the Book of Abraham:

> My name is Jehova, and I know the end from the beginning; therefore my hand shall be over thee. And I will make of thee a great nation, and I will bless thee above measure, and make thy name great among all nations, and thou shalt be a blessing unto thy seed after thee, that in their hands they shall bear this ministry and Priesthood unto all nations; and I will bless them through thy name; for as many as receive this Gospel shall be called after thy name, and shall be accounted thy seed, and shall rise up and bless thee, as their father; and I will bless them that bless thee, and curse them that curse thee; and in thee (that is, in thy Priesthood) and in thy seed (that is, thy Priesthood), for I give unto thee a promise that this right shall continue in thee, and in thy seed after thee (that is to say, the literal seed, or the seed of the body) shall all the families of the earth be blessed, even with the blessings of the Gospel, which are the blessings of salvation, even of life eternal. (The Pearl of Great Price, Abraham 2:8-11)

It is obvious, in the light of this scripture, why Paul taught that Gentiles who are justified by faith become "Abraham's seed and heirs according to the promise." *The Doctrine and Covenants* also points out that those (including Gentiles) who obtain the Aaronic and Melchizedek Priesthoods and magnify their calling "are sanctified by the Spirit unto the renewing of their bodies. They become the sons of Moses and of Aaron and the seed of Abraham, and the church and kingdom, and the elect of God." (84:33-34) *The Doctrine and Covenants* here seems to be a real advance on the doctrine of Paul as expressed in Galatians, in that it reveals the fact that the actual heirship or adoption does not become complete until after (in the case of men) they receive the Priesthood and magnify it, thus being sanctified "by the Spirit unto the renewing of their bodies." Paul doubtless understood this fact and had explained it previously to the Galatians; hence he did not feel it necessary to go into the detail we have given here.

Chapter 14

PAUL'S THIRD MISSIONARY JOURNEY
(Continued)

THE EPISTLE TO THE ROMANS

Some Facts Bearing on the Epistle.—It was now the early part of the year A.D. 58, possibly February, when Paul, foreseeing his early departure from Corinth, felt it necessary to write to the Roman branch of the Church. It is not hard to discover reasons why the Apostle wanted to write the Roman saints. We have already learned that he had thoughts of visiting Spain, and doubtless he felt that Rome would be a good base of operations in carrying the Gospel to the West. Rome was also the capital of the Empire, and Paul recognized the value of the imperial system of administration in bringing peace, order, security, and prosperity to a harassed and bewildered world. He and his fellow missionaries owed much to the Empire for the protection they received and for its relatively good communication facilities, ease of travel by land and sea, and many other benefits of lesser importance. It is possible that Paul felt it wise to make the members of the Roman branch of the Church better acquainted with himself and the Spirit that actuated him in his preaching. He would need their active cooperation in his projected missionary campaigns, and to write them a good letter would help assure himself of a warm welcome from them. Then, too, the Apostle was well aware of the fact that the influence of the Judaizers was still at work in the Church, casting aspersions upon his character, denying the validity of his teachings, rejecting his Apostleship, and in other ways undermining his influence. He felt that his letter needed to give a systematic exposition of certain doctrines that he taught in order to offset the effects of any enemy influence that may have been felt in the Roman branch. It was also important that the Roman members be exhorted to remain united and free from uncharitable contentions and divisions that could easily develop into serious difficulties. Paul's troubles with the Corinthian and Galatian saints had seriously impeded his work, and he would therefore counsel his Roman friends to remain united in the faith for their own spiritual well-being. Last, but not least, Paul seems to have had many good friends in Rome, some of them being of Jewish origin (e.g., Priscilla and Aquila, Andronicus, Junias and Herodion, his kinsmen, the members of the household of Aristobulus); others of Greek extraction (e.g., Epaenetus, Asyncritus, Plegon, Hermas, Patrobas, Hermes, Philologus, etc.); and still others of Latin descent (e.g., the household of Narcissus, Ampliatus, Urbanus, Rufus, Julia). (See Romans 16.) The names given do not exhaust the list. Doubtless these friends of Paul's in Rome were a "must" on his list of those to whom he felt he owed greetings. If it be asked why so many of Paul's acquaintances were in Rome, the answer may be that the capital was the focal point for business interests, affairs of state, and the like which drew them for one reason or another. It should be noticed that at the time Paul wrote the Epistle the greater number of Roman saints were of pagan extraction (cf. Rom. 1:5-6, 13-15; 11:13; 15:16), but a group of Jewish members formed an important minority (cf. Rom. 4:1; 6:15-17; 7:1-6; 8:15). It may be pointed out that from A.D. 49, the date of Claudius' edict expelling the Jews from Rome, until its repeal by Nero in A.D. 54, conversions to the Church would come mainly from the ranks of the Gentiles.

That the branch of the Church in Rome to which Paul wrote had been long established and well organized would seem quite certain from the tone of his Letter and from his long-standing desire to visit the saints there. (1:8, 10-15; 15:22-24, 28, 29) Unfortunately, we know little concerning the early history of the branch, and Paul tells us nothing about its origin and about the men who were first responsible for setting it up. There is good reason for believing that the first Church members in Rome were Jews who had been converted in Palestine. In 63 B.C., after Pompey had taken Jerusalem, many Jews flocked to Rome to take advantage of the kindness and protection of Caesar, but they kept in close touch with their brethren in Jerusalem, especially in religious matters. Accordingly, they came up to Jerusalem at intervals to the regular feasts, just as Latter-day Saints come up to General Conference. In Acts 2:10 we are told that "strangers of Rome, Jews and proselytes" were present on the great day of Pentecost when such wonderful manifestations of the Holy Ghost were enjoyed. Many of them were doubtless converted and returned to Rome with the "good news" at an early date in the history of the Church. These converts spread the message, and it would not be long before the Church Authorities in Jerusalem would be apprised of the necessity of sending brethren to Rome with the necessary authority to organize a branch of the Church and actively preach in that great capital city of the Empire. But the actual facts concerning the establishment of the Church branch in Rome, we emphasize, are not known. The Catholics claim that the unanimous decision of antiquity (Clement of Rome, St. Ignatius, Eusebius, St. Irenaeus, St. Jerome, Orosius, etc.) is that Peter the Apostle was the founder and organizer of the Church branch in Rome. According to Eusebius *(Chron. ad ann. 43)*, St. Jerome (De Viris illust. i. 8), and others, Peter came to Rome during the early years of Claudius, about A.D. 42, very probably soon after his miraculous escape from prison in Jerusalem (Acts 12:17), and "most likely" (Callan) remained in the imperial city until the edict of Claudius

(A.D. 49), when all Jews were expelled, and he then returned to Jerusalem. Many Protestant scholars hold that Peter did not establish and organize the branch at Rome. But whatever the facts about Peter, it must be recognized that when Paul was in Corinth during his Third Missionary Journey the Church in Rome was thriving, and the Apostle was anxious to write its members and visit them.

Outline of the Epistle.—The Epistle to the Romans contains an introduction, the body of the Epistle in two sections, and a conclusion.

 I. Introduction (1:1-17).
  A. Paul, a servant and Apostle of Jesus Christ, from whom he has received grace and a commission to win souls from among all the Gentiles sends greetings (1:1-7).
  B. The Apostle thanks God through Christ for the Roman saints, the report of whose faith is spreading through the world. He makes mention of them in his prayers and trusts that by some means God may make clear the way for him to come to them and impart some spiritual help and strength to them. He had intended to come to them many a time—but until now had been prevented—that he might gather some fruit from his labors among them. He is eager to preach the Gospel in Rome to Greek and non-Greek (1:8-15).
  C. The theme of Paul's Epistle: that justification comes from faith in Christ, and not from observance of the works of the Law of Moses. As an Apostle he is not ashamed of the Gospel of Christ, for it is the power of God working for men's salvation everywhere (1:16-17; contains Mutual Slogan for 1955).

II. Justification through faith, and the moral obligations of Christians (1:18-15:18).

A. The doctrine of justification by faith in Christ
(1:18-11:36).

1. The need of justification (1:18-3:20).

a. Despite the fact that they had knowledge of God, the pagans in their wickedness have not glorified Him nor rendered Him thanks, but have boasted of
their wisdom and have lapsed into
idolatry. Thus they have incurred God's
wrath (1:18-23).

b. God has given up the Gentiles to vile
passions such as sodomy, and since they
did not think fit to retain knowledge of
Him, their hearts are filled with dis-
honesty, mischief, greed, malice, envy,
bloodthirstiness, insolence, faithlessness,
and the like. Though knowing well the
sentence God pronounces against these
things, they not only do them but ap-
plaud those who practice them (1:24-
32).

c. All men are sinners, and those who pass
judgment on their neighbors will feel
God's judgment, for they commit the
same misdeeds. God rewards men according to their deeds, and if the pagans
do not follow the light they have, yet
are responsible for their sins, how much
more will the Jews with their greater
light be held accountable and feel God's
wrath and anger. They are in a more
serious condition than the pagans whom

they condemn. God shows no favoritism (2:1-11).

d. Inasmuch as God has no respect of persons, He will judge the Gentiles by the natural law which they knew, and the Jews by the Mosaic Law which they professed but did not practice (2:12-24).

e. Paul explains what makes a true Israelite, by pointing out that the circumcised Jew who does not observe the requirements of the Law amounts to nothing, but that the uncircumcised pagan who obeys the natural law merits God's praise. The true Jew is one inwardly (2:25-29).

f. The Jews did have an advantage over other peoples in that they were entrusted with God's oracles, but their faithlessness will not nullify God's faithfulness. God's righteousness will only shine forth in a clearer light. The sins of the Jews which serve to manifest God's glory will not go unpunished (3:1-8).

g. The Scriptures prove that both Jews and Gentiles are in bondage to sin, that the failure of the Jews to make proper use of their privileges indicts them equally with the Gentiles (3:9-20).

2. The way to justification (3:21-4:25).

a. Since all men, Jew and Gentile alike, have sinned, all may through God's grace be justified (acquitted) by faith in Jesus Christ, who redeemed us by the shedding of His blood (3:21-31).

b. By citing the case of Abraham, who was declared just or righteous by the Scripture (Gen. 15:16), Paul proves that the Old Testament had already taught that man is justified by faith and not by works. The Apostle demonstrates that Abraham did not acquire justification as a reward for his works, but as a gratuitous gift through his faith in God. Paul also cites David (Ps. 32:1-2), who tells of the blessedness of the man whom God credits with righteousness apart from his actions (4:1-8).

c. The Apostle proves the universality of the doctrine of justification by faith by citing the example of Abraham (Gen. 15:6), who was justified before circumcision, not after. Abraham received circumcision as a seal of the righteousness which was his by faith while still uncircumcised, that he might be the father of all those who believe even though uncircumcised—in order that this righteousness might be credited to them. The promise given Abraham (or posterity) that he should inherit the world did not come through Law, but through righteousness depending on faith. If those who rely on Law are heirs, then faith is useless and the promise to Abraham counts for nothing (4:9-17).

d. Paul describes the perfect and unwavering faith that must be possessed by all those who would partake of the promised blessings. The Scriptures record Abraham's faith for our benefit, that we, by imitating it, may be justified, believing in Him who raised Jesus from the dead, Jesus who was delivered up because of our offenses and was raised to life for our justification (4:18-25).

3. The first fruits and blessings of justification (5:1-8:39).

   a. Justified by faith, man enjoys peace with God and has the hope of seeing His glory, which rests upon the Divine love manifested in Christ's death for us as sinners (5:1-11).

   b. Through Adam, sin and death entered into the world, but through Jesus Christ, grace and life are given to mankind. Just as the result of a single transgression was the condemnation of all mankind, so also the result of a single deed of righteousness brought about a life-giving acquittal for all mankind (5:12-21).

   c. Another fruit of justification is dominion over sin and freedom from its tyranny. Through baptism we were buried with Christ in death, in order that, as Christ was raised from the dead by the Father's glorious power, we also should live an entirely new life. Our old self was nailed to the cross with Him, in order that our sinful nature might be neutralized and we should no longer be the slaves of sin. Christians are not to let sin reign in their mortal bodies, causing them to be subject to their passions; they are no longer to offer their faculties as instruments of wickedness for sin to use. Sin is not to be lord over them, since they are subjects, not of Law, but of grace (6:1-14).

d. Paul exhorts his readers to be ever on their guard against sin. They are pledged to live Christ-like lives and are not to think that, being freed from the slavery of the Law, they may sin with impunity. Now, emancipated from sin, they have their reward in holiness, with eternal life as the result. The wages of sin is death; but the gift of God is eternal life through Jesus Christ our Lord (6:15-23).

e. A third fruit of justification is freedom from the bondage of the Mosaic Law. Men become dead to the Law (which occasioned sin), through the body of Christ, that they may belong to Him in a newness of life. Union with the Christ frees men from the Law (7:1-6).

f. The Law of Moses, although good in itself, being holy and just, was the occasion of new sins. It afforded sin the occasion to muster force for man's destruction (7:7-12).

g. Sin, not the Law, is the cause of death. Under the Law, men are carnal, sold under sin, but now they are spiritual. The Law was impotent in the struggle between the flesh and the spirit, but it made man become conscious of his sins, and he yearned for deliverance (7:13-25; cf. all of Chap. 7 in "Inspired" revision of the Bible).

h. A fourth fruit of justification is the happiness which it brings to regenerated man. Men who have been regenerated in Christ Jesus are no longer under condemnation; for the newness of life effected in them by the Spirit delivers them from former tyranny. The shortcomings of the Law, thwarted by human frailty, God made up for by sending His Son to triumph over the flesh, thereby enabling men to live according to the spirit and thus fulfilling the Law in their lives. Those who follow the flesh cannot do this last, because flesh and spirit are mutually opposing agencies. If the Spirit of Him who raised up Jesus from the dead dwells in men, He who raised Christ from the dead will also quicken their mortal bodies by His Spirit which dwells in them (8:1-11).

i. We are not under obligation to live according to the dictates of the flesh, but are debtors to the Spirit, which enables us to put bodily habits to death, and live. Those who are led by God's Spirit are God's adopted sons and heirs of God; they are joint heirs with Christ and share His glory. The reality of this future glory is shown by the yearning of irrational creatures, by the desire of the saints, by the desire of the Spirit which dwells in us, and by the designs of the Almighty Himself (8:12-30).

j. Having shown the certainty of the future glory of the saints, Paul ends the chapter with a hymn of praise and triumph. The faithful, in face of the evidence of the love of God and Christ, have nothing to fear, for nothing can separate them from the charity or pure love of Christ (8:31-39).

4. The problem facing Paul is Israel's rejection (9:1-11:36).

   a. The Apostle grieves over the rejection of the Jews, his natural kinsfolk, to whom belong adoption by God, His glorious Presence, the Covenants, the giving of the Law, the service (worship?) of God, and the Promises. Also, from their lineage came the Christ (9:1-5).

   b. Mere physical descent from Abraham does not give the Jews a claim to be recipients of God's promises, because these promises had limitations. Not all who have sprung from Israel count as Israel, nor because they spring from Abraham are they necessarily all His. Even in the Old Testament Scriptures (Gen. 25:23; Mal. 1:2-3), election came through God's free choice (9:6-13).

   c. Paul defends God's right to freedom of action. God is not unjust if He prefers one to another. The Jews have no right to object if God prefers the Gentiles to them, because they (the Jews) did not receive His call. The Scriptures

(Exo. 23:19; 9:16; Isa. 29:16) prove that God gives His favors to whom He pleases, and hardens whom He will. God, though patient with the wicked, may show forth His anger as well as His goodness (9:14-24).

d. Paul cites the Old Testament prophets (Hos. 2:23; Isa. 10:22; 18:22; 1:9) to prove the fact that the call of the Gentiles and the rejection of the Jews had been foretold (9:25-29).

e. The Apostle comes to the conclusion that the Gentiles, who were not in pursuit of righteousness, grasped it —a righteousness dependent on faith; while the children of Israel, in pursuit of a Law that could give righteousness, did not attain it, because they misunderstood God's plan, were scandalized at Christ, and sought salvation in a way that God had not ordained. He quotes Isa. 8:14; 28:16. They sought to bring about their own method of justification based upon external observances of the Mosaic Law, instead of attempting to find justification through faith in Christ; i.e., they refused to believe in the Gospel (9:30-10:21).

f. God has only partly cast off His people which He foreknew. At the time Paul writes, there is a remnant left according to the election of grace (11:1-10).

g. Israel's rejection is but temporary; the Israelites have not stumbled irretrievably, and by their lapse, salvation comes to the Gentiles in order to arouse their jealousy. Paul as an Apostle to the Gentiles takes pride in his ministry, trying to arouse his fellow-Jews to jealousy and save some of them. If the Gentiles, compared to the branches of the wild olive, have been grafted on the natural branches of the olive (Israel), they are not to be proud. It is not the Gentiles that uphold the root: the root upholds them (11:11-24).

h. Partial blindness has fallen upon Israel until the fulness of the Gentiles shall come in. (See D. & C. 45:28-30; P. of G. P., Joseph Smith, 2:41.) Then all Israel as a nation will be saved (11:25-29).

i. This mystery of God's wisdom is incomprehensible. His judgments are inscrutable, His footsteps are trackless (11:30-36).

B. The moral obligations of Christians (12:1-15:18).

1. Obligations of brethren to God (12:1-8).

a. Brethren should completely dedicate or consecrate themselves to God's service in order that He may accomplish His purpose on earth. Their minds are not to be conformed to the present world, but are to be transformed and renewed, that they may clearly discern what that good, acceptable, and perfect will of God is (12:1-2).

b. Through the grace (authority) given

Paul, he warns every individual not to esteem himself more than is his due. Just as the human body has many organs, and these organs have not all the same function, so collectively the saints form one body in Christ, while individually they serve as organs for one another. In the Church each member has his special office and gifts, with which he should be content and which he should use for the good of the entire body of the Church. Union with the one Christ forbids pride on the part of the individual member of the Church (12:3-8).

2. Duties of the saints to their neighbors (12:9-13:10).

    a. They are to exercise charity one to the other. As the Lord's servants they are to be full of joyful hope, patient under affliction, persistent in prayer; they are also to relieve the necessities of each other, practice hospitality, be sympathetic, and pay back to no man evil for evil (12:9-21).

    b. Paul gives general instructions concerning the obedience due to the civil authority. Saints are to be obedient to the ruling authorities. There is no authority not under God's control, and under His control existing authorities have been constituted. The man who rebels does so against God's appointment. Civil superiors are divinely appointed for the promotion of good and the repression of evil. Civil authority is to be obeyed, not only for fear of punishment, but also for the sake of one's conscience. The faithful are to pay their taxes to tax-gatherers as if to the servants of God (13:1-7).

   c. Charity as a social obligation. The saints are to have no debt to any man, except the standing debt of love or charity. He who loves his fellow-man has fulfilled the Law. Love avoids wronging one's neighbor and is therefore the fulfilment of the Law (13:8-10).

3. Duties of a man to himself: The believer should rouse himself from sleep; for salvation is now nearer than at the time of conversion. He should lay aside deeds of darkness and put on the armor of light. He is to behave becomingly, not indulging in revelry and drunkenness, nor in unlawful sexual intercourse and wantonness, nor in quarrelling and envy. He is to put on the Lord Jesus Christ and not spend time in planning how to satisfy carnal lusts (13: 11-14).

4. The pattern that saints under Christian liberty should exhibit toward their weaker brethren (14:1-15:13).

   a. Harsh criticism is to be avoided. The brother whose faith is weak should be welcomed, but not in order for others to pass judgment on his doubts. There are conscientious differences of opinions. One man's faith allows him to eat anything, while a man of weaker faith thinks it necessary to be a vegetarian. Paul gives other illustrations. The man who judges his brother must also stand at God's bar (14:1-11).

b. Scandal must be avoided. Church members are not to put any obstacles or stumbling-blocks in the path of their brethren. No one's spiritual progress is to be hindered. Brotherly love limits one's freedom of action. Brethren are to aim at whatever makes for peace and the spiritual upbuilding of one another. The saints are to keep their own stronger faith secretly between themselves and God (14:12-23).

c. The stronger members of the Church ought to bear the infirmities of the weak, and not seek their own pleasure. Each is to act so as to please his neighbor, aiming at his spiritual upbuilding. Christ, as the Scriptures prove, did not seek His own pleasure (Ps. 69:9). The saints are to welcome one another, as Christ welcomed them, to promote God's glory. Christ became a servant to the Jews in order to fulfil the divine promises made to the Patriarchs—and to make the Gentiles glorify God for His mercy (15:1-13).

III. Conclusion (15:14-16:27; an epilogue dealing with personal matters only).

A. Paul is convinced of the goodness of his readers, not to mention their knowledge of the Gospel and competency to advise each other. He speaks of the boldness of his letter and

justifies himself as an Apostle to the Gentiles who wishes to make known in Rome the nature of his preaching to other Gentiles. Paul anticipates a visit to Rome and Spain and tells about the collection for the poor in Jerusalem. He requests his readers to join with him in a prayer in his behalf while in Judea and hopes to enjoy a time of rest with them when he comes (15:14-33).

B. The Apostle commends Phoebe of Cenchreae to the saints in Rome. (Apparently she was to be the bearer of the letter.) She had befriended many, including Paul. He sends his personal greetings to many friends in Rome and warns them of men who would cause divisions and trouble among them. Greetings of brethren in Corinth (16:1-24).

C. Paul closes his Epistle with a sublime doxology (16:25-27).

The Authenticity of Paul's Epistle to the Romans.— Most modern scholars accept the Epistle as being genuine. The external evidence for its genuineness is unusually strong. Some of the earliest Christian writings seem to disclose an acquaintance with the Epistle. I Peter, Hebrews and James are such, and the doxology of Jude (vss. 24-25) is thought by some to bear a strong resemblance to the doxology in Romans 16:25-27, a resemblance which only a good knowledge of the latter could explain. The Epistle was evidently known to Polycarp, Justin Martyr, and Clement of Rome. Irenaeus, Clement of Alexandria, and Tertullian all cite it, and it appears in the Muratorian Fragment. Marcion, Basilides and Valentine, heretics of the second century, not only admitted its authenticity but used it to advance their own causes. By the end of the second century the Epistle was generally recognized as having Apostolic authority and was freely used.

The internal evidence in favor of the Epistle is so strong as to be considered irrefutable. The style, contents, and vocabulary are so obviously Paul's that few critics have ever had the temerity to question its genuineness. One has only to compare the Epistle with Galatians and I and 2 Corinthians to realize that all four possess the same stylistic features and must have had a common author.

The Unity and Integrity of Romans.—Although very few critics have questioned or have seriously attacked the main body of the Epistle, certain textual phenomena found in Chapters 15 and 16 have caused many scholars to reject these chapters as not being part of the original text. The main reasons given by the critics for believing that the last two chapters of Romans are not part of the original Epistle are these:

(1) The heretic Marcion, who made the first collection of Paul's Epistles, omitted entirely these two chapters from his edition of the Epistle.

(2) Such early writers as Irenaeus, Cyprian, and Tertullian, who cite Romans freely, never quote from Chapters 15 and 16.

(3) The Epistle seems to have four terminations in these two chapters (15:33; 16:20, 24, and 27). These terminations would indicate a compilation, perhaps by extractions from other of Paul's letters.

(4) The position of the doxology in 16:25-27 varies strangely in different Mss.,—a circumstance which tends to cast suspicion upon its genuineness. In some of the so-called "best" Mss. it appears at the end of the Epistle, as in our familiar English version, but in others it is inserted at the end of Chapter 14. Some Mss. insert it in both places,

and two or three of them omit it altogether. The Chester Beatty papyrus, which is commonly dated from about A.D. 200, places it at the end of Chapter 15.

Before dealing with these points, we should explain that Chapter 16 is looked upon by many scholars as a small but independent Epistle. They believe that it was originally sent to Ephesus and for some reason or another was later attached to the Epistle to the Romans. The reason for this belief is that the Chapter contains individual greetings to twenty-six Church members, among whom Aquila and Priscilla (Rom. 16:3; Acts 18:18-19; I Cor. 16:19; 2 Tim. 4:19) as well as Epaenetus ("the first fruits of Asia," Rom. 16:5) are enumerated. It will be remembered that Aquila and Priscilla labored with Paul during the greater part of his sojourn in Ephesus. And authorities tend to believe that Paul would be more likely to have been well acquainted with these twenty-six persons in Ephesus, where his friends would be many, than in Rome, where he had never set foot. This view of Chapter 16 has never appealed to the author, because it assumes that Paul's friends could not get about freely, whereas we know that travel between Rome and Asia was common and relatively easy in Paul's time. And witness the frequency with which Jews in the days of the Apostle made trips to Jerusalem for religious purposes from all parts of the Mediterranean world. Furthermore, Paul made friends and converts in many places, and it should not seem strange that numbers of them should return to their homes in Rome or sojourn there for one reason or another, inasmuch as it was the capital of the empire.

In rejecting the view that Chapters 15 and 16 were not originally part of the Epistle to the Romans, the writer does so for several good reasons. First, he does so because a careful reading of the chapters in question gives him the personal impression that they are Paul's and could well be part of the original Epistle. Second, the preponderance of the manuscript evidence seems to be in favor of the integrity and unity of the Epistle as it stands. And third,—and this reason must be deemed very important in the eyes of most Latter-day Saints—the prophet Joseph Smith did not cast out these chapters when he revised the New Testament by the spirit of revelation. Keep in mind that he did cast out the Song of Songs from the books of the Old Testament. These are general reasons for accepting the two chapters as they stand. Now, let us examine the objections raised in the four classifications cited above.

(1) Marcion's omission of the two chapters may simply be due to the fact that he did not consider them important for his purposes, or they did not comport with his heretical teachings. He did not hesitate to mutilate other portions of the New Testament when they did not agree with his heresies (Irenaeus, *Adv. Haer.* III. XII.12; XIV. 4).

(2) It may be admitted that the failure of Irenaeus, Cyprian, and Tertullian to quote from Chapters 15 and 16 is strange, but their failure to do so may be because the subject matter did not suit their purposes. At any rate their failure to quote from the chapters in question is not compelling evidence that they were not part of the original Epistle. The presence of these chapters in many of the best and most ancient Mss. is evidence of that.

(3) Nor are the four terminations compelling evidence that the two chapters are not part of the original Epistle. Letter writers today often add several postscripts to their communications. Almost all of us have seen such letters. The first termination in 15:33 following the main body of the Epistle seems quite natural, and little can be said against it.

Then Paul adds a commendation of Phoebe and a few salutations, followed by some warnings and a promise, as a postscript, and again proceeds to close the letter (16:20). This, again, does not seem difficult to understand. However, the termination in 16:24 is almost precisely the same as that in 16:20, and may appear more difficult to explain. But notice that Tertius, Paul's amanuensis, is mentioned in vs. 22, and Gaius, his host, is named in vs. 23. This suggests that the brethren cited in vss. 21-23 were all in the room with him when his Epistle was being finished, or were very close by. Their salutation, the Apostle felt, should be added to the others. Then a similar postscript to that in vs. 20 followed. The termination in vs. 27 is a doxology and is perfectly justified.

(4)   Objections to the authenticity of the doxology and its present position in the Epistle are far outweighed by the testimony of the great Bible manuscripts and by the intimate relationship which the doxology has in thought and style with the beginning, object and circumstances of the Epistle. It is probable that lectionaries[1] were responsible for the transfer of the doxology to the end of Chapter 14. They would not contain the last two chapters of the Epistle, since these would be considered as unsuitable for public reading because of their very personal nature.

The Historical and Theological Importance of the Epistle to the Romans.—Paul's Epistle to the Romans has exercised a very profound influence upon men through the centuries. Theologians of many schools of thought, notably Augustine, Anselm, Luther, Calvin, and John Wesley, have given it their closest attention. Although it is a true letter,

---

[1]A lectionary is a book or table of lessons for church service.

its theological value is of the highest and merits the attention of all men. Its central doctrine is justification by faith, and the other important doctrines which it treats, such as the Atonement, Sanctification, and Election (see Rom. 9), are dealt with because they are closely linked with the central doctrine.

Chapter 15

PAUL'S THIRD MISSIONARY JOURNEY
(Concluded)

Paul's Journey to Jerusalem.—It was possibly late in February, A.D. 58, following his three-month visit in Corinth, when Paul felt that he had better leave from there immediately if he was to arrive in Jerusalem in ample time for the Feast of the Passover, which was to be celebrated early in April. In his Epistle to the Romans he had said, "But now I go unto Jerusalem to minister unto the saints." (Rom. 15:25) In this connection he told the Roman saints of his intention of delivering the collection for the Jerusalem poor which had been contributed by the Church members in Macedonia and Achaia. The plan of the Apostle was to sail directly to Syria (Acts 20:3), most probably from the port of Cenchreae, and then go immediately to Jerusalem. But before he could set sail, notice of a Jewish plot came to his ears, and he had to make a change of plans. It was apparently the intention of his enemies to let him board the vessel, take his life by night, and dispose of the body in the sea. So the Apostle seems to have frustrated the evil intentions of the Jews by having his friends, Sopater of Beroea, the Thessalonians Aristarchus and Secundus, Gaius of Derbe, Timotheus, and Tychicus and Trophimus of Asia, enter into the ship; but he and Luke remained behind and made their way overland to Philippi in Macedonia. The plan was for all of the members of the party to come together again in Troas. (Acts 20:5) The change in plans was costly as to time, and Paul and Luke were not able to sail from Neapolis, the port of Philippi, until after the Passover. After five days, they reached Troas, where they rejoined their friends and remained a week. (Acts 20:6; notice the "we," indicating Luke's presence.)

On the Sabbath evening preceding the day appointed for the ship to sail, the members of the Church assembled for a sacrament meeting in an upper room lighted by many lamps. Here Paul preached to them and continued his remarks until midnight, possibly impressed that his present opportunity might never again recur. (Acts 20:7-8) A certain young fellow by the name of Eutychus was sitting in a window of the room, when, overcome by weariness and the heat of the crowded place, he fell asleep and fell three stories to the floor below. He was taken up dead (Acts 20:9), to the great sorrow and consternation of the saints in attendance. But Paul went down and embraced the body, saying to the bystanders, "Trouble not yourselves; for his life is in him." (Acts 20:10) The original language would seem to indicate that the life of the lad returned to him,—a real miracle had been performed—and not that he had been merely rendered unconscious by the fall. The joyful saints returned to the upper room, where they broke bread and ate, and the Apostle conversed with them until the break of day. (Acts 20:11-12)

The party of travelers, Paul excepted, now boarded their waiting ship and sailed for Assos. For some reasons of his own the Apostle traversed the twenty or more miles separating Troas and Assos to the south on foot; at Assos he boarded the waiting ship and sailed with his friends to Mitylene, on the southeastern part of the island of Lesbos (Acts 20:13-14). Another day's sail brought them opposite Chios; the next day they touched Samos and proceeded to lay to for the night at Trogyllium, a nearby town on the west coast of Asia Minor. An anchorage at the place is still called St. Paul's Port. From Trogyllium the next day the party sailed the short distance southeast to the seaport of

Miletus, the ancient capital of Ionia, about thirty miles south of Ephesus. (Acts 20:15) Miletus was renowned for its great temple of Apollo and for the fact that it was the birthplace of the noted philosophers Thales and Anaximander. Here Paul and his companions landed, and though being anxious to reach Jerusalem by the day of Pentecost, the Apostle sent a messenger to Ephesus and called the Elders of the Church to come south and meet him. (Acts 20:16-17) They were quick to obey his summons, and he took his last leave of them in this very affecting and impressive address:

Ye know, from the first day that I came into Asia, after what manner I have been with you at all seasons, serving the Lord with all humility of mind, and with many tears, and temptations, which befell me by the lying in wait of the Jews: and how I kept back nothing that was profitable unto you, but have shewed you, and have taught you publicly, and from house to house, testifying both to the Jews, and also to the Greeks, repentance toward God, and faith toward our Lord Jesus Christ. And now, behold, I go bound in the spirit unto Jerusalem, not knowing the things that shall befall me there: save that the Holy Ghost witnesseth in every city, saying that bonds and afflictions abide me. But none of these things move me, neither count I my life dear unto myself, so that I might finish my course with joy, and the ministry, which I have received of the Lord Jesus, to testify the gospel of the grace of God. And now, behold, I know that ye all, among whom I have gone preaching the kingdom of God, shall see my face no more. Wherefore I take you to record this day, that I am pure from the blood of all men. For I have not shunned to declare unto you all the counsel of God. Take heed therefore unto yourselves, and to all the flock, over the which the Holy Ghost hath made you overseers, to feed the church of God, which he hath purchased with his own blood. For I know this, that after my departing shall grievous wolves enter in among you, not sparing the flock. Also of your own selves shall men arise, speaking perverse things, to draw away disciples after them. Therefore watch, and remember, that by the space of three years I ceased not to warn every one night and day with tears. And now, brethren, I commend you to God, and to the word of his grace, which is able to build you up, and to give you an inheritance among all them which are sanctified. I have coveted no man's silver, or gold, or apparel. Yea, ye yourselves know, that these hands have ministered unto my necessities, and to them that were with me. I have shewed you all things, how that so laboring ye ought to support the weak, and to remember the words of the Lord Jesus, how he said, It is more blessed to give than to receive. (Acts 20:18-35)

The reader's attention is especially called to Paul's statement concerning the fact that after his departure grievous wolves should come among them, not sparing the flock. Paul, as well as the other Apostles, knew of the great Apostasy that should come into the Church, leaving it without any authority whatsoever to preach and administer the ordinances of the gospel. (See 2 Thess. 2:3-7; I John 2:18-19)[1] The predicted Apostasy did come and was complete shortly after the passing of the first century. The night of spiritual darkness descended upon the world, only to be dispelled by the promised Restoration of the keys of the Gospel in our own age under the leadership of the modern prophet Joseph Smith.

Having addressed his friends from Ephesus, Paul kneeled down and prayed with them all. The whole company "wept sore" and fell upon his neck and kissed him, sorrowing most of all for the fact that they should see his face no more. (Acts 20:36-37) Following this touching scene, they accompanied him to his ship. The voyage was now resumed, and the ship touched successively at Cos (forty miles south), the Island of Rhodes, and Patara in what was possibly a three-day run. (Acts 21:1) Patara was a maritime city of southwest Lycia, famous for its oracle of Apollo, and was probably the home port of the ship in which the party had been sailing. The party here left the ship but immediately found another bound for Phoenicia and boarded her. It sailed directly for Tyre, passing Cyprus on the left. After what must have been a two-day voyage, the ship reached the port where it was to discharge its cargo. The eventual destination of the vessel, however, was Ptolemais, about twenty miles farther south (Acts 21:7). It

[1]See Sperry, *Themes of the Restored Gospel*, pp. 151-165, for a more detailed treatment of the subject.

would take seven days to discharge and load cargo at Tyre, but Paul, who was well within his schedule, decided to stay with the ship and use the time in calling on the Church members who made up the branch in the maritime city. He did so, and the saints seem to have honored him and to have showed him great kindness. Through the Spirit and through their own knowledge of Jewish feelings toward him, the Tyrian saints warned Paul against going up to Jerusalem, but all to no avail. For when the ship was ready to sail, Paul and his companions resolutely went out toward it. The whole Church population, wives and children included, followed them outside the city. On the shore they all kneeled and prayed. When they had taken their leave of one another, Paul and his party boarded the ship, and the Church members returned home. (Acts 21:4-6) It was a touching demonstration of the love and affection Paul enkindled in the hearts of those who came into close contact with him.

At Ptolemais the party "saluted the brethren, and abode with them one day" (Acts 21:7), and then proceeded, presumably in another coasting vessel, thirty-five miles farther south to Caesarea, where they disembarked and became the guests of Philip the evangelist. (Acts 21:8) Philip is mentioned as having four unmarried daughters who had the spirit of prophecy. (Acts 21:9) Paul and his party stayed with Philip some little time, in the course of which visit Agabus the prophet (cf. Acts 11:28) came down from Judea, took Paul's girdle, bound his own hands and feet, and said, "Thus saith the Holy Ghost, So shall the Jews at Jerusalem bind the man that owneth this girdle, and shall deliver him into the hands of the Gentiles." (Acts 21:11) Paul's party and the other brethren besought him not to go up to Jerusalem. Their entreaties profoundly moved Paul; in fact, they grieved him. The Apostle knew very well that Agabus had prophesied correctly, because he himself had received warnings of the Spirit. (Acts 20:22-23) But he could not be dissuaded from his firm purpose of finishing his mission to Jerusalem, and the brethren ceased remonstrating with him. (Acts 21:14) A few days later the party, including now some disciples from Caesarea, loaded their baggage (apparently on horses), and proceeded on their way to Jerusalem. The sixty-mile journey was broken by an overnight stay at the home of Mnason, a Cyprian, one of the early disciples, in an unnamed village. (Acts 21:15-16) Without further incident the party reached Jerusalem, where the brethren gave Paul and his companions a hearty welcome. (Acts 21:17)

Chapter 16

PAUL'S FIFTH VISIT TO JERUSALEM

Paul Meets the Elders of the Church and Tries to Conciliate the Jewish Christians.—The day following Paul's arrival in Jerusalem (his fifth visit following his conversion), he and his party called on James, the Lord's brother, who seems to have been the authority in charge, all of the original Apostles being absent. Moreover, all of the Elders of the Church came. After exchanging greetings, Paul proceeded to tell in some detail all that God had done among the Gentiles through his ministry during the past four years of his Third Missionary Journey. After hearing Paul's thrilling recital of what had been accomplished, all glorified the Lord. (Acts 21:18-20) But with this part of the meeting finished, Paul was now to be presented by the presiding brethren with a very grave problem that his presence in the city brought to their attention. The brethren seem to have been much concerned with the suspicions and bitterness with which so many Jewish Christians, upholders of the Law of Moses, regarded the Apostle. Here are the words of explanation and advice given by the brethren to Paul:

> Thou seest, brother, how many thousands of Jews there are which believe; and they are all zealous of the law: and they are informed of thee, that thou teachest all the Jews which are among the Gentiles to forsake Moses, saying that they ought not to circumcise their children, neither to walk after the customs. What is it therefore? the multitude must needs come together: for they will hear that thou art come. Do therefore this that we say to thee: We have four men which have a vow on them; them take, and purify thyself with them, and be at charges with them, that they may shave their heads: and all may know that those things, whereof they were informed concerning thee, are nothing; but that thou thyself also walkest orderly, and

keepest the law. As touching the Gentiles which believe, we
have written and concluded that they observe no such thing,
save only that they keep themselves from things offered to idols,
and from blood, and from strangled, and from fornication. (Acts
21:20-25)

This is an amazing statement. As we have earlier
pointed out, here in the year A.D. 58 we find thousands of
Jewish Christians still adhering to the Law of Moses!
Twenty-five years after the death of our Lord, the early
Church Authorities still have not made it clear to a large
portion of the Church membership that the Law of Moses
was done away with upon the Advent of the Master. Those
of us in the Church today have had little conception of the
difficulties that faced the Authorities of the Early Church
with respect to this problem. It is obvious from what Paul
was told that he had been grievously and even mischie-
vously misrepresented by the Judaizers in Palestine. Actually the Apostle contended that circumcision mattered
nothing. Salvation came only through faith in Christ and
not by the rites of the Law of Moses, and Paul would not
impose circumcision on Gentile converts; nevertheless he
never forbade the Jews to practice it. They could practice
it and conform to any Mosaic rites they pleased so long as
they knew that salvation came to them through Christ and
Christ alone. It is a curious fact that the brethren, knowing
Paul's attitude toward the Law, should ask him to give the
appearance that he himself obeyed the Law. But the
Apostle, realizing the gravity of the problem and knowing
that it was important to hold the Jewish and Gentile groups
of the Church together, readily agreed to assume the role
of peacemaker. Paul had previously assumed a Nazirite
vow (p. 107), had even now come up to Pentecost, and
probably felt that he would not compromise his principles
in any serious respect. The Temple rituals would occupy
seven days of purification and sacrifice. Paul would pay for
the four lambs and eight pigeons used for sacrifice and would

attend the four men in their Temple appearances and rituals, which would end in having their heads shaved and their hair burned on the altar. In so doing the Apostle would be obliged to cross the Court of the Gentiles and the Court of the Women, enter the Court of Israel, and finally approach the altar on which burnt offerings were made. He was bound to be in full view of either friend or foe in these Temple areas.

Paul is Seized by a Jewish Mob.—And, indeed, when the seven days were nearly over, certain Jews from Asia who had come to the Feast of Pentecost suddenly recognized Paul in the Temple. They had previously seen Trophimus the Ephesian with him in the streets of the city (Acts 21: 29), and now they imagined that the Apostle had brought his Gentile companion into the Temple, an offense worthy of death, as large signs written in Greek and placed at all the entrances to the Court of the Women made clear. So these Asian Jews, hardened against the Gospel preached by Paul, raised a great cry against him, laid hands on him and cried out,

> Men of Israel, help! This is the man, that teacheth all men everywhere against the people, and the law, and this place: and further brought Greeks also into the temple, and hath polluted this holy place. (Acts 21:28)

We are told that "all the city" (Acts 21:30) was moved against Paul by the fanatical Jewish mobocrats. It mattered little to them that Trophimus was not actually with the Apostle in the Temple. Now was an opportunity to get rid of this troublesome Christian once and for all. Paul was hustled out of the Temple, the doors were shut behind him, and the Jews went about to kill him. (Acts 21:31)

Paul is Rescued by Roman Soldiers Under Claudius Lysias.—Fortunately the Roman soldiers in Jerusalem were alert to the mob, and in a short time Claudius Lysias, the Tribune in command, was on the scene with a few soldiers and their officers. At sight of the troops the mob ceased beating Paul, and the tribune arrested him as the obvious cause of the disturbance. The Apostle was chained to two soldiers, one on each side, while the commander asked men nearby who he was and what he had been doing. Only conflicting answers were forthcoming, so the tribune ordered Paul to be brought into the barracks. (Acts 21:31-34) When they got to the steps of the building, Paul had to be carried by the soldiers because of the violence of the mob which pressed on in the rear, shouting, "Away with him!" (Acts 21:35-36) At this point the harried Apostle got the attention of the tribune and asked whether he might speak to him. The surprised officer said, "Canst thou speak Greek? Art thou not that Egyptian, which before these days madest an uproar, and leddest out into the wilderness four thousand men that were murderers?" (Acts 21:37-38)

To this Paul replied that he was a Jew of Tarsus in Cilicia, a citizen of no unimportant city. Then he requested the privilege of speaking to the mob. (Acts 21:39) The startled tribune seems to have been impressed with Paul's evident culture and quiet demeanor and gave his consent. Anything to quiet the Jewish fanatics.

The Apostle Tells the Mob the Story of His Conversion.—Paul stood on the steps and motioned to the people to be quiet. When they had quieted down, he began speaking to them in Hebrew,—so the text says—but in reality in their native Aramaic. Addressed in the common vernacular, they kept all the more quiet. Paul then gave his defense by telling his persecutors the simple but eloquent story of his early life and conversion. (Acts 21:40-22:20) All went well until he reached the story of his return to Jerusalem and the Lord's injunction to him, "Depart: for I will send thee far hence unto the Gentiles." (Acts 22:21) The mention of his commission to preach the gospel to the heathen was more than the narrow-minded mobocrats could stomach, and with a roar of hate and disapproval they cried, "Away with such a fellow from the earth: for it is not fit that he should live." (Acts 22:22) They continued their demonstration by casting off their clothing and throwing dust into the air. (Acts 22:23) The tribune gave orders that Paul was to be brought into the barracks and examined by being scourged, so that the truth of what the uproar was about could be learned.

Paul Discloses His Roman Citizenship and Prevents the Scourging.—While they were binding Paul and making him ready for the cruel scourging, he turned to the centurion standing by and asked, "Is it lawful for you to scourge a man that is a Roman, and uncondemned?" Roman law being what it was, the centurion immediately took notice and warned the tribune that Paul had Roman citizenship. The officer immediately returned and verified the words of the centurion. Turning to the simply-dressed Paul, who looked anything but rich, he said, "With a great sum obtained I this freedom." (Acts 22:28) The tribune had doubtless paid a large sum of money during the reign of the last emperor, Claudius, when citizenship was sold readily to well-to-do people. The officer's praenomen, "Claudius," does indeed suggest that his citizenship was obtained under that emperor.[1] But to the tribune's words Paul could proudly answer, "But I was born free." (Acts 22:28) Those who were to examine Paul straightway departed, and the embarrassed and frightened tribune— frightened because he had bound a Roman citizen without trial—had to determine what was to be done with him. (Acts 22:29)

Paul's Address Before the Sanhedrin.—The next day the tribune, who wanted to know why Paul was accused by the Jews, loosed his bonds and gave command for the chief priests and all their council to confront the Apostle.

[1]See E. J. Goodspeed, *Paul*, p. 171.

(Acts 22:30) When they were assembled, Paul spoke up and declared that the course pursued by him had been "in all good conscience before God until this day." (Acts 23:1) At these words, presumptuous at least to his Jewish audience, the high priest Ananias commanded those who stood near Paul to strike him on the mouth. If the reader wonders why the tribune did not interfere at this point, let it be remembered that since Paul was a Jew, he was under the jurisdiction of the Sanhedrin. On being struck, Paul replied with righteous indignation:

> God shall smite thee, thou whited wall: for sittest thou to judge me after the Law, and commandest me to be smitten contrary to the Law? (Acts 23:3)

The men close to Paul rebuked him for saying these words. "Revilest thou God's High Priest?" they demanded of him.

Paul's apology was immediately forthcoming: "I wist not, brethren, that he was the High Priest: for it is written, Thou shalt not speak evil of the ruler of thy people." (Acts 23:5)

The Apostle was quick to realize that he would receive no justice in the Sanhedrin. Perceiving from variations in manner of dress that part of the Council were Sadducees and the other Pharisees, he cleverly decided to play upon their differences respecting the doctrine of the resurrection from the dead.

"Men and brethren," he cried out, "I am a Pharisee, the son of a Pharisee: of the hope and resurrection of the dead I am called in question." (Acts 23:6)

Paul's ruse succeeded, as Luke makes clear:

> And when he had so said, there arose a dissension between the Pharisees and the Sadducees: and the multitude was divided. For the Sadducees say that there is no resurrection, neither angel, nor spirit: but the Pharisees confess both. And there arose a great cry: and the scribes that were of the Pharisees' part arose,

and strove, saying, We find no evil in this man: but if a spirit
or an angel hath spoken to him, let us not fight against God.
(Acts 23:7-9)

Paul is Rescued—The Lord Speaks to Him.—So
fierce became the quarrel that arose because of his strata-
gem in dividing the Council that Paul was in danger of
being pulled apart limb from limb. Again Claudius Lysias
saved his life by commanding his soldiers to take him by
force from the Jews and bring him into the barracks again.
This was done, and the following night the courageous Paul
was encouraged by his Lord and Master, who stood by his
side and said, "Be of good cheer, Paul: for as thou hast
testified of Me in Jerusalem, so must thou bear witness also
at Rome." (Acts 23:11)

A Jewish Conspiracy to Kill Paul.—Paul's escape did
not sit well with his implacable enemies, particularly those
of the Sadducee persuasion. More than forty of them, therefore, banded themselves together with an oath neither to eat
nor drink until they had killed Paul. These men conspired
with the chief priests and elders to have Paul brought before
the Sanhedrin again on some pretext that would make it
possible for them to come near enough to the Apostle to
slay him. (Acts 23:12-15)

Fortunately, however, Paul's nephew, the son of his
sister who lived in Jerusalem, was in a position to discover
the plot. Loyal to Paul, he hastened to the barracks and
told him about it. Paul called one of the military officers
and told him to take the young man to the tribune, because
he had information to give him. Out of hearing of others,
Paul's nephew disclosed to Lysias the details of the evil plot.
The tribune then sent the young fellow home, cautioning
him not to let anyone know what he had done. (Acts 23:
16-22)

Chapter 17

PAUL IS SENT TO CAESAREA

Lysias Circumvents the Plot by Sending Paul to Caesarea.—Lysias, the tribune, promptly took measures to safeguard Paul, the Roman citizen, by calling centurions to make ready two hundred foot soldiers, together with seventy horsemen and two hundred spearmen, to march to Caesarea starting at nine o'clock that night. Beasts of burden (generally, horses or mules) were to be provided on which to mount Paul, in order to bring him safely to Felix, the Procurator or Governor. (Acts 23:23-24)

The tribune also dispatched a letter to Felix containing this explanation:

> Claudius Lysias unto the most excellent governor Felix sendeth greeting. This man was taken of the Jews, and should have been killed of them: then came I with an army, and rescued him, having understood that he was a Roman. And when I would have known the cause wherefore they accused him, I brought him forth into their council: whom I perceived to be accused of questions of their law, but to have nothing laid to his charge worthy of death or of bonds. And when it was told me how that the Jews laid wait for the man, I sent straightway to thee, and gave commandment to his accusers also to say before thee what they had against him. Farewell. (Acts 23:26-30)

It will be noticed that Lysias omits in the letter his initial error in sentencing Paul, a Roman citizen, to the scourge, trusting that the Apostle would say nothing about it. The sympathies of the tribune seem to be with Paul.

That night, the soldiers conducted Paul as far as Antipatris, about twenty-five or thirty miles distant. The next day the infantry returned to the barracks, leaving the horsemen to fetch him safely to Caesarea. Felix, after reading the letter, inquired of Paul from what province he hailed; and being told that he was from Cilicia, he said, "I will hear thee when thine accusers are also come." (Acts 23:34-35) The governor then gave command that Paul be detained in custody in Herod's judgment hall.

Thus we see Paul back in Caesarea after only nine days' absence, having been in the hands of the Jews, and now being in the custody of the Gentiles, as Agabus had prophesied. (Acts 21:11)

Paul Before Felix.—So important did it seem to the Jews to get rid of Paul that Ananias the High Priest came down to Caesarea within five days with a number of Elders and a rhetorician or lawyer by the name of Tertullus, to formally present the case before the Roman court. (Acts 24:1) Felix, whose rule had been clouded by lust, cruelty, and tyranny, was a brother of Pallas, the notorious favorite of Emperor Claudius, and was the first freedman ever to be appointed to a procuratorship. He had been governor, so far as we can determine, since A.D. 52, and now held in his hands the future of Paul. Even so, the Apostle had on his side the powerful safeguard of Roman law.

Tertullus opened the trial with a clever speech against Paul. He paid a servile tribute to Felix and then brought three charges against the Apostle. The first was treason, for Paul had been found a source of mischief and an insurrectionist among the Jews throughout the Empire. The second was heresy, because Paul had been a ringleader in the sect of the Nazarenes. And the third was sacrilege, for it was alleged that he attempted to profane the Temple. The Jews in the audience joined in the charge, maintaining that the facts had been presented. (Acts 24:2-9)

At a sign from the governor, Paul began his defense, without the flattery used by the opposition, and continued in these words:

Forasmuch as I know that thou hast been of many years a judge
unto this nation, I do the more cheerfully answer for myself:
because that thou mayest understand, that there are yet but
twelve days since I went up to Jerusalem for to worship. And
they neither found me in the temple disputing with any man,
neither raising up the people, neither in the synagogues, nor
in the city: neither can they prove the things whereof they now
accuse me. But this I confess unto thee, that after the way which
they call heresy, so worship I the God of my fathers, believing
all things which are written in the law and in the prophets:
and have hope toward God, which they themselves also allow,
that there shall be a resurrection of the dead, both of the just
and unjust. And herein do I exercise myself, to have always a
conscience void of offence toward God, and toward men. Now
after many years I came to bring alms to my nation, and offerings. Whereupon certain Jews from Asia found me purified in
the temple, neither with multitude, nor with tumult. Who ought
to have been here before thee, and object, if they had ought
against me. Or else let these same here say, if they have found
any evil doing in me, while I stood before the council, except it
be for this one voice, that I cried standing among them, Touching the resurrection of the dead I am called in question by you
this day. (Acts 24:10-21)

At this point Felix, who was fairly well acquainted
with Christianity, adjourned the trial, telling the Jews that
when the tribune Lysias came down, he would finally decide the case. (Acts 24:22) And he gave orders to the centurion to keep Paul in custody, to treat him with indulgence,
and not prevent his personal friends from showing him kindness. (Acts 24:23) Actually, Felix should have freed the
Apostle; but the governor seems to have kept in mind the
charge of treason made by Tertullus, and resolved to keep
Paul in custody until he could be made sure of his ground
by conferring with Lysias.

Paul Before Felix and Drusilla.—Shortly after the
other hearing, Felix brought along his wife Drusilla, a Jew-
ess, sent for Paul, and listened to his presentation concerning faith in Christ Jesus. Drusilla, the youngest daughter
of Agrippa I, was the third wife of Felix. She had been the
wife of Azizus, King of Emesa, but had been persuaded by
the governor to leave her husband and throw her fortunes

with him, a Gentile and an idolater. It is not surprising, therefore, that when Paul reasoned about righteousness, self-control, and the judgment, the guilty Felix became frightened and said, "Go thy way for this time; when I have a convenient season, I will call for thee." (Acts 24:25) At the same time, like so many disgraceful imperial administrators in the provinces, he hoped that Paul would pay him money as a bribe for his release. Luke tells us that for this reason he sent for him the oftener to converse with him. Thus the time passed until Paul had spent two years in custody. Then, because of a formal complaint lodged by the Jews with Nero, Felix was recalled to stand trial, and Porcius Festus succeeded him. Balked in his attempts to obtain a bribe from Paul, who must have had a considerable sum of money with him, Felix left Paul in prison, hoping to curry favor with the Jews. (Acts 24:26-27)

Festus Becomes Governor and Paul Again Stands Trial.—It was probably about July 1, A.D. 60, when Festus entered upon his duties as governor of the province. With a friendly attitude to the Jews, he went up to Jerusalem; whereupon the Jewish authorities immediately made representations to him against Paul and asked as a favor that he be brought to Jerusalem. They were planning an ambush and hoped to kill him on the way. But the prudent and honorable Festus replied that Paul was in custody in Caesarea; he himself would shortly go back, he said, and he assured the Jews that their influential men could accompany him and impeach the Apostle, if there was anything amiss in him. (Acts 25:1-5)

After spending about ten days in Jerusalem, Festus returned to Caesarea. The next day, taking his seat on the tribunal, he ordered Paul to be brought in. The Jewish deputation from Jerusalem brought against him many weighty charges which they were not able to substantiate. Paul assured Festus that he had committed no offense whatever against the Jewish Law, the Temple, or Caesar. (Acts 25:6-8)

But the harried governor, relatively unacquainted with Jewish customs and institutions and wishing to do the Jewish leaders a favor, asked Paul whether he would be willing to go up to Jerusalem and stand trial before him on the charges as preferred. (Acts 25:9) Festus doubtless felt that his proposal of referring the case to Jerusalem—or was it to the Sanhedrin itself?—with himself sitting in at the trial was eminently fair. But Paul, knowing the dangers involved and also knowing that the Jews would not give him a fair break at any trial, not to mention the fact that the question of Festus implied a possible deprival of his rights as a Roman citizen, refused to go.

> Then said Paul, I stand at Caesar's judgment seat, where I ought to be judged: to the Jews have I done no wrong, as thou very well knowest. For if I be an offender, or have committed any thing worthy of death, I refuse not to die: but if there be none of these things whereof these accuse me, no man may deliver me unto them. I appeal unto Caesar. (Acts 25:10-11)

Paul's firm decision to invoke his right as a Roman citizen was probably an unpleasant one to Festus. It was embarrassing enough for a procurator ever to have his decisions appealed to Caesar, but to have his first administrative decision thus appealed was to prejudice the imperial government against him. But after conferring with the Council, composed of administrative legal advisers, Festus decided that Paul's appeal was a valid one. He turned to the Apostle and said, "Hast thou appealed unto Caesar? unto Caesar shalt thou go." (Acts 25:12)

Festus Confers With Agrippa Concerning Paul.— Although Paul had appealed to Caesar, it was still up to Festus to forward to Rome all the documents dealing with the trial, together with his own judgment in the case. But unacquainted as he was with Jewish theology and institutions, Festus felt himself incompetent in the matter and wondered how he would state the charges against Paul (see Acts 25:27), not to mention what kind of a recommendation he ought to make regarding the final disposition of the Apostle.

Fortunately for Festus, as the new procurator he was paid a formal visit by King Agrippa II and his sister Bernice, who came from the region of Galilee. The pair were Drusilla's brother and sister, being children of King Agrippa I and great grandchildren of King Herod the Great, the tyrant of Judea when the Christ was born in Bethlehem. Agrippa II was king of the region about the Sea of Galilee, a position which he was to retain until near the close of the first century. Agrippa had been given the right by the Emperor Claudius of appointing the high priest in Jerusalem and was well versed in matters pertaining to the Jews. Not only was he a Jew himself, but through his great-grandmother Mariamne he was a descendant of the Maccabean family. Festus took advantage of King Agrippa's stay to lay Paul's case before him. (Acts 25:13-21) Agrippa expressed his interest in hearing from Paul, and Festus assured him that he should do so on the morrow.

Paul Before Agrippa.—The next day, Agrippa and Bernice came in state into the Audience Hall and took their seats, attended by the tribunes and men of high rank in the city. At the command of Festus, Paul was brought in. The governor then gave this explanation:

> King Agrippa, and all men which are here present with us, ye see this man, about whom all the multitude of the Jews have dealt with me, both at Jerusalem, and also here, crying that he ought not to live any longer. But when I found that he had committed nothing worthy of death, and that he himself hath appealed to Augustus, I have determined to send him. Of whom I have no certain thing to write unto my lord. Wherefore I have brought him forth before you, and specially before thee, O king Agrippa, that, after examination had, I might have somewhat to write. For it seemeth to me unreasonable to send a prisoner, and not withal to signify the crimes laid against him. (Acts 25: 24-27)

The explanation of Festus completed, King Agrippa told Paul to speak for himself. (Acts 26:1) In his preliminary statement, Paul expressed himself as fortunate in being able to defend himself before one like King Agrippa, who was so conversant with Jewish customs and questions. (Acts 26:2-3) He then launched eloquently into the story of his life, of his early Pharisaic training, of his hostility to the Christians, of his conversion, and of subsequent events. But when Paul began to speak of Christ rising from the dead (Acts 26:23), the Roman Governor was so far beyond his depth that he cried out in a loud voice, "Paul, thou art beside thyself; much learning doth make thee mad." (Acts 26:24) Let us continue the account:

> I am not mad, most noble Festus; but speak forth the words of truth and soberness. For the king knoweth of these things, before whom also I speak freely: for I am persuaded that none of these things are hidden from him; for this thing was not done in a corner. King Agrippa, believest thou the prophets? I know that thou believest. Then Agrippa said unto Paul, Almost thou persuadest me to be a Christian. And Paul said, I would to God, that not only thou, but also all that hear me this day, were both almost, and altogether such as I am, except these bonds. (Acts 26:25-29)

With these words of Paul's, the hearing was over, and so the King, the Governor, Bernice, and the others arose. They retired and discussed the case, agreeing that Paul had done nothing for which he deserved death or imprisonment. Agrippa said to Festus, "This man might have been set at liberty, if he had not appealed to Caesar." (Acts 26:32)

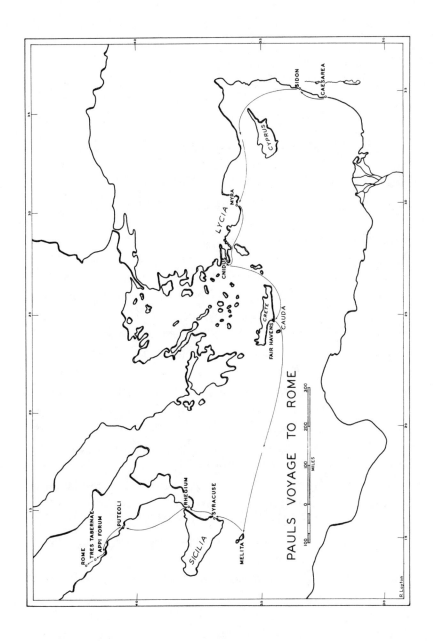

PAULS VOYAGE TO ROME

MILES
100   0   100   200   300

R. Layton

CAESAREA
SIDON
CYPRUS
MYRA
LYCIA
CNIDUS
CRETE
FAIR HAVENS
CAUDA
MELITA
SYRACUSE
RHEGIUM
SICILIA
PUTEOLI
APPI FORUM
TRES TABERNAE
ROME

Chapter 18

PAUL'S DIFFICULT JOURNEY FROM
CAESAREA TO ROME

Paul Begins the Journey to Rome.—When it was
decided that Paul should be sent to Italy, he with a few
other prisoners was handed into the custody of Julius, a
centurion of the Augustan or Imperial Cohort. The prisoners were placed on board a ship in the harbor of Caesarea,
whose home port was Adramyttium, on the south coast of
Mysia. In all probability the vessel was preparing to carry
a cargo to ports along the coast of the Province of Asia, and
it was thought that a ship to Rome might be sailing from
one of them in which the prisoners could obtain passage.
It is interesting that both Luke and Aristarchus, the Macedonian, were allowed to accompany Paul. Perhaps both
were passing as Paul's slaves. After one day's voyage the
ship put in at Sidon, about eighty miles north of Caesarea.
Julius, the centurion, treated Paul very courteously and
allowed him to visit his friends and enjoy their attentions.
When the ship put to sea again, the winds were against it,
and they sailed along the coast of Cilicia and Pamphylia,
finally putting in at Myra in Lycia. In that port Julius
found an Alexandrian ship bound for Italy and put his
prisoners on board her. Such ships were large; this one carried two hundred seventy-six persons and a cargo of wheat.
(Acts 27:37-38) From Myra the ship proceeded slowly and
with great difficulty some one hundred and forty miles west
to Cnidus. Unable to sail directly across the Aegean Sea
from this point, the vessel was forced by the contrary winds
to the south and west. Eventually it rounded Cape Salmone

on the eastern side of Crete, and coasting along the south side of the island with difficulty, it finally reached the bay of Fair Havens, near the town of Lasaea. (Acts 27:1-8)

Luke mentions the fact that the voyage had by now occupied a long time and that navigation was unsafe because the Fast was already over. (Acts 27:9) The party had probably left Caesarea about the middle of August, and Luke's mention of the Fast (of the Day of Atonement) would indicate the early part of October, when navigation was considered dangerous. Paul earnestly tried to warn the officers of the vessel about the dangers of leaving Fair Havens and addressed them in prophetic vein:

> Sirs, I perceive that this voyage will be with hurt and much damage, not only of the lading and ship, but also of our lives. (Acts 27:10)

Unfortunately, Julius, who seems to have been in charge because the ship was in the service of the Roman government, let himself be persuaded by the pilot and the owner rather than by Paul. Fair Havens was thought to be an inconvenient harbor to winter in, and the majority favored putting out to sea, in an endeavor to reach Phoenix, a land-locked bay about fifty miles farther west. A light breeze from the south had now sprung up, so that the ship's officers felt sure of accomplishing their purpose. They weighed anchor and ran along the coast of Crete, keeping close to the shore. (Acts 27:11-13)

The Storm and Shipwreck.—The ensuing account by Luke of what happened to the ship is a masterpiece and should be read by all. Scarcely had the ship rounded Cape Matala, which juts in a southerly direction from Crete, when a furious northeaster struck it and carried her out of her course. Unable to make any headway against the gale, the sailors simply let the vessel drive. About forty miles southwest of Fair Havens, they ran under the lee of the

little island of Cauda or Clauda, where they managed to
hoist on board the ship's dinghy, and also succeeded in
undergirding the vessel with frapping-cables to hold her
hull together. Afraid of being driven on the Syrtis quick-
sands off the coast of Africa, the ship's crew struck sail and
lay to. But even this was not sufficient. The next day they
had to lighten the ship, and the day following they had to
throw her spare gear overboard. Finally, when neither sun
nor stars could be seen for several days and the terrific gale
still continued, the last ray of hope seemed to be vanishing.
(Acts 27:14-20)

Under these conditions, a long time passed during
which the crew and passengers had little opportunity to take
food. Paul, knowing their weary and dispirited condition,
not to mention their hunger, stood among them and said:

> Sirs, ye should have hearkened unto me, and not have loosed
> from Crete, and to have gained this harm and loss. And now I
> exhort you to be of good cheer: for there shall be no loss of any
> man's life among you, but of the ship. For there stood by me
> this night the angel of God, whose I am, and whom I serve,
> saying, Fear not, Paul; thou must be brought before Caesar:
> and, lo, God hath given thee all them that sail with thee. Where-
> fore, sirs, be of good cheer: for I believe God, that it shall be
> even as it was told me. Howbeit we must be cast upon a cer-
> tain island. (Acts 27:21-26)

We do not know what effect this wonderful prophetic
speech of Paul's had upon the exhausted people, but it
must have given some of them courage to face their trials,
in view of the Apostle's prediction in Fair Havens. The
storm, indeed, continued with unabated violence, but upon
the fourteenth night, as the ship floundered through the
Sea of Adria (Adriatic), the sailors suspected, possibly from
the roar of the breakers, that land was near at hand. So
they sounded and found water of twenty fathoms depth;
and after a brief interval they sounded again and found
waters of fifteen fathoms. Fearful lest the ship run on the
rocks, they cast four anchors from its stern and waited for

daybreak. The sailors wanted to escape from the vessel and leave the passengers to their fate; lowering the dinghy into the sea, they pretended that they were going to put out anchors from the bow. But Paul, whose stature had been increased in the eyes of Julius and the soldiers by recent events, warned them of the sailor's intentions by saying:

> Except these abide in the ship, ye cannot be saved. (Acts 27:31)

The soldiers quickly cut the ropes of the ship's boat and let it fall off.

As day dawned, Paul stood up and urged all on board to partake of food:

> This day is the fourteenth day that ye have tarried and continued fasting, having taken nothing. Wherefore I pray you to take some meat: for this is for your health: for there shall not an hair fall from the head of any of you. (Acts 27:33-34)

And leading out, Paul took some bread, gave thanks to God before them all, broke it in pieces, and began to eat. Everyone was cheered by his action and took food. After eating, they lightened the ship by throwing overboard its cargo of wheat. (Acts 27:35-38)

When daylight finally came, no one could recognize the coastline. But noticing an inlet with a sandy beach, the crew hoped, if possible, to run their ship aground there. To this end they cut away the anchors, unloosed the bands which secured the paddle—rudders (steering-gear consisting of two large paddles, one on each quarter), and hoisted the foresail to the wind. The ship apparently ran into a sunken reef, where the bow stuck fast, while the stern began to break in pieces under the pounding it received from the sea. (Acts 27:39-41)

The soldiers, who were held accountable with their lives for the safe custody of their prisoners, were afraid that some of them would escape after swimming ashore. They proposed, therefore, that they be put to death, but their centurion, intent on Paul's safety, would have none of it and gave orders that those who could swim should jump overboard and get to land. The rest were to follow, some on planks or whatever they could find on the ship that would float. Eventually all got safely to shore, as Paul had predicted they would. (Acts 27:42-44)

Paul's Experiences in Malta.—This shipwreck was Paul's fourth. (See 2 Cor. 11:25) He could well lay claim to being an experienced voyager. In the harrowing days since leaving Fair Havens, he and his fellow passengers had drifted over six hundred miles, well over an average of forty miles per day. Having come ashore, the worn and weary passengers discovered from the native population that they had alighted on the island of Melita (Malta). Luke calls the natives *barbarians* (Acts 28:2), but by this he means merely that they were not Greeks. They showed the ship-wrecked people unusual kindness, for they kindled a fire and sheltered them from the pelting rain and the cold. Paul himself gathered a bundle of sticks, and when he had thrown them on the fire, a viper, driven by the heat, fastened itself on his hand. On seeing this, the natives said one to another in their superstitious manner, "No doubt this man is a murderer, whom, though he hath escaped the sea, yet vengeance suffereth not to live." (Acts 28:4) But Paul with great assurance shook off the reptile into the fire and was unhurt. After watching the Apostle for some time and seeing that he did not swell or fall down dead, the natives concluded that he was a god. (Acts 28:5-6)

The governor or "primate" of the island invited Paul and his friends to his house, and for three days generously made them his guests. The father of Publius—that was the governor's name—was lying ill of dysentery and an inter-mittent fever; so Luke the physician describes the case. Paul went to see the sick man and, after praying, laid his hands on him and cured him. On hearing of this miraculous cure, all the other sick people on the island came and were cured. So Paul manifested the gifts of the Spirit that follow the true Church of Christ. (I Cor. 12:9) The grateful people honored the Apostle and his companions greatly, and when they were able to set sail, the people of Melita also put many things on board for the travelers' use. (Acts 28:7-10)

Paul Finally Arrives in Rome.—Paul and his company were obliged to pass three months on the island of Malta before they could resume their journey. It may have been early in February when they set sail in another Alexandrian grainship which had wintered at the island. It was "The Twin Brothers," named after Castor and Pollux, the patrons of seamen. The ship sailed almost due north and put in for three days at Syracuse on the southeast part of Sicily. From there the vessel made its way to Rhegium, a city of Greek origin on the extremity of the toe of Italy's boot. A day later a south wind brought the ship to Puteoli, on the north shore of the Bay of Naples. The old name of Puteoli still exists, with very little change, as Pozzuoli. Puteoli was the regular port into which the Egyptian grainships brought their passengers and discharged their cargoes. Travelers on their way to Rome would proceed by the Appian Road. Julius the centurion would have to communicate with his superiors before he could leave the port. In the meantime, Paul and his companions searched out brethren in the town who urged them to remain with them for a week. After this sojourn the party began its march to Rome and eventually reached the Imperial City. But at two places, before Paul reached Rome, contingents of Church members who had heard of his coming went out to meet the famous Apostle whose letter had reached them about three years earlier. The first group met him at Appii Forum, thirty-nine miles away, and the second at Tres Tabernae ("Three Taverns"), about thirty miles out of the city. As they greeted him warmly, Paul thanked God and took courage. Upon his arrival in Rome, he was accorded the privilege, doubtless upon the recommendation of Festus, of living in a private place outside of the military barracks, guarded by a soldier. (Acts 28:11-16)

Chapter 19

PAUL'S FIRST ROMAN IMPRISONMENT

Paul Invites Leading Jews in Rome to Meet With Him.—When Julius delivered Paul to his superiors in Rome, the Apostle was probably in the charge of the commander of the imperial guards, the Prefect of the Praetorians, and was doubtless in his constant jurisdiction throughout the two years of his imprisonment. Paul would, in accordance with Roman custom, be chained to the soldier who was assigned to guard him, and would never be left alone day or night. The guard would be relieved at regular intervals, and thus many of the praetorians would come in close contact with him.

Paul had rested only three days in his new environment when he asked the leading Jews in Rome to meet him. The Apostle doubtless felt it important to gain their sympathy and, if possible, remove any prejudices they might have against him because of the circumstances under which he had been brought into Rome. Not only that, but he was very anxious to win over such Jews into the service of the Church. When the Jews had gathered to where Paul was in chains, he said to them:

> Men and brethren, though I have committed nothing against the people, or customs or our fathers, yet was I delivered prisoner from Jerusalem into the hands of the Romans. Who, when they had examined me, would have let me go, because there was no cause of death in me. But when the Jews spake against it, I was constrained to appeal unto Caesar; not that I had ought to accuse my nation of. For this cause therefore have I called for you, to see you, and to speak with you: because that for the hope of Israel I am bound with this chain. (Acts 28:17-20)

To Paul's words the Jewish leaders replied:

We neither received letters out of Judea concerning thee, neither
any of the brethren that came shewed or spake any harm of
thee. But we desire to hear of thee what thou thinkest: for as
concerning this sect, we know that every where it is spoken
against. (Acts 28:21-22)

It is obvious from their remarks that the Jews were
courteous, if somewhat cool, and that they were aware that
Paul belonged to a sect which was very unpopular. They
desired to hear what his views were before making any
final pronouncements. Paul could not be too hopeful of
winning them over, but at least they made arrangements
to hear him out. On the appointed day many came to his
lodging. The Apostle used the entire day in expounding to
them and testifying concerning "the kingdom of God,
persuading them concerning Jesus, both out of the law of
Moses, and out of the prophets." (Acts 28:23) The result
was as might have been expected: there was a division
among his hearers. Some believed the words he spoke, and
some disbelieved. (Acts 28:24) To the unbelievers Paul
addressed these words before they departed:

Well spake the Holy Ghost by Esaias the prophet unto our
fathers, saying, Go unto this people, and say, Hearing ye shall
hear, and shall not understand; and seeing ye shall see, and not
perceive: for the heart of this people is waxed gross, and their
ears are dull of hearing, and their eyes have they closed; lest
they should see with their eyes, and hear with their ears, and
understand with their heart, and should be converted, and I
should heal them. Be it known therefore unto you, that the salvation of God is sent unto the Gentiles, and that they will hear it.
(Acts 28:25-28)

As usual, the great Apostle had given the Jews the
first opportunity to receive the Gospel from his lips. We are
not informed how many believers were made. At any rate,
the Jews had been given something really to think about,
and when they departed they were warmly debating among
themselves. (Acts 28:29)

The Delay in Paul's Trial.—Following the incidents
with the Jewish leaders, Luke tells us little more concerning
Paul other than this:

> And Paul dwelt two whole years in his own hired house, and
> received all that came in unto him, preaching the kingdom of
> God, and teaching those things which concern the Lord Jesus
> Christ, with all confidence, no man forbidding him. (Acts 28:
> 30-31)

Many scholars have wondered why Luke didn't tell us more about the great Apostle to the Gentiles; they have speculated at some length as to why he didn't give us some details about Paul's "two whole years in his own hired house," not to mention what his intentions were after finishing the Acts. Frankly, we do not know Luke's reasons for doing what he did, other than the fact that he was writing for the benefit of his friend Theophilus. (Acts 1:1) He was not writing especially for our benefit, and, having accomplished his purposes, he finished the Acts presumably as we now have it. Possibly Paul's two years under guard were not especially eventful, but we are concerned as to why he did not come up for trial during such a long period. Day after day the Apostle must have awaited anxiously for word that he would soon be called up for his hearing. (See Phil. 2:23-24; Philem. 22) But even in bonds Paul did not waste his time, for he probably brought many into the Church. Notice what he says about it:

> But I would ye should understand, brethren, that the things
> which happened unto me have fallen out rather unto the fur-
> therance of the gospel; so that my bonds in Christ are manifest
> in all the palace, and in all other places; and many of the breth-
> ren in the Lord, waxing confident by my bonds, are much more
> bold to speak the word without fear. (Phil. 1:12-14; see also
> Philem. 10)

As for the trial itself, it would have to await the whim of Nero or of the Praetorian Prefect. It is not known before whom Paul finally appeared. Nero did not get down to business; in fact, he was a known creature of caprice and impulse. But even allowing for this, the actual preparation for Paul's hearing would take a long time. It is possible that in the great storm and shipwreck Julius had lost many of the necessary papers for the trial. Others would then have to be prepared in Caesarea and sent on to Rome. Paul's accusers would have to come from Palestine, and the personal presence of the prosecutor was required under Roman law. Sir William Ramsay has suggested that the Apostle's opponents, knowing how flimsy their case against him was, would attempt to put off the trial as long as possible.[1] Moreover, a corrupt judge—Felix is a good example—had ways of postponing trials for one reason or another. The accusers could have postponed the trial of Paul for a long time, on the grounds that witnesses had to be brought from all the provinces wherever he had preached, in order to prove the charges of sedition. Even if they couldn't bring about the Apostle's death, they could partially accomplish their vile purposes by preventing him from preaching in public.

Some of Paul's Friends Who Were With Him During His Imprisonment.—Many of Paul's friends who are unknown to us must have visited him during his period of confinement, but of those who are known we call attention to these: Luke, the beloved physician, and esteemed companion (Col. 4:14; Philem. 24); Aristarchus of Macedonia (Col. 4:10; cf. Acts 27:2); Timothy, a favorite disciple (Philem. 1; Col. 1:1; Phil. 1:1); John Mark, with whom Paul seems to have been reconciled (Col. 4:10; cf. 2 Tim. 4:11); Tychicus (Col. 4:7; cf. Acts 20:4); Demas, faithful at the time (Col. 4:14; Philem. 24), but later to fall away (2 Tim. 4:10); Epaphras of Colossae (Col. 1:7); Jesus-Justus (Col. 4:11); and Onesimus, originally a slave of Philemon, a church member of Colossae, who fled to Rome and was converted by Paul. (Philem. 10-11)

These brethren must have been most useful to Paul during his first imprisonment. The Apostle could do much, even though imprisoned, to further the cause of the Church,

[1]*St. Paul the Traveller*, p. 356.

because these men, and doubtless the other unknown brethren by whom he was surrounded, were willing to carry out his orders and assignments. Thus with their help he was enabled to communicate with many branches of the Church, even those at a distance.

Epistles of the First Roman Imprisonment.—There are four letters of Paul's that are known as the *Captivity Epistles,* because the Apostle was in bonds when he wrote them—most probably in Rome. That they were written there (A.D. 61-63) is the traditional view; we shall assume it in this book. They are Ephesians, Philippians, Colossians, and Philemon. The order of these epistles has been a matter of dispute, but there is no doubt that three of them, Colossians, Philemon, and Ephesians, were sent at the same time. Onesimus carried Paul's letter to Philemon (10) and, with Tychicus, that to the Colossians. (4:7-9) Tychicus also bore the letter to the Ephesians. (6:21) Scholars are in disagreement as to whether Philippians was written before or after this group of three.

There is a marked similarity in vocabulary and style in these four epistles. Moreover, their subject matter is quite similar, and in all four the condition of the Apostle is much the same. He says that he is in prison in behalf of the Gentiles. (Col. 1:24; 4:3; Eph. 3:1, 13; Philemon 1, 9-13, 23; Phil. 1:7; 2:17)

For our purposes here we shall assume that Paul wrote these four epistles in this order: Colossians, Ephesians, Philemon, and Philippians.

THE EPISTLE TO THE COLOSSIANS

Some Facts About the Epistle.—That Paul wrote the Epistle to the Colossians before the one to the Ephesians may be deduced from a comparison of certain statements made in each. In Ephesians we read, "But that ye also may know my affairs, and how I do, Tychicus, a beloved brother and faithful minister in the Lord, shall make known to you all things" (6:21); whereas in Colossians we read this: "All my state shall Tychicus declare unto you." (4:7) The phrase "ye also" in Ephesians would seem to presuppose the previous letter to the Colossians.

Colossae was an ancient city located in southwestern Phrygia in the Roman Province of Asia. It was situated on the southern bank of the Lycus River, about one hundred miles as the crow flies east of Ephesus and on the great highway of trade linking the East and the West of the ancient world. It was not far from the towns of Laodicea and Hierapolis. Long before Paul's day, Colossae had been a town of considerable importance, but with the founding and growth of Laodicea, about ten miles west, it had steadily declined from about the middle of the third century B.C. Earthquakes had contributed to the decline of Colossae, not to mention the fame and attractiveness of Hierapolis, which was located about thirteen miles to the northwest. According to the geographer Strabo (died A.D. 24; cf. XII, 8) Colossae was but "a small town," and it was of little commercial importance.

As far as we know, Paul had never visited Colossae, and it is probable that the branch of the Church there had been established by Epaphras, a possible convert of the Apostle's while in Ephesus. (Col. 1:6-8; 4:13) Epaphras was a native of Colossae (4:12) and had doubtless been much aided in his labors by Philemon, also a native of the town and a good friend of Paul's. (Philem. 2-3) Epaphras seems to have been a very active man in carrying the Gospel to his whole district, for the Apostle speaks of him in these words:

> For I bear him record, that he hath a great zeal for you, and them that are in Laodicea, and them in Hierapolis. (Col. 4:13)

Most of the Church members were probably converts from paganism (Col. 1:13, 21; 2:13; 3:6-7), but there may have been a few Jewish members there, too, for it is a known fact (Josephus, *Antiq.*, XII, 3, 4) that Jewish people had been settled in Phrygia and Lydia by Antiochus the Great (223-187 B.C.).

The occasion and purpose of Paul's Epistle to the Colossians is this: during the years of the Apostle's absence from Asia, it appears that certain false teachers had made a distinct impression upon many of the members of the branch in Colossae. We don't know just who these teachers were, nor do we know the details of their doctrines, but it seems possible to gather the main outlines of their errors from the Epistle. (Col. 2:8-23) The heretical teachings are thought by some scholars to be mainly Jewish in origin; others believe that pagan mystery-cults had a part in them, and still others hold that Greek philosophy played a role. At any rate, we may note at least three distinct elements of interest: (1) The Jewish element, in which Paul makes reference to circumcision, meats and drinks, feast days, new moons, and sabbaths (Col. 2:11-16); (2) the ascetic element, as revealed in his reference to ordinances, "touch not; taste not; handle not" (Col. 2:20-23); and (3) the speculative element, as seen in his warning against "philosophy and vain deceit" (Col. 2:8). This latter may have reference to errors of a semignostic type which tended to detract from the dignity of Christ (Col. 2:9; cf. 1:19), and which held that the angels were superior to or at least equal to Him, and that they may act as intermediaries through whom we may have access to God (Col. 2:18-19). These false teachings were given a Christian coloring and foisted upon the saints.

It is probable that Epaphras was alarmed at the situation, and he hastened to Rome to give Paul a full report of what was taking place. Nor was his report completely

one of alarm and apprehension. The charity and faith of
the Colossian saints were such to win Paul's express commendation. (Col. 1:8; 2:5) The report of Epaphras determined the Apostle to write a letter to the Colossians, not
only to encourage them, but also to check the spread of
false doctrine among them. The letter he sends by Tychicus
and Onesimus (Col. 4:7-9), inasmuch as Epaphras, for
some reason which we do not know, could not return at
once. (Col. 4:12; Philem. 23)

Outline of the Epistle.—The Epistle to the Colossians
consists of an introduction, the body of the Epistle with
two sections, and a conclusion.

    I. The introduction (1:1-14).

        A. The greeting of Paul, "an Apostle," and Tim-
othy, to the saints and the believing brethren
at Colossae (1:1-2).

        B. Paul gives thanks to God for the Colossians,
praying for them, because of their faith in
Christ and because of their love toward all the
saints following the preaching of Epaphras,
who informs the Apostle of their love (1:3-8).

        C. The Apostle prays for their spiritual perfection,
so that they may bear fruit in every good work
and increase in the knowledge of God. They
are to thank the Almighty for making them
members of the kingdom of His beloved Son,
in whom they have their redemption through
His blood, even the forgiveness of sins (1:9-14).

   II. Christ's pre-eminence above all creatures, and the
Christian's new life (1:15-4:6).

        A. Christ's pre-eminence above all creatures (1:15
-2:23).

           1. Christ's supremacy as Creator and Re-
deemer (1:15-23).

    a. He is in the image of the Father (1:15a).

    b. He is the first-born of every creature, the creator of all things that are in heaven and earth, visible and invisible. He is before all things, and by Him all things consist (1:15b-17).

    c. He is the head of the Church, the first-born from the dead. It pleased the Father that in Him should all fulness dwell. God purposed through Him to reconcile all things to himself, whether in earth or in heaven (1:18-20).

    d. Through Christ the Colossians have found salvation. If they hold firmly to the faith, the Savior will bring them holy, faultless, and irreproachable to God (1:21-23).

2. Paul's sufferings for the Colossians are a source of joy to him, for his afflictions help the Church make its contribution toward Christ's sufferings. God has given Paul a responsibility to make known the long-hidden mystery that Gentiles [as well as Jews] may be members of the Church of Christ and become heirs of heavenly glory. The Apostle's endeavor and teaching was to present every man perfect in Christ Jesus. The end and purpose of his labors, through the power of Christ, was to render every man perfect in Christ. Paul wants the Colossians to know of his strenuous struggles for their welfare and that of the Laodiceans. He desires to cheer their hearts and have them welded together in love and advancing towards an abounding

wealth of understanding—to the knowledge of the secret of God. In Him are all the
treasures of wisdom and knowledge stored
up, hidden from view (1:24-2:3).

3. The Colossians are warned against false
teachers (2:4-23).

   a. What Paul had said just previously was
to put them on guard against any one's
plausible sophistry. He is delighted with
the good discipline of the Colossians
and the solid front presented by their
faith in Christ. Inasmuch as they have
received the Christ, Paul wants them
to live and act in vital union with Him.
Rooted and built up in Him and confirmed in the faith, they are to over-
flow with thanks (2:4-7).

   b. The Colossians are warned not to be
cheated by philosophy and empty de-
ceitfulness, following human tradition
and the world's elementary (crude) notions, instead of Christ. In Him dwells
the fulness of the Godhead bodily. They
can find in Him all they need for their
salvation and perfection. He is the head
of all principalities and authority. [He
is therefore over all angels.] In Him
they have received the real, spiritual
circumcision by which they have thrown
off their sinful nature; they have been
buried with Christ in baptism, and
raised with Him through faith produced by God, who raised Him from
the dead. Christ has given them life
with Him, having forgiven their trans-

gressions. [In this Paul implies that physical circumcision is unnecessary.] The
Savior, through His death on the cross,
has blotted out Satan's decrees against
men, by making possible an atonement
for sin and transgressions (2:8-15).

4. The Colossians are warned to avoid Jewish observances under the Law of Moses,
the superstitious worship of angels, and
false asceticism. Obedience to outward
rules is of little value in combating the
indulgence of our lower natures (2:16-23).

B. The Christian's new life (3:1-4:6).

1. The Colossians are to exhibit a newness of
life in union with Christ (3:1-17).

a. If they have risen with Christ, they are
to seek for things above, not for earthly
things. They have died [through baptism to earthly things], and their lives
are hidden with Christ in God. When
Christ appears—their true life—they
will appear with Him in glory (3:1-4).

b. Their newness of life means a complete
break with sins common to the pagan
world; fornication, impurity, sensuality,
evil desire, and greediness. They are to
rid themselves of every kind of sin:
anger, bad temper, malice, slander,
foul language, and the like. They are
not to lie, for they have stripped off the
old self with its doings and have clothed
themselves with the new self. In their
new state of regeneration the old dis-
tinctions between races and conditions

of men are wiped out, all being united in Christ (3:5-11).

    c. Their newness of life requires them to manifest by their actions those Christian virtues in keeping with their privileged state, particularly charity (the pure love of Christ), which is the bond of perfection. They are to clothe themselves with tender-heartedness, kindness, lowliness of mind, meekness and long suffering; bearing with one another, and forgiving each other. Over all of these is charity, the love spoken of above. The word of Christ is to remain as a rich treasure of their hearts, and whatever they do, in word or deed, is to be done in the name of the Lord Jesus. Through Him thanks is to be given to the Father (3:12-17).

2. The admonition of Paul concerning domestic life (3:18-4:1).

    a. Wives are to be submissive to their husbands, as is fitting in the Lord. Husbands are to love their wives, and not be resentful or bitter toward them (3:18-19).

    b. Children are to be obedient to their parents in everything; for this is pleasing to the Lord. Fathers are not to fret or irritate their children, so as to make them lose heart or become despondent (3:20-21).

    c. Slaves are to be obedient to their secular masters in every way, not as menpleasers, but with simplicity of purpose, because they fear the Lord. Their hearts are to be in their work, for from the Lord they will receive the inheritance as their reward. Masters are to deal justly and equitably with their slaves, knowing that they too have a Master in heaven (3:22-4:1).

3. The Colossians are urged to continue stead-fastly in prayer, being intent on it and in giving thanks. Paul requests prayers in his behalf, that the Lord may open a door for his preaching of Christ, for whose sake he is in bonds. They are to be prudent and discreet in dealing with outsiders, making the best use of their opportunities. Their speech is to be gracious and so well reasoned out that they may know how to give every man a fitting answer (4:2-6).

III. The conclusion (4:7-18).

A. Tychicus, Paul's loved assistant and fellow servant, will convey to the Colossians all necessary information about him and his welfare. He will also cheer their hearts; and with him the Apostle will send Onesimus [slave of Philemon, whom Paul converted at Rome], "faithful and beloved brother." The two of them will inform the brethren of everything going on where Paul is (4:7-9).

B. He conveys greetings from Aristarchus (fellow prisoner), Mark, Jesus, called Justus, Epaphras (fellow Colossian, who has deep interest in them and the brethren at Laodicea and Hierapolis), Luke, and Demas (4:10-14).

C. Paul sends greetings to the brethren at Laodicea, especially to Nymphas, at whose home
the branch meets. When this letter has been
read by the Colossians, it is to be read by the
Laodiceans. The epistle to the Laodiceans is
to be read, in turn, by the Colossians. Archippus [probably the son of Philemon (Philem.
2)] was to be told to discharge carefully his
duties as a servant of the Lord (4:15-17).

D. Paul adds his final greeting to his own handwriting. He asks the brethren to remember his
bonds (4:18).

The Authenticity of the Epistle to the Colossians.—
The ancients were practically unanimous in favor of the
Epistle as being Paul's. Most New Testament scholars accept
it as being genuine. The external evidence is very strong.
The Muratorian Fragment expressly attributes it to Paul,
and it was quoted by Irenaeus, Justin Martyr, Clement of
Alexandria, Origen, and Tertullian. The early versions,
such as the Itala and the Peshitto, contain it. It is also to
be found in the earliest collections of Paul's Epistles. The
heretics of the second century, such as Marcion, Valentine,
and the Docetae, quoted it as Scripture. Allusions to it are
to be found in Clement of Rome, Barnabas, Ignatius of
Antioch, Polycarp, Theophilus of Antioch, and in Justin
Martyr.

The internal evidence in favor of the authenticity of
the Epistle is also very strong. There are linguistic peculiarities in the Epistles, to be sure, but they are in accordance
with the nature of the subject matter treated. The style
and doctrine are certainly Paul's. The style differs somewhat from that of his earlier epistles in that his sentences
are longer and more involved, the movement of thought
is slower, and the tone is loftier; but the difference in subject
matter and the lack of urgency resulting from the absence

of any personal opponent probably explain the stylistic differences. The doctrine expounded by the Apostle is in perfect agreement with that which we find in his other Epistles.

PAUL'S EPISTLE TO THE EPHESIANS

Some Facts About the Epistle.—In our discussion of Paul's Third Missionary Journey, we have already emphasized the importance of the city of Ephesus, which was located on the Cayster River and which was the sea terminal of the great highway of trade between the East and the West. The capital of Proconsular Asia, Ephesus under Roman rule was indeed one of the most important cities of ancient times.

It was probably about A.D. 62 when Paul wrote his Epistle to the Ephesians, along with that to the Colossians and Philemon—the three were sent together, it will be remembered. Offhand, it would seem quite natural for Paul to write a letter to the Ephesian saints, inasmuch as Tychicus and Onesimus, the bearers of the other two letters, would probably land at the port of Ephesus before proceeding overland to Colossae. But it has been difficult for scholars to decide for whom the letter was intended. In favor of the traditional opinion that it was to the saints at Ephesus are these facts: (1) most MSS. containing Paul's Epistles have the reading "at Ephesus." in 1:1; (2) the title "to the Ephesians" is given to the Epistle by practically every known MS.; (3) the most ancient versions, dating to the middle of the second century, which have following the MSS. the reading "at Ephesus" in 1:1, seem to indicate that this reading was already old when they were produced; (4) the Muratorian Fragment, Clement of Alexandria, Irenaeus in Gaul, and Tertullian in Africa give their support on the authority of tradition, not on the evidence of MSS.

Against the traditional opinion we have these facts: (1) Codexes Vaticanus and Sinaiticus and some lesser MSS. omit "at Ephesus" in 1:1; (2) Marcion the heretic (middle of second century) said the letter was sent to the Laodiceans and, since he had no particular axe to grind on this score, may have reflected the reading of some ancient codex; (3) Tertullian, in his argument against Marcion for the Ephesian destination, seems to have used MSS. which made no reference to the words "at Ephesus" in 1:1; (4) Origen and St. Basil seem to have used MSS. in which the phrase "at Ephesus" was missing, and St. Jerome explicitly states that these words are absent in some MSS.

In addition, this evidence of an internal nature is urged against the traditional view: (1) the lack of personal greetings of any kind, so unlike Paul and so hard to understand if he was writing to Ephesus where he had so many friends; (2) the formal and distant tone of the letter, not to mention the absences of terms of familiarity and endearment; (3) the fact that Paul seems to be personally unknown to his readers (1:15; 3:2-3; 4:20-21), a fact hard to reconcile if he was addressing readers at Ephesus only.

In view of these arguments against the traditional opinion, many authorities maintain that the Epistle was a circular letter addressed, not only to the saints in Ephesus, but (Colossae excluded) to many branches of the Church in Asia, including Laodicea. In this way they can accept the traditional views as to who were the recipients of the letter and at the same time give a plausible reason for its formal and distant tone and its lack of special greetings.

A few scholars have adopted the view of Marcion, that the Epistle was addressed to the Laodiceans. And Colossians 4:16 indicates that Paul wrote such a letter.

In this book we shall hold to the traditional opinion respecting the destination of the Epistle. It is not without difficulties, but it seems to be supported by the prophet Joseph Smith in the "Inspired" revision of the Bible.

It is possible that Epaphras, in his report to Paul concerning the Colossians (1:7-8), may have also reported on what he knew about the branch of the Church in Ephesus. What the report consisted of we do not know exactly, but it seems clear that some difficulties in the branch prompted the letter, as well as the mere fact that Tychicus would probably pass through Ephesus. Ephesians seems to follow the same general line of argument as the Epistle to the Colossians, but with the difference that it does so with less passion and with a greater intellectual and spiritual grasp. Chapters 1-3 of Ephesians have been pronounced by some writers as the most profound passage in all Christian literature.[2] In the Epistle Paul stresses the unity of the Church, which its members are not to imperil by sin or possible errors.

Outline of the Epistle.—The Epistle to the Ephesians contains an introduction, a body with two sections, and a conclusion.

    I. The introduction: Greeting of Paul, an Apostle of Jesus Christ (1:1-2).

   II. Paul's praise to God for blessings bestowed on the world through Christ, and the character of Christian life (1:3-6:20).

      A. Paul's praise to God for blessings bestowed on the world through Christ (1:3-3:21).

         1. Praise for blessings which we receive through Christ (1:3-14).

           a. Before the foundation of the world, God foreordained us for adoption to Himself through Jesus Christ, and we were to be holy and without blame before him in love (1:3-6).

[2]See A. T. Robertson, *Epochs in the Life of Paul*, p. 287.

    b. Through Christ's blood we have redemption and forgiveness of sins, according to His grace. He has made known to us the mystery that in the dispensation of the fulness of times He will gather together in one all things in Christ, in whom we have obtained an inheritance. We are foreordained according to His purpose that we should be to the praise of His glory. In Him, says Paul, the Ephesians also trusted, after hearing the gospel of their salvation (1:7-13 a).

    c. The Holy Spirit of promise is the pledge or security of our final blessedness or eternal inheritance (1:13b-14).

  2. The Church is a unity with Christ (1:15-2:22).

    a. Having heard of the faith of the Ephesians, Paul gives thanks for them, praying that God may give them wisdom and revelation in the knowledge of Him; the eyes of their understanding being enlightened, that they may know the hope of His calling, the wealth of the glory of His inheritance in the saints, and the transcendent greatness of His power in those who believe as seen in the working of His infinite might (1:15-19).

    b. The great power of God was manifested in raising Christ from the dead and in setting him above all things including the Church, which is His body (1:20-23).

    c. Through God's grace the faithful have been quickened (who were dead in trespasses and sins, according to the prince of the power of the air) and are saved through faith in Christ. Men are His workmanship, created in Christ Jesus unto good works, in which God has ordained that they should walk (2:1-10).

    d. The Ephesians, who are Gentiles, have become heirs through Christ to the same blessings as the commonwealth of Israel. Through the cross both Jews and Gentiles have been reconciled to God and have access by one Spirit unto the Father. They are no longer strangers and foreigners, but are fellow-citizens with the saints and the household of God, being built upon the foundation of the apostles and prophets, with Jesus Christ himself the chief cornerstone. Thus they belong to the spiritual temple of God (2:11-22).

3. The Gospel plan is extended to the Gentiles through Paul's preaching (3:1-21).

    a. Through revelation the mystery that Jews and Gentiles should be a unity in the Church was made known to Paul. In past ages this was not made known to men as it now is to apostles and prophets by the Spirit (3:1-6).

    b. To the Apostle was grace given by God to announce this mystery to the Gentiles, the unsearchable riches of Christ (3:7-13).

    c. Paul beseeches God that the Ephesians might be strengthened by His Spirit with power in their inner selves; that Christ might dwell in their hearts by faith; that being grounded in love they might be able with all saints to comprehend the breadth, depth, length, and height of Christ's love, which surpasses knowledge; that they might be filled with all the fulness of God. The Apostle ascribes praise to God through Christ (3:14-21).

B. The character of Christian life (4:1-6:20).

    1. Paul exhorts the Ephesians to preserve, by lowliness and meekness and loving forbearance, the spirit of unity given them by the Holy Ghost. There is but one Spirit, one Lord, one faith, one baptism, one God and Father of all. Everyone is given grace according to the measure of the gift of Christ. He "led captivity captive" and gave gifts to men. (Ps. 68:18) He placed various officers in the Church such as apostles, prophets, evangelists, pastors and teachers, in order to perfect the saints, to work in the ministry, and edify the body (Church) of Christ. These officers will remain until the saints, in the unity of the faith, all come to the knowledge of the Son of God, unto a perfect man, unto the measure of the stature of the fulness of Christ. (See "Inspired" revision.) Henceforth they will no longer be children tossed to and fro by every wind of doctrine or by man's craftiness, but will grow in perfection

to resemble Christ in all things. The Church will grow and increase as it is united to Christ in love (4:1-16).

2. The Ephesians are to renounce and put away the Gentile vices which they followed through ignorance and put on the new man, that better self that is created in God's likeness in genuine righteousness and holiness (4:17-24).

3. The Apostle shows in a practical way how they are to put on the new man; he lists the vices and sins by which the Holy Spirit is grieved and which are to be avoided, and the Christian virtues which are to be practiced (4:25-5:20).

4. Paul's admonitions concerning domestic life (5:21-6:9).

   a. The Ephesians are to submit themselves one to another in the fear of the Lord. Wives are to submit themselves unto their husbands, as unto the Lord, for the husband is the head of the wife, even as Christ is head of the Church. Husbands are to love their wives, even as Christ loved the Church and gave Himself for it; that He might sanctify and cleanse it with the washing of water by the word, that He might present it to Himself without spot, wrinkle, or blemish. So ought men to love their wives as their own bodies. He that loves his wife loves himself. Each man is to love his own wife, and a married woman is to treat her husband with respect (5:21-23).

    b. Children are to be obedient unto their parents. Paul quotes Exo. 20:12. Fathers are not to provoke their children, but are to bring them up tenderly in the discipline and admonition of the Lord (6:1-4).

    c. Slaves are to be obedient to their earthly masters, and be eager to please them. Whatever right thing any one does will be reciprocated by the Lord, whether he be a slave or a free man. Masters are to act toward their slaves on the same principles and refrain from threats. For they know that in heaven there is One who is their Master; neither is there respect of persons with Him. (6:5-9).

  5. The Apostle admonishes the Ephesians to be prepared for the warfare which must be waged against the enemies of their salvation. They are to put on the complete armor of God, so as to stand firm against all the stratagems of the devil. They are to be able to stand their ground on the evil day, and, having fought to the end, to remain victors on the field. They are to pray unceasingly on behalf of all the saints and ask, also, that Paul may be given words to make known with boldness the mystery of the Gospel, for which he is an ambassador in chains (6:10-20).

III. The conclusion (6:21-24).

  A. The beloved and faithful Tychicus will inform Paul's readers concerning all that is happening to the Apostle. He is sent for the very purpose of informing and encouraging them (6: 21-22).

B. The Apostle sends his farewell blessing of peace, and love combined with faith, to the saints (6:23-24).

The Authenticity of the Epistle to the Ephesians.— Paul's Epistle to the Ephesians was not too well known and circulated by the end of the first century, but by the end of the second century it was widely known, and it was always ascribed to the Apostle. Irenaeus makes explicit and repeated reference to the Epistle. The Muratorian Fragment includes Ephesus as one of the Church branches to which Paul wrote letters. Tertullian, Clement of Alexandria, Origen, and Basil are equally explicit in making reference to Paul's authorship. Eusebius, the church historian, includes the Epistle as among those which were accepted without hesitation as being sacred. Ignatius Martyr, Polycarp, Tatian, Clement of Rome, The Teaching of the Twelve Apostles, the Epistle of Barnabas, Ignatius of Antioch, the Shepherd of Hermas, Pseudo-Clement, and Justin all indicate that Ephesians was known in early times.

Even the early heretics such as Marcion, Valentine, Basilides, and Theodotus recognized Paul's authorship of the Epistle.

But in spite of the evidence from early times, many modern scholars deny the authenticity of Ephesians. Their chief objections to Paul's authorship are based chiefly on internal evidence such as its vocabulary and style, its doctrine, and its similarity to Colossians.

Let us look for a moment at the argument based on vocabulary and style. If it be objected that Ephesians contains about forty unusual Greek words found nowhere else in the New Testament, attention is called to the fact that such peculiarities are found more or less in all of Paul's

Epistles, and about as frequently in those whose authenticity is admitted by the critics as in the others. It is alleged
by the critics that the style of Ephesians is "dull and
sluggish," containing long and involved sentences; that it
is "overtaxed with phrases, clauses, synonyms ,and quali-
fying epithets; and that it is lacking in the sharpness, vigor,
and overpowering eloquence so characteristic of St. Paul."[3]
To this criticism of style it may be pointed out that long and
involved sentences may also be found in both Romans and
Colossians; they are not peculiar to Ephesians. Moreover,
it is unsound criticism to assume that an author's style
must be uniform through the years. In the Epistle to the
Ephesians the style perhaps varies from that of his other
epistles, because he is dealing not with controversial matters
but with universal ideas, and so adapts his style to suit the
sublime theme which he is treating. And further, a consideration of the time, place, and conditions under which
Paul wrote the Epistle, as well as the circumstances of the
Ephesians to whom it was addressed, helps us to understand its peculiarities of style.

The critics have said that Ephesians presents entirely
new doctrines or that the doctrine of the Epistle is un-
Pauline. The author has to dissent from the conclusions of
the critics in this respect. In fact, many scholars dissent.[4]
They cannot agree that the doctrine concerning God, the
angels, and the universal Church set forth in this Epistle
differs substantially from that which Paul expounded in his
other Epistles. And in the Epistle we meet certain of the
Apostle's familiar themes found in his other writings—for
example, justification (i.e., new creation) in Christ through
faith without the works of the Law (Eph. 2:8 ff.), the
universality of salvation (Eph. 2:1 ff.), and the necessity of

[3]See Callan, *The Epistles of St. Paul*, II, 14. By permission of Joseph F. Wagner (Inc.),
Publisher, New York.
[4]See, e.g., Steinmueller, *A Companion to Scripture Studies*, III, 320; Henshaw, *New Testament
Literature*, p. 305.

grace. (Eph. 2:5, 7, 10) In view of the disagreement of men on the subject of doctrine in the Epistle, it is difficult to see how doctrinal matters can be used in any decisive way to prove that Paul didn't write the Epistle.

The critics have held that there are similarities so many and striking between Ephesians and Colossians that they are forced to conclude that some author other than Paul imitated and enlarged upon Colossians. But are the critics justified in such a course? Most of us will agree that the resemblances between the two Epistles are many and striking. But such similarities are to be expected in letters written by the Apostle at about the same time to two branches of the Church in the same general area and in practically the same spiritual environment. And though we grant many striking resemblances between the two Epistles, we call attention to some notable differences. Whereas Colossians is personal, concrete, and polemic, Ephesians is impersonal, general, calm and poetical. Colossians stresses Christ's pre-eminence, whereas Ephesians is didactic, dealing with and emphasizing the greatness and sublimity of universal salvation in Christ. Callan thinks of Ephesians as the ecclesiastical Epistle, treating of the relation between Christ and the Church.[5] He also points to the fact that Ephesians makes references to the Holy Ghost, whereas there is only one in Colossians; Ephesians has nine quotations from the Old Testament, but none are found in Colossians.

In view of the over-all evidence, there is no compelling reason for rejecting the traditional view that Paul wrote the Epistle to the Ephesians.

[5]Op. cit., p. 14.

Chapter 20

PAUL'S FIRST ROMAN IMPRISONMENT
(Concluded)

THE EPISTLE TO PHILEMON

Some Facts About the Epistle.—The Epistle to Philemon is one of Paul's most interesting and beautiful letters. During the Apostle's imprisonment in Rome, a runaway slave by the name of Onesimus ("useful," "profitable") somehow got in touch with Paul there and was converted by him to the Church. (Philem. 10-11) It so happened that Onesimus had belonged to Philemon, a well-to-do resident of Colossae and friend of Paul's. Philemon was a member of the Church and owed his conversion to Paul. (Philem. 19) It is probable that Philemon had been converted during the Apostle's long residence in Ephesus, and it may have been while visiting in that metropolis that Onesimus, his slave, had first met Paul. At any rate, Onesimus ran away from his master, perhaps after stealing from him. (Philem. 18) He eventually found his way to Rome, where there was a large population and where there was a good chance that he would never be identified. Just what the situation was that caused him to seek out Paul no one knows, but the Apostle was not averse to winning a slave to the service of the Master. He thought so much of Onesimus that he would gladly have retained him for Church service in Rome (Philem. 10, 13), but facing him was the grim fact that the new convert was a slave. He was the property of his friend Philemon, and under the customs of the time death was commonly meted out to a runaway slave. It is a well-known fact that slavery was one of the worst curses in ancient times.

One scholar has estimated that there were at least 60,000,000 slaves in the Roman Empire. In those days a slave was completely at the mercy of his owner; for trivial offenses he could be cruelly whipped, crucified, or even thrown to wild beasts. Christianity was, of course, against slavery, but Paul as well as the other Apostles had to make the best of an evil situation. Had they opposed it openly, the Church would have been destroyed in short order. Under the circumstances Paul was content to advise both slaves and masters to be kind and considerate to each other. (Eph. 6:5-9; Col. 3:22-4:1) The Apostle did not deal with the problem of slavery in his Epistle to Philemon, but realizing that the first duty of Onesimus was to his master, he sent him back to Colossae with a note—the Epistle is hardly more than that—urging with tact and delicate humor that Philemon take him back not merely as a slave, but as "a brother beloved." (Philem. 16) Paul asks that Philemon receive Onesimus "as myself," (Philem. 17) and requests that if his former slave has wronged him or owes him anything, to charge it to his (Paul's) account. (Philem. 18) And in verse 21 the Apostle even hints at the emancipation of Onesimus.

Throughout the letter, Paul addresses Philemon as his dear and intimate friend (Philem. 13, 17, 22) and fellow worker. (Philem. 1) Greetings are sent not only from the Apostle but also from Timothy and are directed to Apphia, Archippus, and the Church members at Colossae as well as to Philemon. (Philem. 1-2) Apphia is supposed to be Philemon's wife, and Archippus is generally regarded as his son. According to Colossians 4:17, Archippus was advised to take heed to his ministry in the Church.

There is an ancient tradition to the effect that Philemon became Bishop of Colossae and, during the Neronian persecution, was martyred there in company with Apphia, Archippus, and Onesimus.

Armed with the letter, Onesimus went back to his master Philemon at Colossae accompanied, as we have learned previously, by Tychicus. The date, we repeat, was about A.D. 62.

An Outline of the Epistle.—The Epistle may be divided into an introduction, the body of the letter, and a conclusion. Because of the brevity of the Epistle, we shall quote its entire text in the outline.

I. The introduction (1-7).

A. The address and greeting from Paul and Timothy.

> Paul, a prisoner of Jesus Christ, and Timothy our brother, unto Philemon our dearly beloved, and fellow laborer, and to our beloved Apphia and Archippus our fellow soldier, and to the church in thy house: grace to you, and peace, from God our Father and the Lord Jesus Christ (1-3).

B. Paul gives thanks for Philemon's love and faith.

> I thank my God, making mention of thee always in my prayers, hearing of thy love and faith, which thou hast toward the Lord Jesus, and toward all saints; that the communication of thy faith may become effectual by the acknowledging of every good thing which is in you in Christ Jesus. For we have great joy and consolation in thy love, because the bowels of the saints are refreshed by thee, brother (4-7).

II. The body of the Epistle (8-22).

A. Paul entreats in behalf of Onesimus, his converted slave friend.

Wherefore, though I might be much bold in Christ to enjoin thee that which is convenient, yet for love's sake I rather beseech thee, being such an one as Paul the aged, and now also a prisoner of Jesus Christ. I beseech thee for my son Onesimus, whom I have begotten in my bonds: which in times past was to thee unprofitable, but now profitable to thee and to me: whom I have sent again: thou therefore receive him, that is, mine own bowels: whom I would have retained with me, that in thy stead he might have ministered unto me in the bonds of the gospel: but without thy mind would I do nothing; that thy benefit should not be as it were of necessity, but willingly. For perhaps he therefore departed for a season, that thou shouldest receive him for ever; not now as a servant, but above a servant, a brother beloved, specially to me, but how much more unto thee, both in the flesh, and in the Lord? If thou count me therefore a partner, receive him as myself (8-17).

B. Philemon is assured by Paul that his friendly reception of Onesimus will be pleasing to him. The Apostle hopes that he may be permitted to visit Colossae at some future time.

If he hath wronged thee, or oweth thee ought, put that on mine account; I Paul have written it with mine own hand, I will repay it: albeit I do not say to thee how thou owest unto me

even thine own self besides. Yea, brother, let me have joy of thee in the Lord;
refresh my bowels in the Lord. Having
confidence in thy obedience I wrote
unto thee, knowing that thou wilt also
do more than I say. But withal prepare
me also a lodging: for I trust that
through your prayers I shall be given
unto you (18-22).

III. The conclusion: The Apostle sends greetings from
brethren with him, and he includes a blessing.

There salute thee Epaphras, my fellow-
prisoner in Christ Jesus; Marcus, Aristarchus, Demas, Lucas, my fellowlabor-
ers. The grace of our Lord Jesus Christ
be with your spirit. Amen (23-25).

The Authenticity of the Epistle to Philemon.—In
spite of the fact that the Epistle is brief, personal, and non-
doctrinal in character, thus precluding any extensive quotation from it by the Apostolic Fathers, the external evidence in favor of its authenticity is so strong as hardly to
be questioned. The Epistle is found not only in the Muratorian Fragment, but also in the Syriac and Old Latin Versions. Ignatius seems to allude to it. Tertullian knew it, as
did Origen, Eusebius, St. Jerome and Chrysostom. The
heretic Marcion included it in his Canon; it is also found
in the oldest collections of the Epistles of Paul.

The internal evidence is such that few scholars have
ever questioned the authenticity of the Epistle on that score.
The style and spirit of the letter are so characteristic of Paul
that it is universally acknowledged to be the Apostle's work.

PAUL'S EPISTLE TO THE PHILIPPIANS

Some Background to the Epistle.—In this book, as
we have earlier pointed out, it will be assumed that Paul's

Epistle to the Philippians was the last written during his First Roman Imprisonment. We may date it about A.D. 63.

In Chapter 8 we discussed briefly the city of Philippi, in which Paul first labored during his European ministry. Situated in Eastern Macedonia at the foot of Mount Pangaeus and between the Nestus and Strymon rivers, it was a prosperous trading center because of its location on the famous Egnatian Road, which linked the Aegean and Adriatic Seas. The Apostle seemed to have a special affection for the converts he made in this city, and they readily reciprocated it. The trust which Paul had in the Philippian saints is shown in the fact that he on several occasions allowed them to send him gifts of money (2 Cor. 8:9; Phil. 4:15, 16, 18), although it was usual for him to make his own way through tent-making.

It was one of these gifts from the Philippians during his imprisonment which caused the Apostle to write the Epistle. Knowing that Paul was in prison and presumably in need of funds, the thoughtful Philippians sent him a gift of money by the hand of Epaphroditus, one of their number. (Phil. 2:25; 4:14-18) It was their apparent intention that Epaphroditus should not only deliver the money, but stay and assist Paul in whatever way that he could. In his characteristic manner, the Apostle calls him "my brother, and companion in labor, and fellow-soldier, but your messenger, and he that ministered to my wants." (Phil. 2:25) Epaphroditus administered to Paul's needs with zeal and devotion, but his health failed and he became very ill—indeed, "nigh unto death." (Phil. 2:27) Through the Lord's mercy his life was spared, lest Paul "should have sorrow upon sorrow." *(Ibid.)* When he recovered, Epaphroditus grew homesick and "was full of heaviness" because his friends in Philippi had heard that he had been sick. (Phil. 2:26) Paul thereupon allowed him to return to his home and at the same time seized upon the opportunity to send his friends a letter by him. In it the Apostle thanked the Philippians for their kindness, commended Epaphroditus for his devoted service, and exhorted them to receive him with joy and honor. (Phil. 2:26-30)

Epaphroditus may have reported to Paul, when he first arrived in Rome, that there was some tendency to disunion in the branch at Philippi, that some members were pessimistic about the future in view of the Apostle's imprisonment, and that the Judaizers and Libertines were stirring up trouble. It is possible that Paul had received a letter about these and other facts at a more recent time (Phil. 1:12, 19, 25, 26; 3:2; 4:10-13) and so was also using this letter to counsel the Philippians in these matters and to encourage them. He tells them that their difficulties will pass by if they live their religion and carry out in their lives the teachings of Christ. His watchword in the Epistle is "joy." However difficult their task may be, the Philippians are not to give way to despair. They are to meet and solve their hardships bravely, with stout hearts. In this joyful vein, Paul closes his exhortation: "Rejoice in the Lord alway: and again I say, Rejoice." (Phil. 4:4)

In the Epistle, Paul seems to express faith that his trial will result in his acquittal and consequent ability to visit them shortly. (Phil. 1:25-26) Timothy was with him at the time of writing.

An Outline of the Epistle.—The Epistle is not very orderly but may be divided into the introduction, the body of the Epistle, and the conclusion.

    I. The introduction (1:1-11).

        A. Paul and Timothy, "the servants of Jesus Christ," greet the Philippian saints, bishops, and deacons (1:1-2).

        B. The Apostle expresses his thankfulness and joy to God for the cooperation of the Philippians in spreading the gospel. He has them in his heart, inasmuch as in his bonds, and in the defense and confirmation of the gospel, they are all partakers of his grace. He yearns for them with the tender affection of Christ (1:3-8).

C. Paul prays that their love may grow richer in knowledge and discernment, that they may approve (test) better things and be uncontaminated and without offense unto the day of Christ (judgment). They are to be filled with the fruit of divine righteousness to the glory and praise of God (1:9-11).

II. The body of the Epistle (1:12-49).

A. The Apostle gives personal news concerning his imprisonment (1:12-26).

1. He assures his readers that what he has gone through has not hindered but has furthered the Gospel cause. Among the imperial guard and everybody else it has become well known that he is a prisoner for the sake of Christ. The brethren, now made confident, declare God's word more fearlessly than ever. Some preach Christ out of envy, but others from good will; the first do so to add difficulties to Paul, the latter because of love for him. In any case, it doesn't matter as long as Christ is preached. The prayers of the saints and the supply of the Spirit will contribute also to the salvation of Paul (1:12-20).

2. Paul describes his dilemma. His own desire is to depart (die) and be with Christ, but for the sake of the saints it is more impor-

tant, despite the extra labor which a longer life on earth will entail, that he still remain in the body. He is convinced that he will remain to work side by side with them and promote their advancement and joy in the faith (1:21-26).

B. The Apostle exhorts the Philippians to unity and faithfulness (1:27-2:18).

1. Paul urges the Church members to conduct themselves as becomes followers of Christ, standing firm in one spirit and one mind, striving together for the faith of the Gospel (1:27-30).

2. He pleads with them to make his joy complete by being of one mind, never acting for their own private ends or from vanity, but with due consideration for their neighbors. They are to let the very spirit which was in Christ be in them also. Though He had the nature of God, He humbled Himself and took on the nature of a bondservant by becoming a man, and became obedient to death, even the death of the cross. Wherefore God has highly exalted Him, and has given Him a name above all others. The Philippians are, therefore, to "work out their own salvation with fear and trembling," (Phil. 2:12) doing all things without a grumbling and contentious spirit. They are to be blameless and without spot in the midst of a crooked and perverted generation. It will then be Paul's glory, on the day of Christ, that he will not have run his race in vain, neither will he have labored in vain. Even if his life is

sacrificed upon the service of their faith, he will joy and rejoice with them all. (2:1-18).

C. Paul hopes to send Timothy to Philippi shortly after the departure of Epaphroditus (2:19-30).

   1. The Apostle is sending Timothy to the Philippians before long, in order that Paul, in turn, may receive news of them. Paul reminds the saints of Timothy's approved worth. The Apostle himself has hopes of coming to them before long (2:19-24).

   2. Paul is sending Epaphroditus, their messenger, and his brother and companion in labor. Epaphroditus longs for his friends at home and is distressed because they have heard of his illness. He was sick nigh unto death, but God had pity upon him and Paul, who would have had extreme sorrow if he had died. The Philippians are to receive him with joy and honor, because it was for the sake of Christ's work that he so nearly died (2:25-30).

D. The Philippians are warned to beware of false teachers (3:1-4:1).

   1. Paul advises the Philippians to be joyful in the Lord, but warns them to beware of the "dogs," evil workers (probably the Judaizers), whose conduct would destroy Christ's work. Their notion of circumcision was false, because it consisted of mere physical mutilation and was devoid of spirituality. The saints are the true circumcision, because they worship God in spirit and rejoice in Christ and have no confidence in purely external ceremonies. If there were any merit

in such, he could claim a right to trust in them because he could boast of an unusual Jewish background (3:1-6).

2. The Apostle gave up the advantages of his Jewish background and reckoned it a loss for Christ's sake. He suffered the loss of all things and reckoned it refuse in order to win the righteousness which is of God through faith. Paul desired to know Christ and the power of His resurrection, share in His sufferings, and attain to the resurrection of the just. The Apostle did not claim to have attained this knowledge or to have gained perfection. His ultimate aim was to press toward the goal for the prize of the high calling of God in Christ Jesus (3:7-16).

3. Paul urges the brethren to imitate him, and not to follow the example of enemies of the cross of Christ. Their end is destruction, their belly is their god, their glory is in their shame, and they are devoted to earthly things. He advises the brethren to stand firm in the Lord (3:17-4:1).

E. Euodia and Syntyche are urged by Paul to reconcile their differences as sisters in Christ should. He begs his true yokefellow, possibly Epaphroditus, to help these women who labored with him (Paul) in the Gospel (4:2-3).

F. Paul urges the Philippians to rejoice, show a forbearing spirit to everyone, and not worry. They are to lay their troubles before the Lord with prayer, pleading, and thanksgiving. So the peace of God, which passes all understanding, will keep their hearts and minds through

Christ Jesus. He advises the brethren to think of whatsoever things are true, honest, just, pure, lovely, of good report, or praiseworthy. (Cf. Article of Faith No. 13.) The Apostle admonishes them to do what they have learned, received, heard, and have seen him do. Then the God of peace will be with them (4:4-9).

III. The conclusion (4:10-23).

    A. Paul thanks the Philippians for their thoughtfulness in providing him with gifts. He does not refer to this because he fears privation, for he has learned to be content whatever his circumstances may be. They are to be praised for sharing his troubles. He is now, thanks to them, fully supplied. The gifts they sent by Epaphroditus are a sweet odor, an acceptable sacrifice, well pleasing to God (4:10-19).

    B. The Apostle's doxology (4:20).

    C. Paul and the brethren with him send their greetings. The Roman saints, especially those of Caesar's court, extend their salutations. Paul closes with a farewell benediction (4:21-23).

The Authenticity and Integrity of the Epistle to the Philippians.—The evidence of antiquity is unanimous in attesting the authenticity and integrity of the Epistle to the Philippians. And, in fact, most modern scholars are also agreed in these matters.

The external evidence shows direct references to Paul's authorship of the Letter in the Muratorian Fragment, Tertullian, Irenaeus, and Clement of Alexandria. The Epistle is included in the Old Latin and Peshitta-Syriac Versions, and even the heretics Marcion, Theodotus, and Valentine make use of it. Indirect references or allusions to the Epistle will be found in Ignatius of Antioch, Polycarp, Clement of Rome, the *Shepherd of Hermas*, the Epistle to the Church of Lyons, and the Martyrdom of St. Polycarp.

The internal evidence amply confirms Paul's authorship of the Epistle. The language and style are characteristic of the Apostle. There are about forty unusual words in the Epistle which are not found in Paul's other Epistles; but this fact proves nothing, since the same phenomenon is found in letters of the Apostle whose authenticity is not questioned.

Only in modern times has the authenticity and integrity of the Epistle been questioned; in the nineteenth century Baur and some other rationalists denied that Paul wrote the Epistle. Some few critics denied the unity of the Letter, asserting that it is a combination of two original documents which were written by Paul at different times and then brought together or fused by some editor after the Apostle's death. Another view is that one of the two epistles which were brought together may have been apocryphal. These views have won little approval even among rationalistic critics.

Chapter 21

BETWEEN THE FIRST AND SECOND ROMAN IMPRISONMENTS

Paul's Presumed Release From His Roman Imprisonment. — When Luke finished the Book of Acts, he said nothing definite about Paul's release from prison. He does intimate that the Apostle was left in captivity for two whole years. (Acts 28:30) There is good reason to believe from the Pastoral Epistles (1 Tim.; 2 Tim.; Titus), from tradition, and from some other facts that Paul was in due time acquitted after he had been imprisoned for two years in Rome: (1) The very latest verses in the Acts (28:30-31) emphasize the comparative freedom accorded the Apostle in carrying out his work, despite his imprisonment. Such freedom would be more likely extended to Paul if the Roman authorities felt that he should be freed. (2) There can be little doubt that Festus and Agrippa were convinced of Paul's innocence, and the report of Festus, not to mention that of Julius the centurion, who conducted the Apostle to Rome, would be favorable to his acquittal. (Acts 25:14-21; 26:31-32; 27:3) (3) Paul seems to have felt confident of release. (Phil. 1:25; 2:17, 24; Philem. 22) (4) It seems probable that the Palestinian Jews did not finally carry their accusations against Paul to Rome, because the leading Jews in that metropolis with whom he met knew nothing of his troubles. (Acts 28:21) (5) The tradition that Paul was released, resumed his missionary journeys, and was again arrested is a very early one. That he went to Spain is definitely implied by Clement of Rome, A.D. 96, who says that the Apostle "reached the limit of the West." The

Muratorian Fragment, A.D. 170, also mentions his trip to Spain. Other witnesses of this are Athanasius, Epiphanius, Jerome, Theodoret, Chrysostom, and St. Gregory the Great. The preparations for Paul's journey to Spain are related in some detail in the first three chapters of the Gnostic *Acts of Peter* (A.D. 200 or earlier). Eusebius (*Hist. Eccl.* ii. 22, 2) reports the common tradition that "after he [Paul] had made his defense, the Apostle was sent again on the ministry of preaching, and a second time having come to the same city [Rome], he suffered martyrdom." (6) The Pastoral Epistles, inasmuch as no place can be found for them in the history of Paul as related by Luke in the Acts, indicate very definitely that Paul was free for a time and was carrying on activities following—so we judge—his First Roman Imprisonment. We shall refer to these activities later in another connection.

It is probable that Paul was released from prison sometime during the year A.D. 63.

THE EPISTLE TO THE HEBREWS

Some Facts About the Epistle.—In this book we shall assume that the Epistle to the Hebrews was written shortly after Paul was freed from his Roman imprisonment. (Heb. 13:19, 23) We hasten to add that the question of the Epistle's authorship has been a vexed one, even from ancient times. But in the "Inspired" revision of the Bible the prophet Joseph Smith accepted the Epistle as Paul's without any question. The question of authorship of the Epistle is so important that we deem it necessary to present the most important facts concerning it. At the outset it should be observed that Protestant scholarship generally rejects the Pauline authorship of the Epistle, but Catholic scholarship accepts it.

The earliest explicit Christian reference to the Epistle by author we know of is that quoted by the Church historian

Eusebius *(Historia Ecclesiae* VI, 14) from Clement of Alexandria. Eusebius writes that Clement in his outlines *(Hypotyposes)* says that

> ... The Epistle is Paul's and that it was written to Hebrews in the Hebrew language, and that Luke translated it with zealous care and published it to the Greeks; whence it is that the same complexion of style is found in the translation of this Epistle and in the Acts. [Further] that the [ordinary] phrase 'Paul an Apostle' was not placed at the head of the Epistle for good reason; for, he says, in writing to Hebrews who had formed a prejudice against him and viewed him with suspicion, he was wise not to repel them at the beginning by setting his name there.[1]

Clement of Alexandria dates from about A.D.155-220. It should be kept in mind that the Epistle was known much earlier but was not referred to by name. In fact, Clement of Rome frequently quotes it and refers to it in his letter to the Corinthians about A.D. 95. Origen, who followed (A.D. 186-253) Clement of Alexandria, is quoted by Eusebius *(Historia Ecclesiae* VI, 25) in his own words. After pointing out that every competent judge of language must admit that the style of Hebrews is not Paul's, but that every one conversant with the Apostle's teaching must agree that the thoughts are marvelous and in no way inferior to his acknowledged writings, Origen, he tells us, after a while continues,

> If I were to express my own opinion I should say that the thoughts are the thoughts of the Apostle, but the language and the composition that of one who recalled from memory and, as it were, made notes of what was said by his master. If therefore any Church holds this Epistle as Paul's, let it be approved for this also [as for holding unquestioned truths], for it was not without reason that the men of old time have handed it down as Paul's [that is, as substantially expressing his thoughts]. But who wrote the Epistle God only knows certainly. The account that has reached us is twofold: some say that Clement, who became bishop of the Romans, wrote the Epistle, others that Luke wrote it, who wrote the Gospel and the Acts. But on this I will say no more.[2]

[1] As quoted in B. F. Westcott, *The Epistle to the Hebrews*, p. lxvi.
[2] *Ibid.*, pp. lxviif.

The words of Clement of Alexandria and Origen will give the reader some idea of early views respecting the authorship, style, and language of the Epistle. Origen even goes so far as to say that he could show that "the Epistle was Paul's" in answer to those "who rejected it as not written by Paul."[3]

We may sum up the main reasons for doubts concerning Paul's authorship of the Epistle under these headings: (1) Paul's name and usual greeting do not appear at the beginning of the Epistle; (2) there are unusual differences in language and style as compared with Paul's other letters; (3) the writer gives the impression that he is not an Apostle, but rather belongs to the second generation of Church members (Heb. 2:3; 13:7); (4) the subject matter of the Epistle differs in many respects from the topics commonly treated in Paul's Epistles.

The early Eastern Church, though "uncritical," to quote one scholar, was almost unanimous in receiving the Epistle as Paul's, but until the middle of the Fourth Century the Latin Fathers were not inclined to accept it. Finally, however, Eastern opinion triumphed, and for over a thousand years both the Eastern and Western churches were one in describing the Epistle to the Hebrews as Paul's. During the Reformation period the question of Paul's authorship began to be debated again, with the result that Protestant scholars generally, as we have already noticed, rejected—and still do reject—the Apostle's authorship. Erasmus, Calvin, and Luther all agreed in holding that Paul did not write it.

In view of the history of the problem, with Catholic and Protestant scholars differing in their opinions—and excellent authorities there are on both sides—what shall the Latter-day Saint position be? I have already hinted at our position, but if the author may be indulged, let him

[3]*Ibid.*, p. lxix.

sum up the evidence and his own position as one Latter-day Saint: (1) The fact that the Epistle to the Hebrews was quoted by Clement of Rome as early as A.D. 95, though the author is not named, may be cited as being presumptive evidence in favor of the Epistle's authenticity as an inspired document. This evidence is, of course, not decisive in the problem of authorship, for the Epistle could have been written by Barnabas, Luke, Apollos, or Timothy (as some have claimed) and still have been inspired. (2) Considerable weight should be given to the fact that the earliest reference to the Epistle by author names Paul explicitly. It is true that the Western Church did not look upon the Epistle as the work of Paul until the Fourth Century, but that was probably because many of its doctrines were not understood because of its rhetorical style. That no less a scholar than Origen said that he was prepared to show that "the Epistle was Paul's" should add a little weight to the view that Paul wrote the Epistle. Add to this the fact that both the Eastern and Western Churches became unanimous in their decision that Paul wrote the Letter. All things considered up to this point, it seems to me that Paul's authorship of the Epistle has a little more to be said in its favor than does the negative view. (3) That the Epistle was written by some inspired person who was well acquainted with the Church and the Holy Priesthood the author accepts without reservation. He denies that its doctrines contradict any commonly treated in the accepted Pauline Epistles. On this last point most Catholic scholars are in full agreement. Paul could well have been the author of the subject matter of the Epistle. (4) The author fails to see in any way that Hebrews 2:3 and 13:7 seem to speak as if the writer were not an Apostle. The language used would be natural if directed to the saints in Palestine. It is true that Paul insisted on the primary, direct, and independent character of the Gospel preached by him (it came to him not by men); but his statements simply exhibit a natural deference to those who

were acquainted with and associated with the Savior during His ministry. (5) The prophet Joseph Smith attributes
the Epistle to Paul's authorship in his "Inspired" revision
of the Bible. (6) On the other hand to the author, the very
great dissimilarity in style or literary form between Hebrews
and the uncontested letters of Paul is by all means the
strongest argument against the Apostle's authorship. Although it is possible for an author to have more than one
style (witness Thomas Mann's earliest and latest books),
nevertheless, there is such a disparity in style between the
Hebrews and the other Pauline Epistles that the author
cannot honestly believe that Paul was its actual writer and
responsible for its literary form.

In view of all the facts thus presented, the author believes along with many other writers ancient and modern,
that Paul was the author responsible for the ideas and doctrines of the Epistle to the Hebrews, but that he was not
the actual writer who was responsible for its literary form.
Possibly the subscription to the Epistle is correct; Timothy
may have written it. But Origen may have been right when
he said, "Who wrote the Epistle God only knows certainly."

That Italy was the country from whence the Epistle
was sent is the belief of many scholars, but the meaning of
Heb. 13:24 is not certain. The Codex Alexandrinus has the
reading at its end of "from Rome," and Rome is the traditional place of origin.

Outline of the Epistle.—The Epistle to the Hebrews
may be divided into an introduction, the body of the Epistle
containing two sections, and a conclusion.

I. The introduction: Paul announces the theme of
the Epistle: The superiority of the revelation of
Christ to all that which had preceded Him.

All the revelation that had preceded had been
fragmentary and of necessity had been imperfect.
Now God had revealed Himself in the perfection

of His Son, who purged the sins of mankind and sat on the right hand of the Majesty on high (1: 1-3).

II. The body of the Epistle (1:4-13:17).

A. The superiority of the New Dispensation to the Old (1:4-10-18).

1. The Savior's superiority to the angels (1:4-2:18).

a. Paul shows by an appeal to the Scriptures that the Savior is superior to the angels. Angels are but ministering spirits, whereas the Son is the Creator and the Lord of all things and was anointed with the oil of gladness above all of His fellows (1:4-14).

b. Because of our Lord's superiority, greater heed should be paid to His doctrines than to those of the Law, which were revealed through angels. If transgression and disobedience were justly punished under the former Dispensation, how shall men escape if they neglect so great a salvation as that now offered by the Lord Himself, and confirmed with miracles, signs, and gifts of the Holy Ghost? (2:1-4).

c. Returning to 1:14, Paul gives additional proof that the Savior is superior to the angels by showing that He is Lord of the world to come. Through Christ's suffering He became temporarily a little lower than the angels (Ps. 8) and tasted death for all men, but now He is crowned with glory and honor. Christ was made perfect through suffering and became the captain of men's salvation. Inasmuch as men are partakers of flesh and blood (i.e., are mortal), He also partook of the same mortal experiences as they do; that through death He might destroy the devil who had the power of death. In all things it behooved Him to be like unto His brethren, that He might become a merciful High Priest in things pertaining to God. In the fact that He suffered and was tempted, He is able to help those who are tempted (2:5-18).

2. The Savior's superiority to Moses (3:1-4:13).

   a. The Apostle and High Priest of our profession is Jesus Christ who was faithful to Him that appointed Him, as also Moses was faithful in all his house [i.e., in teaching and governing Israel]. But Christ is counted worthy of more glory than Moses, who was only a servant *in* the house of God, whereas He is the Son *over* the whole house of God as a son over his own house (3:1-6).

   b. Paul interrupts the line of his argument to make a practical appeal to the saints to remain firm in the faith. They are not to harden their hearts as their fathers did in the wilderness during the Exodus. If they exhibit unbelief and apostasy by departing from the living God, they will not enter into His rest, even as the unbelieving Israelites were

excluded from His rest and from enter-
ing the Promised Land (3:7-4:14).

3. The superiority of the Priesthood possessed
by Christ over the Levitical Priesthood (4:
14-7:28). Introductory: The faithful are
to hold fast their profession as saints because they have a great High Priest, Jesus
Christ, who can appreciate their infirmities
and who was tempted in all points as they
are, yet did not sin. They are to have confidence in Him and find grace (4:14-16).

   a. The qualifications of a High Priest: He
   is appointed to represent men in matters pertaining to God, to offer gifts and
   sacrifices for sin; and he must be able
   to be patient with the ignorant and the
   wayward, because he is also beset with
   weaknesses, moral and physical. No
   one takes this honor to himself, unless
   called of God as was Aaron (5:1-4).

   b. So also Christ was called to be a High
   Priest after the order of Melchizedek
   and met all of its qualifications. Though
   a Son of God, He underwent difficulties in the flesh and was heard when
   He offered up prayers and entreaties;
   He learned obedience by the things
   which He suffered. He was made perfect and became the author of eternal
   salvation to all that obey Him (5:5-10).

   c. Paul indicates that he finds the High
   Priesthood of our Lord hard to expound
   because of its abstruse nature and also
   because of the spiritual obtuseness of
   his readers. At a time when they should

be teachers themselves, they have need
to be taught first principles again; they
have need of milk, and not of strong
(solid) food. But solid food is for adults,
whose spiritual faculties are so trained
as to be able to distinguish both good
and evil (5:11-14).

d. Paul exhorts his readers to advance
beyond rudimentary principles and go
on to perfection. "Therefore not leaving
the principles of the doctrine of Christ,
let us go on unto perfection." ("Inspired" revision of Heb. 6:1) He repeats
the elementary principles of faith, baptism, laying on of hands, the resurrection, and eternal judgment which formed the core of their first instruction,
but he wants them to press on to a more
profound understanding of Gospel principles. They are warned of their respon-
sibilities, however, after they have been
enlightened, have been made partakers
of the Holy Ghost, and have tasted of
the good word of God and the powers
of the world to come. If then they fall
away, crucify the Son of God afresh,
and put Him to an open shame, they
are beyond hope of receiving salvation;
their end is to be burned (6:1-8).

e. But Paul expects better things of his
readers, for God will not forget their
work and labor of love in His behalf.
The Apostle desires that each one show
diligence and not be slothful, but be
followers (imitators) of them who

through faith and patience inherit the promises (6:9-12).

f. Paul shows them how God's promise was fulfilled to Abraham; hence, by this example they may know that their hope of eternal salvation is firmly based (6:13-20).

g. The Apostle compares the Priesthood of our Lord and that of the Levites: (1) Reference is made to Melchizedek, who met Abraham returning from the slaughter of the kings and blessed him. Abraham paid tithes to this great Priest, who was King of Salem and a Priest after the order of the Son of God, which order was without descent, having neither beginning of days nor end of life. (See 7:3 in "Inspired" revision of Bible.) All those who are ordained unto this Priesthood, are made like unto the Son of God, abiding a Priest continually (7:1-3). (2) Melchizedek is shown to be greater than Abraham and the Levites who were his descendants (7:4-10). (3) Perfection could not come through the Levitical Priesthood, for under it Israel received the Law, hence the need of another Priest (Christ) arising after the order of Melchizedek. With the advent of the Melchizedek Priesthood there was a necessity of a change in the Law [salvation could not come by the Law of Moses]. And associated with the change was the Christ who came of the tribe of Judah, not from the tribe of

Levi, members of which ordinarily held the Priesthood. The old Law was weak and ineffective, but now men have a new and better hope by means of which they can draw near to God. Under the Law the priests were continually succeeding each other because of death; their office was transitory. But in Christ there is one who abides forever with an unchangeable Priesthood. He ever lives to make intercession for men (7:11-25). (4) In Christ men have a High Priest who is ideal; He is holy, guileless, undefiled, separated from sinners and exalted above the heavens. He had no sins to expiate and, was, therefore, unlike the priests under the Law, who found it necessary to offer up sacrifices continually, first for their own sins and then for the sins of their people (7:26-28).

4. The sacrifice of Christ is superior to the Mosaic sacrifices (8:1-10:18).

    a. The point that Paul has been making is this: The faithful have a High Priest who has taken His seat at God's right hand and ministers in the true tabernacle built by the Lord and not man. While on earth He offered for a sacrifice his own life for the sins of the people. (See "Inspired" revision of Bible.) On the other hand, the priests under the Law offer gifts, or sacrifices, that are only a shadow and imitation of that in heaven (8:1-5).

b. Christ has obtained a more excellent
ministry and is the Mediator of a new
and better Covenant, as predicted by
Jeremiah. By the Lord saying that He
would ratify a new covenant, He makes
the old one (the Mosaic) out of date
(8:6-13).

c. The greater excellence of Christ's sacrifice: The Apostle contrasts the ancient
Tabernacle, with its furnishings, sacrifices, and worship which could not inwardly qualify the worshiper to approach God, with the better Sanctuary
into which Christ entered and with the
unblemished sacrifice He offered for
men. If sprinkling men (under the old
Law) with the blood of bulls and goats
and with the ashes of a heifer cleanses
them physically, how much more will
the blood of Christ purify their consciences from lifeless works to serve the
living God? Paul shows how necessary
it was that Christ die in order to put
into effect the will and testament He
made. Just as the Old Covenant had to
be instituted or ratified with the sprinkling of the blood of animals, so the
New Testament or Covenant had to be
established by the shedding of Christ's
blood. Without the shedding of blood
there can be no remission of sins. Just
as men are destined to die and after
that to be judged, so Christ, after being
offered in sacrifice once for all to bear
the sins of many, will appear the second

time, without sin, to those that await Him for salvation. The repeated sacrifices under the Mosaic Law were of little value. The blood of bulls and goats is powerless to take away sins. It is not sacrifice that God wants, but the doing of His will. The repeated sacrifices under the Old Covenant are supplanted by Christ's one sacrifice for sins, which is completely sufficient. The New Covenant is to be written in men's hearts and minds. Jeremiah is quoted (31:33-34) to that effect (9:1-10:18).

B. Paul's exhortations of a moral nature (10:19-13:17).

1. The Apostle gives an exhortation to perseverance in faith (10:19-12:13).

a. Since the faithful have free access to the Holy Place by the blood of Jesus, by the new and living way He has opened through the veil of His body, and since they have such a great Priest with authority over the house of God, they are exhorted to draw near to God with sincerity of heart and with perfect faith, with hearts sprinkled from a wicked conscience, and bodies washed with clean water. They are to stimulate one another to brotherly love and good deeds. Paul warns of the awful prospect of judgment that awaits those who wilfully sin after having received the truth (10:19-31).

b. The saints are reminded of their sufferings and persecution after they first received the faith. They also shared the sufferings of those who were treated in the same manner. They are to continue in their confident hope, for it will issue in a great reward. Patient endurance will bring the promised reward (10:32-39).

c. Having shown that faith is necessary for salvation, Paul describes the general nature of faith [he does not attempt a strict definition of it in 11:1, and the translation given in the Authorized Version is practically impossible to be understood by the average reader]. Apparently the Apostle is trying to say that by faith men are *assured* of future things for which they hope, and are *convinced* of the reality and certainty of the things they do not see. Numerous great Old Testament worthies such as Abel, Enoch, Noah, Abraham, Sarah, Isaac, Jacob, Joseph, Moses, etc., are cited as examples to show the unusual results which faith produced in their lives. Through their faith all of these persons won God's approval but did not receive the promises, for the Almighty provided some better things for them through their sufferings; without sufferings they could not be made perfect (11:1-40; see "Inspired" revision).

d. With such a cloud of witnesses, the faithful are exhorted to cast off all entanglements of sin and run with endurance the race that lies before them,

looking unto Jesus, the author and per-
fecter of their faith. Those who would
escape weariness and troubles should
compare their difficulties with His.
Their sufferings are an evidence of
God's love for them, for what father
does not discipline his offspring?
Through pain and suffering men may
become nobler characters, in fact, may
share God's holiness (12:1-13).

2. Paul exhorts the faithful to keep before
them other Christian virtues (12:14-13:17).

a. The Apostle exhorts his readers to strive
for peace with all men and for sanctification, without which no one will see
the Lord. All should seek God's grace
and see to it that no bitter root springs
up through which many may be de-
filed; that there be no fornicator or
profane person like Esau. A comparison
of the Old and New Covenants is made.
The New invites men to a glad and
glorious fellowship. Those who are un-
faithful to it are more guilty than those
who failed to obey the Old Covenant.
Hence the necessity for strict obedience
to Him who speaks to them. The saints
are advised to serve God pleasingly,
with reverence and piety (12:14-29).

b. The faithful are urged to continue brotherly love. They are to show hospitality
to strangers, for angels may be their
guests. Those who are ill-treated or
prisoners are to be remembered. The
marriage relation is to be held sacred;

God will judge fornicators and adulterers. Avarice is to be shunned. Their former leaders—those who brought them the word of God—are to be remembered; their faith is to be imitated. Jesus Christ is forever the same; the saints are to be steadfast and avoid strange doctrines. Christians are to keep to their own altar and sacrifice and not take part in Jewish worship. They are to praise God continually and are not to forget to be helpful and liberal; for God is pleased with sacrifices of that kind. The saints are to be loyal and obedient to their leaders, who are keeping watch for their (the saints') souls (13:1-17).

III. The conclusion (13:18-25).

    A. Paul requests the saints to pray for him, because he has a clear conscience (13:18-19).

    B. The Apostle prays that God will equip his readers with every good work to do His will (13:20-21).

    C. Paul asks the saints to bear with his exhortations; for his letter is but short. They will rejoice to know that Timothy has been set at liberty. The Apostle sends greetings to all the saints and their leaders. The Italian brethren also send their greetings (13:22-25).

Chapter 22

BETWEEN THE FIRST AND SECOND ROMAN IMPRISONMENTS—*(Concluded)*

Other Presumed Activities of Paul Following His First Roman Imprisonment.—We have already pointed out (Chapter 21) some of the evidence that indicates that Paul was released from his First Roman Imprisonment and that he went on his long-anticipated journey to Spain. (Cf. Rom. 15:24, 28.) What the Apostle's immediate itinerary was after his release is impossible now to say. We are left pretty much in the realm of speculation. But it will be remembered that when Paul wrote his letter to the Philippians, he had hoped to come to them shortly. (Phil. 1:26; 2:24) Moreover, when he wrote his Epistle to Philemon at Colossae, he told his friend to prepare him a lodging for his expected visit. (Philem. 22) Let us assume, then, that Paul first went to Macedonia, where he stayed with his Philippian friends and rested for a time after his long years of suffering and privation. Then he probably went on to Ephesus, where he had labored so long and where he had so many friends. Here he doubtless set up his headquarters and thence visited Colossae, Laodicea, Hierapolis, and other branches of the Church in that general area of Asia. No doubt he did all that he could while there to put down false doctrines taught by the Judaizers and other false teachers who had long given him and other leaders of the Church a difficult time. In this activity most of the remainder of the year A.D. 63 was probably spent by the Apostle following his release from the Roman captivity.

Possibly Paul's anticipated visit to Spain was carried out the following year (64). We may suppose (with others) that he spent two years in that land building up the Church in prominent cities along the coast. But let us emphasize that Paul's trip to Spain is assumed on the basis of his expressed intentions (Rom. 15:24-28) and on tradition. Even if he certainly went to that country we are left without any knowledge of his travels or accomplishments.

After he came back from Spain (A.D. 66?), we may believe that he returned to Ephesus and found, to his sorrow, that what he had long ago predicted to the Ephesian Elders at Miletus (Acts 20:28-31) was coming to pass. The grievous wolves he had spoken of had indeed entered their midst and were not sparing the flock. That Paul did come to Ephesus after his Roman imprisonment we may not doubt. (See 1 Tim. 1:3) False leaders such as Hymenaeus, Philetus, and Alexander (1 Tim. 1:20; 2 Tim. 2:17; 4:14-15) were attempting to pervert the simple faith of the saints in that metropolis by teaching false doctrines involving Jewish superstition, Greek philosophy, and Oriental speculation. Apparently Paul had pressing duties elsewhere that called him away from Asia; so, leaving Timothy at Ephesus, he returned to Macedonia. (1 Tim. 1:3) But perhaps fearing that he would be detained longer than he at first supposed (1 Tim. 3:14-15), and knowing well the difficulties that would face his beloved missionary companion, he wrote to him the Epistle we know as 1 Timothy. In this letter he wrote to assist Timothy in combating false teachers, to give him counsel regarding the choice of officers in the Church, and to remind him of the main duties devolving upon one engaged in the ministry. (1 Tim. 1:2-3; 3:14-15; 4:7, 13-16; 6:1-6)

This is the point at which we might logically consider 1 Timothy, but it may be better first to say a word about the Pastoral Epistles (of which 1 Tim. is one) as a group.

The Pastoral Epistles.—The title "Pastoral Epistles" was given to 1 and 2 Timothy and Titus in Paul Anton's time (1726), because in them the great Apostle is supposed to give his two younger missionary companions, Timothy and Titus, private instructions concerning their duties as heads of branches of the Church of which they had been given charge during his absence. The title is not sufficiently broad to cover all the matters covered by the Epistles, but it has remained in general use on the grounds of convenience, since it designates a group of Epistles that are closely connected in thought, style, and vocabulary. The Pastoral Epistles are very valuable because of the insight they give us (1) into primitive church organization and discipline, (2) into the qualifications that church leaders and teachers should possess, (3) into the duties of the church leaders, (4) into the heresies that arose in the Church, (5) into the ideals that should animate those who hold the Priesthood, and (6) into the activities of Paul in his last years of life.

The three Epistles are so closely linked together in style, thought, and phraseology, and in the historical situation presupposed by them, that we are justified in assigning the writing of them within a short time of each other. The Pauline authorship of the Pastoral Epistles was never questioned in ancient times, with the exception of the heretic Marcion (A.D. 140), who denied the Pauline authorship of all three, and Tatian (A.D. 110-172), who denied that of the two Epistles to Timothy. But as to these two men, we have the testimonies of Jerome, Clement of Alexandria, and Tertullian to the effect that their rejections of Pauline authorship was due to the teachings of these books. So with few dissents Paul's authorship of the Pastorals was never questioned until modern times, when, in 1801, Schmidt denied the genuineness of 1 Timothy. Since that time these Epistles have been under fierce fire and have been more generally rejected by Protestant scholars than any of Paul's letters except Hebrews. The position of Catholic scholarship has been consistently to accept them as genuine works of Paul. The critics reject the Pastorals in general because of the differences between them and the accepted Pauline literature in style, content, and vocabulary. A full discussion of the objections to the Pauline authorship is beyond the scope of this book. We refer the student interested in the subject to C. J. Callan's *The Epistles of St. Paul*, I, 249-253. Professor Callan cites ten objections in his excellent discussion and gives solid answers to them.

On the positive side we find the external evidence of ancient times lined up in this way: Clement of Rome and the Epistle of Barnabas (near the end of the first century), Ignatius, Bishop of Antioch (*circa*, A.D. 110), Polycarp (c. 117), Justin Martyr (c. 140), Heracleon (c. 165), Hegesippus (c. 170), Athenagoras of Athens (c. 176), and Theophilus of Antioch (c. 181) all make allusions to their wording or quotations from the Pastorals. And such men as Tertullian, Irenaeus, Clement of Alexandria, and Origen unhesitatingly accepted these writings as Paul's. Add to these the testimony of the Muratorian Fragment and the old Latin and Syriac versions, not to mention the Pauline Epistles accepted by Eusebius the church historian, and we find an imposing array of external authority in favor of Paul's authorship.

The internal evidence is also very strong and appears clearly when the objections to the genuineness of the Pastorals are answered. For this we refer the student to Professor Callan's work cited above.

The author believes these Epistles are without any doubt genuine. Latter-day Saints will, of course, notice that the prophet Joseph Smith accepted the Pastorals as Paul's work. (See "Inspired" revision of the Bible.) If citation of great New Testament scholars who believed the Pastorals to be Paul's will bolster the faith of any timid souls, we point to Hort, Sanday, Lightfoot, Plummer,

Adeney, Farrar, Alford, Ramsay, Godet, Findlay, Lange, Zahn, Schaff, Wiesinger, and Weiss. An imposing array indeed! And if it be maintained that imposing names can be pointed out who deny Paul's authorship, or who take a middle point of view (i.e., holding the Pastorals to be partly Pauline), we do not deny it, but hasten to point out that one under the circumstances (i.e., having the doctors divided) had better get a testimony of the Holy Spirit concerning the truth of the matter.

THE FIRST EPISTLE TO TIMOTHY

The Place and Date of Composition.—Reverting back to what we had said about Paul's first letter to Timothy before taking up the problem of the Pastorals, it will be remembered that we had the Apostle writing the Epistle from Macedonia. But there is an old tradition that he wrote it from Laodicea. (See subscription in Authorized Version.) No matter where the Apostle wrote the Letter, our understanding of it will be little changed.

Paul possibly wrote 1 Timothy in 66 or 67 A.D.

Outline of the Epistle.—For purposes of analysis we may divide the Epistle into an introduction, the body of the Letter, and a conclusion.

    I. The introduction: Paul's greeting to Timothy (1: 1-2).

    II. The body of the Epistle (1:3-6:19).

        A. Paul reminds Timothy that he had previously charged him to prevent certain people from teaching erroneous doctrines and from giving heed to fables [Jewish legends?] and endless genealogies [extravagant legends concerning the ancient patriarchs?] which only tended to lead the saints from the faith. The true precepts of the Gospel lead to charity from a pure heart, a clear conscience, and faith unfeigned. Those who deviate from this teaching turn to empty talk; they want to be teachers of the Law without understanding what they say or what they strongly affirm. The Apostle points out the true purpose of the Law and expresses his gratitude to the Lord for deeming him worthy to be in His service. Paul exhorts Timothy to fight the good fight by holding to the faith and a clear conscience, in agreement with the prophecies made concerning him (Timothy) at an earlier time. The Apostle commits Hymenaeus and Alexander to Satan because of their blasphemy (1:3-20).

B.   The Apostle exhorts that supplications, prayers, petitions, and thanksgiving be offered up for all men, especially for kings and men high in authority; this is pleasing to God, who wishes all men to be saved and come to a knowledge of the truth. Christ is the Mediator between God and man. He gave Himself as a ransom for all men. Of this fact Paul says that he was made a herald and an Apostle. Men everywhere are to pray, lifting to God holy hands without anger and contention. Women are to dress modestly and are not to teach or to domineer over men. Adam was first formed, then Eve; Adam was not deceived [in the Garden of Eden], but the woman being deceived was in transgression. She will be saved through childbearing, if she continues in faith, love, and holiness. Paul outlines the personal and moral qualifications of a bishop. He must be without reproach, the husband of one wife, sober, discreet, decorous, hospitable, apt in

teaching, not given to wine, not pugnacious,
not greedy, but gentle, not contentious, not
loving money, but ruling his own house well.
He ought not to be a recent convert, lest he
become puffed up. Men who are to serve as
deacons should be serious, not double-tongued,
not given to much wine, not greedy of base
gain, but are to hold the mystery of the faith
with a pure conscience. Their wives are to be
honorable, sober, faithful in all things. Deacons
are to be husbands of one wife and should
rule their children and household well (2:1-
3:13).

C. Paul hopes to see Timothy before long, but
writes as he does in order that Timothy may
know how to conduct himself in the household
of God. Timothy is told that in latter times
there will be an apostasy, a falling away from
the faith, in which some will yield to deceiving
spirits and teachings of devils, whose consciences
will be seared as with a hot iron. He is to lay
these facts before the brethren and thus be a
a good servant of Jesus Christ. The Apostle
also urges him to train himself in godliness,
for while physical training is of some benefit,
godliness is beneficial all around. Paul advises
Timothy not to let anyone despise his youth,
but in word, in conduct, in love, in the Spirit,
in faith, and in purity he is to be an example
of those who believe. Until the Apostle arrives,
he is advised to give heed to reading, to exhortation, and to teaching. He is not to neglect
the gifts with which he was endowed by prophecy and by the laying on of the hands of the
elders of the Church. Timothy is to meditate

on these matters so that his advancement may
be manifest to all (3:14-4:16).

D. Paul advises Timothy not to rebuke an older
man, but to entreat him as a father; the elder
women as mothers, and the younger women
as sisters. Timothy is next counseled concerning the treatment of widows. Destitute widows
without relatives are to receive help from the
Church, but if a widow has relatives, these are
to take care of her. A pleasure-loving widow
is dead while she lives. No widow is to be put
on the Church roll if she is under sixty years
of age, and if on the roll she must be known
for her good deeds. Younger widows are not
to be enrolled; as soon as their affections stray
wantonly from Christ, they want to marry,
and they become restive, learn to be idle, and
become gossips and busybodies. Younger
women should marry, bear children, manage
their houses, and act circumspectly. If a believing man has widows depending on him,
he is to take care of them and not burden the
Church, which desires to take care of the really
destitute widows. Elders of the Church who
preside or rule well are worthy of double honor,
particularly those who labor in preaching and
teaching. An Elder is not to be accused unless
there are two or three witnesses. Paul solemnly
charges Timothy to carry out his instructions
without prejudice; he is not to act by reason
of favoritism. He is not to lay hands on any
man suddenly [i.e., not ordain anyone without
due consideration], nor is he to be a partaker
of other men's sins; he is to keep himself pure.
Because of Timothy's delicate health he is not

to drink water, but is to take a little wine for his stomach's sake and for his "often" (5:25) infirmities. Paul gives Timothy some advice on how to judge men's characters, presumably to help him in choosing persons to hold Church office. The Apostle advises slaves to honor their masters so that the name of God will not be spoken against. Slaves who have believing masters should show due respect to them because they are brethren, and should serve them all the more. Paul gives a sharp rebuke to false teachers and the difficulties they cause. He warns against greediness. Godliness is a great gain if it is accompanied with contentment. Men bring nothing into the world and they can take nothing out of it. They should be satisfied with food and clothing, for people who want to be rich fall into temptation and snares. Men of God are to flee these things and follow after righteousness, godliness, faith, love, patience, and meekness. They are to fight the good fight of faith and lay hold on eternal life. Timothy is to advise the rich not to be haughty, but to use their wealth in doing good to others; laying up in store for themselves a good foundation for a time to come, that they may lay hold of eternal life (5:1-6:19).

III. The conclusion: Paul exhorts Timothy to be true to his trust, avoiding profane and vain babblings and oppositions of science, falsely so-called. He adds a benediction (6:20-21).

Paul Travels to Crete With Titus.—Returning to Paul's travels, we will recall that when he wrote his First Epistle to Timothy he expressed the hope of shortly returning to Timothy. (1 Tim. 3:14) Whether the Apostle actually returned to Ephesus at this time we do not know, but it is certain that he took Titus with him to Crete. (Titus 1:5) The branches of the Church there seem to have been founded already, by whom we do not know. These branches —some at least—needed better organizing (*ibid.*) and false teachers seemed to be troubling them, particularly Jews. (1:10-16). Inasmuch as Paul seems to have been unable to remain in Crete long, he doubtless left Titus on the island, as he had left Timothy at Ephesus, to complete the organizing of the Church branches and to confront the false teachers who were causing difficulty. Apparently Paul wrote his Epistle to Titus shortly after reaching Ephesus. Possibly the letter was written from there, for in 2 Tim. 4:20 he speaks of leaving Trophimus sick at Miletus, which is near the metropolis. But there is an old tradition that the Letter was written from Nicopolis of Macedonia, where Paul hoped to winter. (See Titus 3:12 and subscription in Authorized Version.) Let us now examine the Epistle to Titus.

THE EPISTLE TO TITUS

Outline of the Epistle.—We may divide the Letter into an introduction, the body of the Epistle, and a conclusion.

    I. The introduction (1:1-4).

        A. Paul, an "Apostle," indicates his authority which the Savior had committed to him (1:1-3).

        B. The Apostle sends a greeting of grace, mercy, and peace to Titus, his "own son after the common faith" (1:4).

    II. The body of the Epistle (1:5-11).

        A. Paul reminds Titus that he left him in Crete to set in order the Church, ordain Elders in every city, etc., as he had directed him. An Elder is to be blameless, be the husband of one wife, and have children that are not un-ruly. A bishop is to be blameless as God's steward; not self-willed or hot-tempered, not given to wine, not pugnacious, nor fond of base gain. He is to be hospitable, a lover of good, discreet, just, holy, temperate, and ortho-dox (i.e., holding fast to the faithful word as he has been taught). He is to encourage others by his teaching, as well as refute his oppo-nents. Titus is to stop the mouths of those who are refractory and given to troublemaking, particularly those who are Judaizers. The Apostle tells of the traditional perversity of the Cretans. They are to be corrected (1:5-16).

B. The Apostle gives Titus advice to speak things that become sound teaching; he then gives instructions applying to different classes of people: (1) aged men and women, (2) young men, and (3) slaves. Above all, Titus is to give a pattern of good works; in his teaching he is to be sound in doctrine, grave, and sin-cere; and his speech is to be discreet and un-impeachable, so that his opponents will be ashamed, having no evil thing to say of him. The grace of God, which brings salvation to all men, teaches us to renounce godlessness and worldly passions, to live discreetly, right-eously, and piously, and to look for the hope and glorious appearance of Jesus Christ, who gave Himself for us, that He might redeem us from all iniquity and purify for Himself a special people, zealous of good works. Titus is to speak these things and exhort and reprove with full authority. He is to let no one esteem him lightly (2:1-15).

C. Titus is told to counsel the Cretan saints to be obedient to their rulers. [Cretans were notorious for their seditious tendencies.] They are to exercise charity and consideration for others, remembering their own sinful state before God's love and grace found them and made them heirs of eternal life. They are to maintain good works and avoid foolish disputes, legends, and unfruitful wranglings concerning the Law. Heretics are to be avoided (3:1-11).

III. The conclusion (3:12-15).

A. Paul requests Titus to lose no time in coming to Nicopolis (where the Apostle was to spend the winter) after he has sent either Artemas or Tychicus to take his place. Titus is also requested to speed Zenas the lawyer and Apollos on their journey, so that nothing will be wanting to them. The Cretan saints are to apply themselves to honest work so as to supply their needs and be productive (3:12-14).

B. The Apostle and those with him send greetings. Titus is to greet the faithful in Crete in behalf of Paul and his companions (3:15).

Paul's Activities in Ephesus Before Leaving for Nicopolis.—How long Paul remained in Ephesus before leaving for Nicopolis we do not know, but he apparently made visits from the metropolis in Syria to various Church branches in the course of his labors. One of these visits was to Troas where he left, inadvertently or otherwise, his cloak, books, and parchments. (2 Tim. 4:13) The Apostle's many friends doubtless assisted him in numerous ways. One of them he mentions later whose name was Onesiphorous. "In how many things he ministered unto me at Ephesus, thou knowest very well." (2 Tim. 1:18) Onesiphorous was still to administer to Paul after the Apostle again fell into

Roman hands. (2 Tim. 1:16-17) When the time came for
Paul to sail from Ephesus, those who were to accompany
him were probably Luke, Tychicus, Erastus, and Trophimus. There may have been others.

Paul Leaves for Nicopolis.—On leaving Ephesus, the
Apostle stopped at Miletus, as we have already seen, where
he left Trophimus, who seems to have suddenly turned ill.
(2 Tim. 4:20) When the travelers reached Corinth, Erastus,
the city-treasurer (Rom. 16:23), whom we have met with
earlier, left the party. (2 Tim. 4:20) From Corinth Paul
probably went directly to the town of Nicopolis (Greek:
"city of victory"), located in Epirus, four miles from the
city of Actium, which Augustus founded in 30 B.C. in com-
memoration of his victory. It was possibly the winter of
67-68 that Paul had hoped to spend in this town. When
he got settled, he possibly sent Tychicus on a quick errand
to Crete along with Zenas and Apollos, with instructions
to have Titus come and join him at once. (Titus 3:12-13)

Chapter 23

PAUL'S SECOND ROMAN IMPRISONMENT
AND DEATH

The Apostle's Probable Arrest in Nicopolis and Imprisonment in Rome.—If Paul got comfortably settled in Nicopolis, he possibly rested for a time and then began his customary missionary activities. But by this time the Romans could readily distinguish Christians from Jews, particularly since the burning of Rome in A.D. 64, much of the blame for which was placed on the hated sect that believed in Christ. Therefore any activity of Paul, the noted Christian leader, would draw the attention of enemies everywhere, particularly from Jewish ranks. Although specific information is lacking, it is not at all improbable that some informer brought about the Apostle's arrest, either late in 67 or before the Spring of 68. In order to please Nero, such an important Christian would be forwarded to Rome immediately and placed in close confinement. The terror caused by the Apostle's arrest caused many to desert him. Paul himself said:

> Demas hath forsaken me, having loved this present world, and is departed to Thessalonica; Crescens to Galatia, Titus unto Dalmatia. Only Luke is with me. (2 Tim. 4:10-11)

So he wrote to Timothy from his prison cell. It is hard to believe that Titus forsook him; it may be that the Apostle sent him to Dalmatia. Certainly he sent Tychicus back to Ephesus. (2 Tim. 4:12)

In his first imprisonment, Paul had been well treated, partly because he had been accused by Jews of offenses that the Romans took somewhat lightly. Now the Jews in Palestine were in definite disfavor because of their rebellion; and Paul the Jew was in prison for a pretended offense against the Romans. The Apostle was even chained to his prison as a criminal. (2 Tim. 2:9) It is true that his friends were allowed to see him, but he seems to have done no preaching. Even some of his friends found it difficult, if not dangerous, to find him; Onesiphorous seems to have had that experience. (2 Tim. 1:16-17) He may have come especially from Ephesus to see Paul. (Cf. 2 Tim. 1:18) So perilous was Paul's situation that no one dared to stand by him at his first hearing or at the first stage of his trial, called by the Romans the *primo actio*. (2 Tim. 4:16) But the Lord stood by him, as he says, and at his first hearing the Apostle did so well that he was "delivered out of the mouth of the lion." (2 Tim. 4:17) It was possibly at this hearing that Alexander the coppersmith did him much evil; for he must have been one of the informers who got the Apostle in trouble. "The Lord reward him according to his works," says Paul to Timothy. (2 Tim. 4:14)

But after Paul had been remanded back to prison to await the second hearing of his case, he knew that his fate was sealed. Apparently he thought it might be some time before the hearing, because in his letter to Timothy he urged him to come before winter (2 Tim. 4:21); nevertheless, "the time of his departure was at hand." (2 Tim. 4:6) Paul's nobility and greatness are shown by these additional words:

> I have fought a good fight, I have finished my course, I have kept the faith: henceforth there is laid up for me a crown of righteousness, which the Lord, the righteous judge, shall give me at that day: and not to me only, but unto all them also that love his appearing. (2 Tim. 4:7-8)

But Paul's second hearing possibly took place in May, contrary to his expectations.

Despite the cheering presence of Luke and Onesiphorous (2 Tim. 1:16, 17; 4:11), and occasional visits from others such as Eubulus, Pudens, Linus, and Claudia (2 Tim. 4:21), Paul seems to have longed for the presence of his young bosom friend Timothy. Timothy was probably in Ephesus —of his presence there we cannot be sure from 2 Timothy —engaged in his Church duties, but Paul bade him come with all dispatch. (2 Tim. 4:9) Whether Timothy got to Rome in time to see the Apostle before his death and to bring him his cloak, books, and parchments, which he had left in Troas with Carpus (2 Tim. 4:13), we do not know. Now let us look in some detail at Paul's Second Epistle to his favorite missionary companion.

THE SECOND EPISTLE TO TIMOTHY

An Outline of the Epistle.—This is the last of Paul's three Pastoral Epistles. For convenience we may divide the Letter into an introduction, the body of the Epistle, and the conclusion.

   I. The introduction (1:1-5).

      A. Paul, "an Apostle of Jesus Christ," sends greetings to Timothy (1:1-2).

      B. The Apostle thanks God that unceasingly he remembers Timothy in his daily prayers, and, greatly desiring to see him, he calls to remembrance the younger man's faith, which first dwelt in his grandmother Lois and in his mother Eunice (1:3-5).

   II. The body of the Epistle (1:6-4:18).

      A. Paul exhorts Timothy to faithfulness and endurance (1:6-2:13).

         1. The Apostle admonishes Timothy to stir up the gift of God which he received at his ordination by the laying on of Paul's hands. Timothy is not to be ashamed of the testi-

mony of the Lord, nor of Paul His prisoner. The Apostle bears testimony of the Lord's work in abolishing death and in bringing life and immortality to light through the Gospel. Timothy is advised to hold fast to the pattern of sound words which he has heard from Paul, in the faith and love which is in Christ Jesus; that good treasure which is committed to him he is to guard by the Holy Spirit which dwells in the faithful (1:6-14).

2. Because of an apostasy or defection in Asia, including Phygellus and Hermogenes, Timothy is urged to hand on to faithful men what he had been taught by Paul. (The Apostle prays that mercy will be extended to the house of Onesiphorous, who was so faithful to him in Rome.) Timothy is exhorted to be like a good soldier who pleases the officer who enlisted him. Anyone who takes part in an athletic contest gets no prize or crown unless he follows the rules governing the contest. Timothy is to remember the Christ and His resurrection, and his duties will be clear. If men suffer for the Lord, they will also reign with Him (1:15-2:13).

B. Paul's further counsels to Timothy (2:14-4:5).

1. Timothy is admonished to charge men not to engage in wordy disputes, which are unprofitable and which tend only to upset the listeners. He is to do his utmost to show to God that he is an approved workman, who has no reason to be ashamed. He is to hold himself aloof from unspiritual (secu-

lar), empty chattering which only leads
people further on into godlessness and
spreads like gangrene. Hymenaeus and
Philetus are men who talk like that and
have gone astray when they say that the
resurrection has already taken place. In so
doing they have overthrown the faith of
some. Nevertheless, God's foundation stands
sure. Paul compares Church members to
two kinds of articles used in a large house.
Some are of gold and silver, others of wood
and earthenware; some are for honorable
use, and others for ignoble or common
use. The faithful will keep themselves for
honorable use, dedicated, and fit for the
Master's use, prepared for every good work.
Timothy is urged to flee from youthful
lusts and strive to follow righteousness,
faith, love, and peace, in company with
all those who call on the Lord with pure
hearts. He is to avoid foolish discussions
that beget contention; he is to be gentle,
apt to teach, forbearing; disciplining his
opponents in meekness, trusting that God
will grant them repentance leading to ac-
knowledgment of the truth, and that they
may wake up out of the devil's snare (2:
14-26).

2. Paul warns Timothy of the perilous nature
of the coming apostasy in the Church. He
tells of the personal sins of men, of false
teachers, of foolish women, and of men of
debased minds, and reprobates so far as
faith is concerned. But Timothy has known
of Paul's doctrine, of his manner of life, and

of the persecutions he endured and from
which the Lord delivered him; from the
Apostle's example and teachings, and from
the Scriptures he has known since child-
hood, Timothy will be fully equipped to
meet the coming dangers. The Apostle
charges him strongly and solemnly to
preach the word incessantly, to reprove,
rebuke, exhort, watch in all things, endure
afflictions, and fully carry out his ministry
(3:1-4:5).

C. Some personal messages of Paul (4:6-18).

   1. The Apostle indicates that his death is close
at hand, that he is "now ready to be offered." He has fought a good fight, and a
crown of righteousness awaits him. He bids
Timothy to come to him speedily. Demas
has forsaken him; Crescens has gone to
Galatia, and Titus to Dalmatia. Only Luke
is with him. Paul requests that Timothy
bring Mark with him, for he is profitable
to the Apostle for the ministry. Paul indicates that he has sent Tychicus to Ephesus.
He requests that Timothy bring to him the
cloak, books, and parchments that he had
left at Troas with Carpus. Alexander the
coppersmith, Paul says, did him much evil
[probably as an informer]; the Lord reward
according to his works. Timothy is told to
beware of him, because he withstood their
words (4:6-15).

   2. At Paul's first hearing, no man stood with
him; all men forsook him. He prays that
God will not lay it to their charge. But the
Lord was with him, that all the Gentiles

might hear his preaching; and he was "delivered out of the mouth of the lion." The Lord will deliver him from every evil work and will preserve him for His heavenly kingdom (4:16-18).

III. The conclusion: Paul greets a number of persons at Ephesus, requests Timothy to come to him before winter, and adds his blessing (4:19-22).

The Tradition Concerning Paul's Final Hearing and Execution.—At the time of Paul's first hearing before the Roman court, it is said that Nero was absent in Greece. What the charge against Paul was we do not know, but it was probably one involving sedition. Nor do we know what happened at the second hearing. Apparently Nero had returned, and his displeasure sealed the Apostle's doom. The Roman Senate had passed an ordinance to the effect that ten days should elapse between the condemnation of a criminal and his execution in order that the Emperor might, if so disposed, grant him a pardon. It was the custom, especially if a demonstration might take place, to take the criminal outside of the city to be executed. The tradition is that Paul was conducted about two miles from Rome on the Ostian Way, southwest of the city, where he was beheaded by the sword. His Roman citizenship saved him from the suffering sustained by many Christians in being crucified or in being smeared with pitch and set on fire. According to the testimony of St. Jerome, Paul met his death in the fourteenth year of Nero's reign, that is, sometime between October 13, 67 A.D. and June 9, 68 A.D.[1]

[1]The traditions regarding Paul's death may be seen in the *Martyrdom of Saint Paul* (c. A.D. 150) and the *Acts of Peter and Paul* (later date) in *Acta Apostolorum Apocrypha*, as edited by R. A. Lipsius and M. Bonnet, Vol. 1, Leipzig, 1881.

BIBLIOGRAPHY

Following are a few of the many books which the author has found useful in studying Paul. Not many titles on Paul's Epistles are cited here.

ATLAS AND DICTIONARY

Wright, G. E. and Filson, F. V. *The Westminster Historical Atlas to the Bible*. Philadelphia: The Westminster Press, 1946. Pp. 114. For New Testament see pp. 70-114.

The Westminster Dictionary of the Bible. John D. Davis, Editor. Fifth Edition revised and rewritten by Henry S. Gehman, Philadelphia: The Westminster Press, 1944.

GENERAL REFERENCE BOOKS

Bouquet, A. C. *Everyday Life in New Testament Times*. New York: Charles Scribner's Sons, 1954. Pp. xix, 236. A very readable and useful work.

Friedlander, L. *Roman Life and Manners Under the Early Empire*. 4 Vols. Authorized Translation of the 7th enlarged and revised edition of the Sittengeschichte Roms by L. A. Magnus. Second Edition. New York: Dutton, n.d.

Moore, George Foot. *Judaism in the First Centuries of the Christian Era—The Age of the Tannaim*. Two volumes. Cambridge: Harvard University Press, 1927. Very useful to the scholar.

Tucker, G. T. *Life in the Roman World of Nero and St. Paul*. New York: The Macmillan Company, 1924. Pp. xix, 453.

INTRODUCTIONS TO THE NEW TESTAMENT

Goodspeed, Edgar J. *An Introduction to the New Testament*. Chicago: The University of Chicago Press, 1937. Pp. xiii, 362. Liberal.

Henshaw, T. *New Testament Literature*. London: George Allen and Unwin Ltd., 1952. Pp. 454. Liberal in viewpoint.

Lake, Kirsopp and Silva. *An Introduction to the New Testament*. New York and London: Harper & Brothers Publishers, 1947. Pp. x, 302. Liberal.

McNeile, A. H. *An Introduction to the Study of the New Testament*. Second Edition revised by C. S. C. Williams. Oxford: The Clarendon Press, 1953. Pp. 486. Liberal critical views. Contains lists of books and articles.

Salmon, George. *A Historical Introduction to the Study of the Books of the New Testament*. Ninth Edition. London: J. Murray, 1899. Pp. xxxi, 643. Conservative.

Scott, Ernest Findlay. *The Literature of the New Testament*. New York: Columbia University Press, 1932. Pp. xiii, 312. Liberal.

Steinmueller, John E. *A Companion to Scripture Studies*. Volume III. Special Introduction to the New Testament. New York: Joseph F. Wagner, Inc., 1943. Pp. vii, 409. By a good Catholic scholar. Very useful to students. Contains good bibliographies. Conservative.

Tenney, Merrill C. *The New Testament*. Grand Rapids, Mich.: Wm. B. Eerdmans Publishing Co., 1954. Pp. 474. Conservative. Contains a useful bibliography.

Thiessen, Henry C. *Introduction to the New Testament*. Grand Rapids, Mich.: Wm. B. Eerdmans Publishing Co., 1951. Pp. xx, 347. Conservative.

Zahn, Theodor B. *Introduction to the New Testament*. Translated from the third German edition, ed. by J. M. Trout, W. A. Mather, and others. Three volumes Edinburgh: T. & T. Clark, 1909. Grand Rapids: Kregel Publications, 1953. Possibly the best advanced conservative introduction.

LIVES OF PAUL

Conybeare, W. J. and Howson, J. S. *The Life and Epistles of St. Paul.* Now published in Grand Rapids: Wm. B. Eerdmans Publishing Company, 1950. Pp. xxi, 850, plus maps. A great classical work. Conservative.

Farrar, F. W. *The Life and Work of St. Paul.* New York: E. P. Dutton & Co., 1902. Pp. xx, 781. Conservative. Still very useful.

Goodspeed, Edgar J. *Paul.* Philadelphia: The John C. Winston Company, 1947. Pp. 246. Liberal. Contains useful notes.

Goodwin, Frank J. *A Harmony of the Life of St. Paul.* Grand Rapids, Mich.: Baker Book House, 1950. Pp. 240. A very useful work for students. Conservative views.

Hayes, Doremus A. *Paul and His Epistles.* New York and Cincinnati: The Methodist Book Concern, c. 1915. Pp. 508. Liberal. Contains a useful bibliography.

Moe, Olaf. *The Apostle Paul.* Translated by L. A. Vigness. Minneapolis, Minn.: Augsburg Publishing House, c. 1950. Pp. 578. By a conservative scholar.

Nock, Arthur Darby. *St. Paul.* New York: Harper & Brothers, Publishers, 1938. Pp. 256. Liberal. Contains a useful bibliography.

Ramsay, W. M. *St. Paul the Traveller and the Roman Citizen.* New York: G. P. Putnam's Sons, 1897. Pp. xvi, 394. A great classical work.

Robertson, A. T. *Epochs in the Life of Paul.* New York: Charles Scribner's Sons, 1909. Pp. xi, 337. By a great conservative scholar. Contains a useful bibliography.

Smith, David. *The Life and Letters of St. Paul.* New York: Harper & Brothers, n.d. Pp. xv, 704. Formerly by G. H. Doran Co., 1920. A classical work by a fairly conservative scholar.

Spencer, F. A. *Beyond Damascus.* New York: Harper & Brothers, 1934. Pp. viii, 466. Liberal. Useful for background material. Notes are very useful. Written in racy style. L.D.S. teachers should use with care.

TITLES ON SPECIAL TOPICS

Callan, C. J. *The Epistles of St. Paul.* Two volumes. New York: Joseph F. Wagner (Inc.), 1922. A very fine work by a great Catholic scholar. Its introductions and commentary are generally valuable. Latter-day Saints will not, of course, always agree. Conservative.

Enslin, Morton Scott. *The Ethics of Paul.* New York: Harper & Brothers, Publishers, 1930. Pp. xix, 335. Useful in many respects. Liberal.

Machen, J. Gresham. *The Origin of Paul's Religion.* New York: The Macmillan Company, 1936, Pp. 329. Eerdmans Publishing Company, 1947. Conservative views by a great scholar.

Morton, H. V. *In the Steps of St. Paul.* New York: Dodd, Mead & Company, 1936. Pp. xi, 499. A very interesting and useful work by a modern traveler who retraced Paul's journeys. Contains a useful bibliography.

Prat, Fernand. *The Theology of St. Paul.* Two volumes. Translated from the Eleventh French Edition by John L. Stoddard. Westminister, Md.: The Newman Bookshop, 1926. By a great Catholic scholar. Its introductions and theological discussions will prove of value to trained L.D.S. scholars.

Ramsay, W. M. *Pictures of the Apostolic Church.* Philadelphia: The Sunday School Times Company, 1910. Useful and interesting.

Ramsay, W. M. *The Cities of St. Paul.* London: Hodder and Stoughton, 1907. Pp. xv, 452. A great classical work with useful notes.

Westcott, Brooke Foss. *The Epistle to the Hebrews.* Second Edition. Grand Rapids, Mich.: Wm. B. Eerdmans Publishing Co., 1955. lxxxiv, 504. Greek text.

INDEX

INDEX

A

Aaron, 177
Abel, 281
Abinadi, 70
Abraham, 57, 150, 164, 165, 175, 177, 185, 189, 277, 281
Achaia, 81
Achaicus, 118, 138, 158
Acro-Corinthus, 90
Acropolis, 86
Actium, 296
Acts of Peter, Gnostic, 268
Adam, 289
Adeney, 288
Adramyttium, 222
Adria (Adriatic), 224
Adultery, 283
Aegean Sea, 72
Agabus, 30, 33, 34, 205, 215
Agrippa I, 216
Agrippa II, 218, 219, 220, 267
Alexander, 111, 285, 289
Alexander the Coppersmith, 298, 302
Alexander the Great, 74
Alexandria, 32
Alexandrians, 11
Alford, 288
Alma the Younger, 20
Amphipolis, 74, 76
Ampliatus, 180
Amyntas, 159
Ananias, 21, 22, 23
Ananias (high priest), 212, 215
Anastasis, 87, 89
Anaximander, 203
Ancyra, 159
Andronicus, 180
Anselm, 199
Antioch, 26, 30, 31, 32, 33, 34, 37, 38
Antioch in Pisidia, 43, 45, 47, 51, 52, 70, 71, 72, 159
Antioch in Syria, 52, 53, 54, 55, 57, 66
Antiochus the Great, 235; kingdom of, 70
Antipater, 5
Antipatris, 214
Anton, Paul, 286
Antony, 74
Aphrodite worship, 91
Apollo, 204
Apollonia, 80
Apollos, 110, 118, 119, 271, 295, 296
Apologists, 106
Apostasy, 103, 105, 204, 301
Apostle(s), 24, 27, 28, 36, 37, 38, 48, 58, 59, 61, 63, 69
Apostolic fathers, 98, 106
Appeles, 111
Apphia, 255, 256

Appian Road, 227
Appii Forum, 227
Aquila, 91, 107, 111, 112, 180, 197
Arabia, 23, 24, 26
Aramaic, 6, 210
Archedamus, 5
Archippus, 255, 256
Architecture, 86
Archons, 48
Areopagus, 87
Aretas, 26
Aristarchus, 140, 157, 201, 222, 232, 258
Aristobulus, 180
Artemidorus, 5
Artemis, 41, 111
Article of Faith, 265
Asia, 72
Assos, 202
Astrologer, 40
Asyncritus, 180
Athanasius, 268
Athenagoras of Athens, 287
Athenodorus, 5
Athenodorus Cordulio, 5
Athens, 85, 86, 87, 90
Atonement, 200
Attaleia, 41, 52
Augustine, 199
Augustus, 5, 39, 47, 74, 157, 219, 296
Authorities, Church, 32
Authorized Version, 18, 40, 51, 105, 123
Azizus, 216

B

Baptism, 22, 23, 38, 186; for dead, Paul's reference to, 134
Bar-jesus, 40
Barnabas, 27, 28, 31-54, 57-61, 62, 66, 85, 271; tradition concerning death of, 66; epistle of, 287
Basilides, 136, 153, 195, 251
Bauer, B., 170
Baur, 266
Bernice, 219, 220
Beroea, 82, 84
Beroeans, 83
Bishop of Antioch, 287
Bishop, character of a, 294
Bishop of Colossae, 255
Bithynia, 72
Blasphemy, 49
Bleek, 158
Book of Abraham, 177
Book of Mormon, 3
Bonnet, M., 303
Brutus, 74